New Releases from
Thomson Executive Press

BUILDING COMMUNITY: THE HUMAN SIDE OF WORK
by George Manning, Kent Curtis and Steve McMillen

Building community between people is the focus of this engaging book. It is written for the work setting, but is applicable to any situation where communication, teamwork and valuing diversity are important. *Building Community* uses applications and experiential learning to help the reader achieve new skills.

Resource Guide for trainers and instructors is also available, containing chapter learning objectives, teaching notes, discussion questions and activities, transparencies and study quizzes.

CUSTOMER VALUE TOOLKIT
by Earl Naumann and The Mescon Multimedia Group

The definitive source for the new business paradigm of customer value. Includes Earl Naumann's groundbreaking book, *Creating Customer Value: The Path to Sustainable Competitive Advantage*, plus the Mescon Multimedia Group's CD-ROM, *Customer Driven Companies,* providing the user a hands-on tool for applying the principles of Naumann's book.

This package shows you why business must go beyond product quality and integrate customers throughout their decision-making processes. Includes case studies from Baldrige Award winners such as Motorola, Hewlett-Packard, and Xerox.

THE BUCK STARTS HERE: PROFIT-BASED SALES AND MARKETING MADE EASY
by Mary Molloy and Mike Molloy

A "must have" for anyone who needs to sell or market a product or service profitably. *The Buck Starts Here* focuses on how to stop spending money on sales and marketing activities that cannot be evaluated and start investing money in programs that accomplish specific, quantified, measurable business objectives.

Includes perforated workbook section containing all the blank forms discussed in the book—ready for use in your own business enterprise.

RULES OF THE GAME: GLOBAL BUSINESS PROTOCOL
by Nan Leaptrott

An essential tool for any businessperson in today's global business environment. Author Nan Leaptrott has applied her years of global business experience to present a simple, practical methodology for understanding cultural interaction today. *Rules of the Game* takes you beyond the "dos" and "don'ts" of international business customs to the rationale and reasoning behind these actions. With this thorough understanding of protocol and etiquette, you'll have the confidence to approach any culture and act consistently and effectively in all areas of business transactions.

Resource Guide for trainers and instructors also available.

TP

Thomson Executive Press
A Division of South-Western College Publishing
5101 Madison Road
Cincinnati, Ohio 45227

To order, call the ITP Business, Industry and Government Group at 1-800-347-7707, or contact your local ITP sales representative.

WHY STOCKS GO UP

WILLIAM H. PIKE

SECOND EDITION

(and Down)

THOMSON EXECUTIVE PRESS
A Division of South-Western College Publishing

Sponsoring Editor:	James L. Sitlington
Production Editor:	Holly Terry
Production House:	DPS Associates, Inc.
Internal Design:	Tom Hubbard
Cover Design:	Birdland Design/Larry Hanes
Marketing Manager:	Stephen E. Momper

Copyright © 1996
by THOMSON EXECUTIVE PRESS
Cincinnati, Ohio

I(T)P

International Thomson Publishing
Thomson Executive Press, a division of South-Western College Publishing,
is an ITP Company. The ITP trademark is used under license.

Library of Congress Cataloging-in-Publication Data:

Pike, William H.
    Why stocks go up (and down) / William H. Pike. — 2nd ed.
      p.   cm.
    Includes index.
    ISBN 0-538-86138-X
    1. Investments. 2. Stocks—Prices. 3. Polaroid Corporation
  —Finance—History. I. Title
HF4521.P498 1995   95-40724
332.63'22—dc20   CIP

1 2 3 4 5 6 MT 0 9 8 7 6 5

Printed in the United States of America

ISBN: 0-538-86138-X

TO THE READER

This book is the outgrowth of a course I have taught for the Boston Security Analysts Society for more than fifteen years. Most of my students are newcomers to the investment business who have had little or no experience with accounting, finance, or the stock market. This book has evolved to provide a strong background for these people and prepare them to work with investments every day.

Why Stocks Go Up (and Down) goes well beyond other introductory investment books I've seen. It will not insult your intelligence with oversimplification. In many places, in fact, this book goes into more detail than you may need, but by doing so, two things happen: first, the major concepts will stay with you, and second, you will not end up with more questions than you started with.

To make some concepts more concrete, the book frequently uses the example of the Jones Mousetrap Company, a fictitious company that we follow for a number of years from its inception in 1991 through the present.

Part One introduces the basic principles of business ownership and record keeping. The emphasis on accounting might not seem relevant at first, but stock prices are always related to accounting reports. To *not* write about income statements and balance sheets would be oversimplifying and leave you with major gaps in your knowledge. Part One also deals with what it means to *go public*, and why and how a company does so. This section will clear up many misconceptions that new investors have.

Part Two is about bonds and preferred stock (which is quite different from common stock). Most newspaper or magazine articles that cover a company's stock will say little or nothing about the company's bonds or preferred stock, but to understand a company and its common stock price behavior, you must be familiar with all the company's securities. However, it is possible to skip over Part Two without losing the continuity of the other parts.

Part Three explains more fully how income statements and balance sheets relate to stock prices. When you understand concepts such as write-offs, or the difference between earnings and cash flow, you will be able to understand stock price moves that otherwise would seem the opposite of what one might expect.

Part Four discusses stock price valuation. It will give you a framework for understanding stock price behavior and point to what you should watch for in your investments. It will help you avoid many of the mistakes that new investors make. This part deals with the topics that most interest new investors, but readers will get much more value out of Part Four by reading the other parts first.

A glossary at the end gives succinct definitions of many of the terms used in the book. Readers, however, are encouraged to read the text before referring to the glossary. Succinct definitions without sufficient background knowledge can be confusing. In fact, the material presented in this book has been carefully designed to avoid just that confusion that comes from presenting information for which the reader has not been prepared.

No single book can tell you everything you need to know about the stock market. Even if it did, it would not be sufficient to guarantee successful investing. A complete book about bicycle riding can give you all the background you need, but there is no substitute for getting on the bike and trying it. You will probably fall a few times, but as you gain more experience, you will gain confidence and make fewer mistakes, and bicycle riding will become second nature. So it is with investing. You need to develop the experience of watching your own stocks respond to day-to-day news about your company, the economic environment, and the stock market in general. The background that you take from this book, however, should help you gain that experience much faster.

This book could have been called, "The book that will help you understand all the other investment books." I have seen too many books that deal with one or more aspects of investing without providing the necessary understanding. Such books try to convey wisdom without first conveying adequate knowledge. *Why Stocks Go Up (and Down)* does the opposite. It presents basic fundamental knowledge that all investors should have. In doing so, I believe it also manages to convey considerable wisdom. But equally important, it enables you to get more value from other books that deal with specific aspects or approaches to the stock market.

CONTENTS

Part One

Basics: Starting a Business, Financial Statements, and Common Stock

A company is founded and basic financial statements and terms are introduced.

The company raises new equity money from private investors. The company incorporates and formalizes its ownership equity accounts.

The basic terminology of borrowing is explained, and some new terms are added to the balance sheet.

Part Two

Securities Other Than Common Stock: Bonds and Preferred Stock

The cost of a company's inventory is not as easily determined as one might guess. The LIFO or FIFO assumptions that a company makes in costing its inventory will impact its earnings in the current year and in the future.

Part Four
Why Stocks Go Up (and Down)

Here we look at a stock exchange specialist assisting in a trade, and see how exchange trading differs from NASDAQ and over-the-counter trading.

The price / earnings ratio is the primary measure that investors use in valuing stocks. We look at the price / earnings ratios in a number of ways, and also look at the price / cash-flow ratio. The material in this chapter has helped clear up a lot of my students' misunderstandings about stock prices.

We look at some of the basics of how a mutual fund works and some of the considerations in deciding whether to select your own stock investments or to use mutual funds.

PART 1

Basics: Starting a Business, Financial Statements, and Common Stock

1

Getting Started

Our story begins in late 1990, when Mr. Jones had the inspiration that he could build a better mousetrap. He immediately decided to go into business to see if he could make some money. He was handy in the workshop, and he knew where to buy some wood and metal to make the mousetraps, as well as where to buy a screwdriver, a saw, and other tools. He even had a friend who owned a department store and who would probably be willing to sell his traps. Jones knew that he would have to keep financial records of what he bought and sold and the profit he made, but he recognized that his knowledge of business and accounting was limited. So he asked his good friend, Mr. Greenshades, who had been an accountant for years, if he would advise him. Greenshades was quite willing, knowing that once the business was underway, he would be able to charge a fee for his services. Greenshade's first advice to Jones was to open a separate bank account for his mousetrap business and keep it independent of his personal account. Legally, of course, there is no distinction between Jones's personal account and his business account. For example, if both bank accounts draw interest, Jones would have to pay income tax on both.

On January 1, 1991, Jones deposited $100 into the mousetrap company account and declared himself in business. He named his company the Jones Mousetrap Company, or JMC for short. At this point, JMC is called a *sole proprietorship*. This means the company is owned by one person and is not yet incorporated (see Chapter 2).

3

Greenshades advised Jones to keep accounting records in the same manner as most other companies, which means having two financial statements: a *balance sheet* and an *income statement*. The balance sheet has three major categories, which show, *for a given point in time*: (1) *assets*, which are anything of value that the company owns or has claim to; (2) *liabilities*, which are debts the company owes at the same point in time; and (3) *ownership equity*, which reflects the combination of the amount of money put into the company by the owners plus the total amount of profit it has earned through the years, less any dividends the company has paid through the years.

In the common form of the balance sheet, all assets are recorded on the left side of the balance sheet and liabilities and ownership equity are recorded on the right side:

Assets	Liabilities
	Ownership Equity

Because Jones put $100 into the company on January 1, the balance sheet at that time looked like this:

Assets		Liabilities	
Cash	$100		
		Ownership Equity	
		Jones put in	$100

What this really says is that the company has $100 worth of assets, and Jones (as the sole owner of the company) has a claim, or equity, of $100 in the company. The terms *equity* and *ownership equity* are frequently a source of confusion because, as we will see, they are used in many different contexts. At this point it will be helpful just to memorize the definition above and remember where equity goes on the balance sheet. It will become clearer later. Since JMC has not made or sold any mousetraps, there is no statement of income yet.

After opening the bank account, Jones set out to make his initial purchases. He spent $30 on wood and metal, from which the traps will be made, and another $20 on screwdrivers, saws, and other equipment that will be used to make the traps. The $30 worth of wood and metal is called *inventory*. The $20 worth of tools is called *equipment*. The difference is this: Inventory consists of the raw materials from which the traps will be made; it will be used up and ultimately become part of the mousetraps that are to be sold. Equipment does not become part of the mousetraps; it is only used to make the mousetraps. Equipment will not be used up during the manufacturing process, although it may wear out, get lost, or be disposed of because it became obsolete and was replaced by better equipment.

DEFINITIONS

- **Inventory** is material or materials that will be used and will become part of the products that will ultimately be sold. This may include raw material, partially completed goods, or finished goods waiting to be sold.

- **Equipment** is the tools that are used to help produce the goods that are to be sold. Usually they are expected to last longer than one year.

  At this point, then, the JMC balance sheet looks like this:

Assets		Liabilities	
Cash	$ 50		
Inventory	30		
		Ownership Equity	
Equipment	20	Jones Put In	$100
Total	$100	Total	$100

All that has happened thus far is that one asset (cash) has been changed into two others (inventory and equipment).

It is customary to distinguish on the balance sheet between *current assets*, consisting of cash and items that are expected to be converted into cash within one year, and *long-term assets*, which are expected to be around for more than one year. The most common long-term assets include tools, buildings, company cars and trucks, and the like. We will see other types of long-term assets later. If Jones wanted to build a factory in which to make his traps, the cost of the factory and the cost of the property on which it was built would obviously be long-term assets, because they would be around for well over one year. Buildings, tools, motor vehicles, and so on are often categorized on the balance sheet as *property, plant, and equipment*. Thus, a more formally drawn balance sheet would look like this:

Assets		Liabilities	
Current assets:			
Cash	$ 50		
Inventory	30		
Property, plant, and		**Ownership Equity**	
equipment	20	Jones Put In	$100
Total	$100	Total	$100

At this point, Jones began making mousetraps. After a week's work, he had used up $20 worth of wood and metal and had built ten traps. He brought the traps to the store that had agreed to sell them. The store owner, however, said she would not pay Jones for the traps until they were sold.

If Jones wanted to be more accurate on his balance sheet, he could now separate inventory into two groups:

Inventory:	
Finished goods	$20
Raw materials	10

By the end of January, all ten mousetraps were sold, for $6 each. The store, however, kept $1 per trap as its profit, and owed JMC $5 per trap, or a total of $50. After Jones collected the $50, he decided to redo his balance sheet and draw up his first income statement. What has happened?

1. Sales of $50 were made and the $50 was received in cash.

2. Finished goods worth $20 were sold.

Thus the income statement for the month of January might look like this:

JMC
Statement of Income
From 1/1/91 to 1/31/91

Sales	$50
Less: Cost of goods sold	− 20
Equals: Profit	= $30

Jones knew he would have to pay income tax on his profit. Even though it does not have to be paid until later, tax is a legal liability, so it would be most accurate to put it into the income statement immediately. Since Jones owned the entire company, which was still a sole proprietorship (not yet incorporated), the Internal Revenue Service would treat the profit as part of Jones's total income including his salary from his regular job. Therefore, the actual tax rate paid on the mousetrap profit could vary, depending on Jones's other job salary that year. Since 50 percent is an easy number to work with, we will assume a 50 percent tax rate throughout this book. The income statement, therefore, would be more complete like this:

JMC
Statement of Income
From 1/1/91 to 1/31/91

Sales	$50
Less: Cost of goods sold.............................	− 20
Equals: Profit before tax..............................	= 30
Less: Income tax @ 50 percent..................	− 15
Equals: Net profit after tax	= $15

Since the tax has not yet been paid, but will have to be paid, Jones put the following entry on the balance sheet under Liabilities:

Taxes payable	$15

The liability group on the balance sheet, like the asset group, is usually broken into two parts, *current liabilities* (those due within one year), and *long-term liabilities* (those due after one year). Since taxes are paid quarterly by most businesses and by individuals who don't have their tax deducted from each pay check, *taxes payable* is a current liability.

The net profit of $15 that was earned is classified as *retained earnings* in the ownership equity section of the balance sheet. Thus, the balance sheet now looks like this:

	JMC Balance Sheet 1/31/91	Liabilities and Ownership Equity	
Assets			
Current assets:		Current liabilities:	
Cash	$100	Taxes payable	$ 15
Inventory:		Long-term liabilities	
Raw materials	10		
		Ownership equity:	
Property, plant, and		Jones put in	100
equipment	20	Retained earnings	15
Total	$130	Total	$130

Reviewing the right-hand side of the balance sheet, notice that ownership equity is *not* a liability. Ownership equity is not owed to anybody, except in the sense that the company is "owed to" or belongs to Jones. What actually does belong to Jones? The company has $130 worth of assets, but the United States government has a claim on $15 worth. In other words, if Jones liquidated the company (i.e., sold all the assets for what they were worth), he could not legally pocket the entire $130. He first would have to pay the $15 in taxes, and he would be left with $115. Now one might say Jones's equity (or ownership) in the company is $115, not just the $100 that he put in. Although the total ownership equity is now $115, it is conventional to list separately the amount of money put into the company and the amount of money earned by the company (retained earnings), as just shown on the January 31 balance sheet.

DEFINITIONS

- **Balance sheet**—The balance sheet reflects the financial condition of the company *at a point in time*. It shows what assets are held, what liabilities are owed, what money (or capital) was initially put into the company, and how much was earned by the company. It is sometimes called the "Statement of Financial Condition."

- **Income statement**—The income statement shows the revenue (sales) that the company has made, the expenses that have been incurred to make those sales, and the profit or loss derived therefrom. The income statement shows what has happened *over a period of time.* It should always say "Income Statement from (date) to (date)." This statement is also called the Profit and Loss Statement, or just the "P and L."

- **Book value**—Book value is defined as total assets less total current and long-term liabilities. In other words, JMC's book value is currently $115— exactly equal to the ownership equity account. This is not always so, for reasons that will be seen in later chapters, but book value often closely approximates ownership equity.

Jones was pleased with his successful mousetrap sales and his profit and wanted to make some more, so he bought some more raw materials. During the first week of February, he spent $60 on metal and wood. He also used $30 worth of raw material to build mousetraps, which he brought to the store. At that time, the current assets portion of the balance sheet would have looked as follows:

Currents assets (as of 2/7/91)	
Cash	$40
Inventory:	
Finished goods	30
Raw materials	40

Because Jones planned to take a vacation in the latter part of the month, he hired a trusted friend, Mr. Arbetter, as an employee. Jones agreed to pay Arbetter $4 per hour. Jones expected Arbetter would work 15 hours before the end of the month, so he knew the company would need $60 to pay Arbetter's wages. Since the store owner only pays for the traps after the end of the month, and Arbetter wanted to be paid weekly, it was obvious that JMC would need to borrow some cash to pay Arbetter until the store came through with JMC's money. Jones did not want to put any more of his own money into the company, so he went to a bank. To be on the safe side, and to have enough money for new raw materials, Jones asked to borrow $100 for 30 days, from February 15 to March 15. The bank, however, thought the business was too risky (i.e., if the traps were unable to be sold, it was unlikely the bank could get all its money back). The bank did say, however, that if Jones was willing to put in another

$50 of equity, it would be willing to loan JMC $50 for the month. The bank stipulated, however, that if the traps did not sell, and if the company had no money to pay back the loan at the end of the month, the company would be obligated to sell its equipment and raw materials for whatever they would bring in order to pay back the bank. Actually, in a case like this where JMC is a sole proprietorship (owned entirely by Mr. Jones), he personally would be responsible to the bank. The bank, however, did not know Jones very well and felt safer knowing there were assets that could be sold to raise the money should the company default on the loan (i.e., not pay it back on time). To compensate for the risk of the loan, the bank asked interest of $4 for the month.[1] Jones agreed to the stipulations and the loan was made on February 15. The new balance sheet of February 15 appeared as follows:

JMC
Balance sheet
2/15/91

	Assets			Liabilities and Ownership Equity	
Current assets:			Current liabilities:		
Cash		$140	Taxes payable		$15
Inventory:			Bank debt payable		50
Finished goods		30	Long-term liabilities		
Raw materials		40			
Property, plant, and			Ownership equity:		
equipment:			Jones put in		150
Equipment		20	Retained earnings		15
Total		$230	Total		$230

At the end of February, all the mousetraps (in this case, 15) had been sold. The store owner and Jones, however, had agreed to raise the price, and this time Jones received $6 per trap, or a total of $90. On February 28, the store owner informed JMC that although all the traps had been sold, her store was a little short on cash and would not be able to pay JMC until the 10th of March.

At this point, February 28, Jones wished to set up a new balance sheet and income statement. He had a number of things to enter:

1. Although cash had not yet been received, JMC had a legal claim against the store, so JMC recorded $90 in *Sales*, and set up a new

---

1   The $4 interest on the $50 loan for one month is unrealistically high, just as some other numbers may seem low. The numbers in these examples have been chosen to keep the math simple.

account on the balance sheet, *Accounts receivable* (i.e., money that is owed to the company).

2. *Finished goods* of $30 had been sold, so they must be removed from the balance sheet. Even though the money for the traps had not yet been received, the traps had been sold. So JMC removed the $30 from *finished goods* inventory and recorded the $30 in *Cost of goods sold* for the month of February.

3. Arbetter had worked diligently and had converted another $20 of raw materials into finished goods. He received his $60 for wages as expected. To reflect these wages, JMC lowered *Cash* by $60.

4. Arbetter had spent one-third of his time building mousetraps and two-thirds of his time keeping the books, sweeping the floor, and doing other chores. Therefore, $20 (reflecting his time working on mousetraps) was entered into inventory, specifically *Finished goods*. (None of Arbetter's traps had actually been sold yet. The traps that were sold during February had been built by Jones.) The other $40 of Arbetter's pay was taken directly to the income statement. Since that $40 cannot be attributed to any particular mousetraps, yet was a necessary expense of doing business, it must be recorded as an expense in the period (February) during which it was incurred. Rather than being listed under *Cost of goods sold (CGS)*, it is listed separately as *General and administrative expense (G&A)*.

Note these distinctions carefully:

- *Cost of goods sold* is the dollar cost of the goods that *have actually been sold.*

- The dollar cost of goods that have been manufactured but *not yet sold* is put on the balance sheet as *finished goods*. Even though the cost of their manufacture has been paid for, they are not put on the income statement as cost of goods sold until the goods are actually sold.

- The $40 cost attributable to keeping the books, sweeping the floor, and so on is not attributable to any specific mousetrap. Therefore, it is not put in Cost of goods sold but into General and administrative expense (or something similar) and put on the income statement for the period in which it occurred. General and administrative expense (G&A) is almost never put on the balance sheet. The exceptions are too minor to consider here.

Other things to enter:

5. Of the 30 days the bank loan was to be outstanding, 15 had elapsed.[2]
    Thus, since half of the time had passed, it might be assumed that
    half of the interest had been "earned" by the bank. Since the interest
    had not actually been paid yet, JMC set up a new current liability
    account, *Interest payable*, of $2. Also, since the bank's money was
    used to conduct business, the interest on the money must be consid-
    ered an expense. Accordingly, a new account, *Interest expense*, was
    set up on the income statement in the amount of $2. Again, even
    though the interest had not actually been paid yet, it had been
    "earned" by the bank, so it must be accounted for.

6. *Taxes payable* are increased to reflect the February profit.

Thus, for the month of February, the income statement looked like this:

JMC Statement of Income From 2/1/91 to 2/28/91		
Sales		$90
Expenses:		
CGS	$30	
G&A	40	
Interest expense	2	
	$72	72
Profit before tax		18
Taxes at 50 percent		9
Net profit after tax		$ 9

At this point, Jones decided to take some of the profit out of the company for himself, and he chose to do this by declaring a $5 dividend.
Alternatively, he could have taken out the $5 and called it his salary. If
he had taken the $5 as salary, it would have appeared under *expenses* in
either CGS or G&A, or possibly on the balance sheet as finished goods,
depending on how he attributed the $5 of salary. In fact, he might have
been better off if he had taken the $5 as salary, because if it then ap-
peared as an expense, he would have had higher expenses; therefore, less
profit before tax; and therefore, less tax to pay. However, for illustrative
purposes, let us assume he declared a dividend. Note the difference.

---

2   Actually, February is a shorter month, so not quite 15 days had elapsed. For simplicity, we shall
assume a 30-day month.

Salary is a cost incurred while conducting business and attempting to make a profit. A dividend is something a company *may* choose to pay with the profit it earned. Although $5 gets deducted from cash in either case, the rest of the accounting is quite different. Since Jones decided to pay himself the $5 as a dividend, he deducted $5 from the *Cash* account on the balance sheet and $5 from the *Net profit after tax* account on the income statement. This left only $4 of the profit to add to *Retained earnings*. Retained earnings, for now, means any profit earned by the company that was not paid out as a dividend. The definition will be made more precise later on. Thus Jones could put the following at the bottom of the income statement:

Net profit after tax.........	$9
Less: Dividend	– 5
Retained earnings	= $4

Some companies do not put this on the bottom of the income statement, but leave it as a separate statement called the Statement of Retained Earnings.

As of February 28, the balance sheet looked like this:

JMC
Balance Sheet
2/28/91

Assets		Liabilities and Ownership Equity	
Current assets:		Current liabilities:	
Cash	$ 75	Interest payable...............	$ 2
Accounts receivable	90	Bank debt payable	50
Inventory:		Taxes payable	24
Finished goods.............	40	Total current liabilities	76
Raw materials	20		
Total current assets	225	Long-term liabilities	
		Ownership equity:	
Property, plant, and		Jones put in	150
equipment:		Retained earnings.............	19
Equipment	20	Total liabilities and	
Total assets	$245	owners' equity.................	$245

The $40 under *Finished goods* may present some confusion. It is the dollar cost of the finished goods, which in this case consists of two components: the $20 worth of raw materials used by Arbetter and the $20 worth of labor paid to Arbetter. On the earlier balance sheets, *Finished goods* had only a raw materials component, because Jones was not paying himself any wages. Generally, the cost of finished goods consists of all costs that are normally attributable to making the goods. These almost always include both labor and raw material costs, as well as some other generally smaller items. On the other hand, such costs as interest and wages paid for general and administrative functions usually are not attributed directly to making goods and are therefore *not* included in *Finished goods*. These types of costs, sometimes called *overhead* costs, are not put on the balance sheet but rather are put directly on the income statement as general and administrative expense, or interest expense, or whatever is appropriate.

Note the convention of subtotaling both current assets and current liabilities. It is also conventional to place the current liabilities due first at the top and those due latest at the bottom. Similarly, in current assets, cash comes first, the current asset most easily converted into cash comes second, and so on. The current assets that would be most difficult to convert into cash come last.

Note also that the balance sheet *balances*—that is, the left side and the right side total the same amount. There is absolutely no significance to the actual dollar amount, in this case $245. The only thing that matters is that they balance. If they do not, an error was made someplace.

2

Ownership and Stock

In the month of March, Mr. Jones decided it was time to move the business out of his garage and buy some land to build a small factory. He estimated that buying the land and building and equipping the factory would cost about $500. This seemed like a lot of money for a company this small, but Jones knew the plant would last for years and the land would probably appreciate in value, so he decided to go ahead. But with only $75 in cash—and that needed to buy raw materials, pay wages, and pay off the bank loan—it was clear the company needed more money. Because it was very unlikely that a bank would loan $500 to a new, risky venture with so few assets, Jones decided to raise more equity money (permanent money that does not have to be paid back like a bank loan). Having no desire to risk any more of his own money, he decided to see if his friends would be willing to invest in his company. Why should they risk their money? Because they knew that if the venture was profitable, it would be able to pay them dividends. Should profits grow, so would dividends. Each investor, then, would hope to eventually receive in dividends more than he or she had initially put in as equity money. In fact, many of Jones's friends had faith in his ability to run the mousetrap business successfully, and four of them agreed to put in $75 each. At this point, Jones was afraid that since his friends had put up a total of $300, or two-thirds of the total equity money paid in, they might think they owned two-thirds of the company. (Recall that Jones had only put in $150.) Jones turned to Mr. Greenshades for help. Greenshades first pointed out that percentage ownership in a company does not have to be proportionate to

15

the amount of money put in. It is entirely up to the people putting money into a company to negotiate with the people already owning the company what their percentage will be. Obviously, Jones wanted to maintain as large a percentage of the company as possible. Similarly, his friends wanted as large a share of the company as they could have for their money. There is no law to say who gets what percentage of the company. Percentage ownership in a company does not have to be proportionate to the amount of money put in. In this case, all agreed that since Jones had invented the mousetrap and would be putting a lot of time into the company, he deserved a larger share of the ownership than his proportion of the money put in. It was agreed that Jones would keep 60 percent of the company and the four other investors would get 10 percent each.

Next, Greenshades explained the use of stock as a way to reflect ownership of a company. Very simply, stock represents ownership. A share of stock is a piece of paper that entitles the owner of the paper to whatever portion of the company this share represents. Until now, Jones owned the entire company. Therefore, he owned all the company's stock; he could have had one share worth the entire company, or two shares each worth half the company, or ten shares each worth one-tenth of the company. It made no difference—Jones could have printed up as many shares of stock as he pleased. He owned them all, totaling 100 percent of the company. Now he had agreed to give up 40 percent of the company to his friends. They decided to draw up 100 shares of stock. Jones would keep 60 shares and each of the four investors would get 10 shares. They could just as easily have printed 200 shares and Jones would have kept 120, and the four investors 20 each. It makes no difference how many shares there are as long as each partial owner of the company has the proper proportion.

Finally, Greenshades explained that, with the addition of the four investors, JMC would no longer be a sole proprietorship and would need to be made either a *partnership* or a legal *corporation*. The primary advantage of being a corporation is called the *limited liability* feature, which means that neither Jones nor the partners can be held personally liable for the debts of the company. For example, when the company was a sole proprietorship, if business had been bad and the company was unable to repay the bank loan when it was due, Jones would have had to come up with the money out of his own pocket; or, if the company had become a partnership, the partners would have had to come up with the money from their own pockets. Similarly, if Arbetter had broken his hand while working for the company, he might have sued JMC for medical expenses. If he won and if the company did not have enough cash to pay the settlement, even after having sold off all its assets, Jones (or the partners) would have had to come up with their personal cash. The limited liability feature of a corporation means that neither the bank nor Arbetter would have been able to collect from Jones (or the partners). They could have collected as much as the assets of the company could have been sold for, but beyond that, the owner or owners would have no liability from their personal money for the debts of the corporation. Jones and the four investors readily agreed that incorporation was a good idea. Note that in recent years, new law has enabled people to create *limited liability partnerships*. Such limited liability partnerships enjoy the same limited liability feature of corporations, but are still partnerships.

Another factor that distinguishes a corporation from a sole proprietorship or partnership is the way its profits are taxed. In a sole proprietorship, the profits are taxed as a part of the income of the proprietor. In a partnership, the profits are taxed as part of the partners' income in proportion to their ownership of the partnership. In a corporation, however, profits are taxed at rates based on how much profit the corporation made. Corporate tax rates are independent of the earnings of the owner or owners of the corporation.

Incorporation in most states usually involves no more than filing a simple statement at the statehouse and paying a nominal fee. Thus, JMC became a corporation. The company name was changed to JMC, Incorporated. Greenshades now explained the following to Jones and the four investors.

Every person who owns one or more shares of a company is called a *shareholder*, or a *stockholder* of that company. Each stockholder has the right to attend stockholders' meetings and has as many votes as he or she has shares on all issues that come up before the stockholders at the meeting. In the case of a large company such as IBM or Eastman Kodak, the stock is very widely held and no person is likely to hold more than 1 or 2 percent. Most stockholders own far less. Kodak's ownership, for example, is divided into 330 million shares of stock. Therefore, a person owning one hundred shares owns less than one ten-thousandth of 1 percent of Kodak!

Most corporations have one stockholder meeting each year. The primary purpose of the meeting is to elect the board of directors. Usually, any stockholder can nominate anyone for the board of directors, whether or not that person works for the company and whether or not the person is a stockholder of the company. The board of many companies, however, includes the president and some of the officers. Directors who are not employees of the company are called "outside directors." Typically, a board of directors is made up of between 7 and 13 members. The board's most important functions usually include choosing the president of the company, reviewing the president's performance, and declaring dividends.

If a large number of stockholders are dissatisfied with the way their company is being run, they can elect new directors at the next meeting who can replace the president with someone more acceptable. To do this, of course, requires a large number of unhappy stockholders. As a practical matter, in most large companies the board is similar from year to year with only one or two changes every couple of years. Nevertheless, all directors have to be reelected periodically. In some companies, all directors come up for reelection each year; in other companies, only some of the directorships come up for election (or reelection) each year. There is usually no limit to the number of terms a director can serve.

Stockholders are notified well in advance of the meeting of when and where it will be held. Those who cannot attend are allowed to vote by proxy, which is essentially an absentee ballot. The term *proxy fight*, which is often heard in the financial community, refers to a case where a group of unhappy stockholders wants to elect new directors who the group thinks will more adequately represent them (e.g., make changes in the company that they feel are necessary). Since most stockholders do not actually attend the meeting, the dissident group tries to get the nonattending stockholders to vote their proxies in favor of the dissidents' candidate. The incumbent directors, of course, will endeavor to get the stockholders to vote them in again.

In the case of JMC, Jones owns 60 percent of the stock and he can therefore elect himself as at least 60 percent of the board of directors and appoint himself president. In a closely held company (very few stockholders) the stockholders' meeting might be quite informal, particularly if one shareholder has a majority (over 50 percent) of the shares.

Besides voting, the importance to the four investors of owning as much of the stock as possible is that whenever a dividend is declared, the same amount of dividend will be paid *on each share*. Thus, a person owning 60 shares would receive six times as much as a person owning 10 shares. A stockholder with 10 shares would receive twice as much as a stockholder owning 5 shares. The final reason for wanting to own as many shares as possible is that if the company were dissolved or liquidated (i.e., if all the assets were sold and all the debts paid off), the remaining money would be distributed to the stockholders in proportion to the number of shares owned.

Greenshades now proposed setting up the ownership equity portion of the balance sheet in the format used by most companies, which is as follows:

Ownership Equity

Paid-in capital:
  Common stock (at par value $1 per share) ... $100
  (authorized 100 shares, issued 100 shares,
  outstanding 100 shares)
  Additional paid-in capital 350
Retained earnings 19

Total ownership equity $469

Paid-in capital, Greenshades explained, represents money put into the company in exchange for stock. Since the total capital paid in by the five investors (including Jones) was $450, the items under *Paid-in capital* must, by definition, total $450. *Retained earnings* represents profits earned by the company's operations (i.e., making and selling mousetraps), less the amount of dividends paid.

Par value, Greenshades went on, was an anachronism with little meaning today, but he thought JMC should put it in for formality. *Par value* is an arbitrary dollar value assigned to each share of stock. In this case, the assigned par value was $1 per share. Thus the dollar figure in Common stock (at par value $1 per share) is $100 ($1 times 100 shares outstanding = $100).

Additional paid-in capital is the difference between the total money (capital) paid into the company for stock, less the portion that has been assigned to par value. Therefore:

  Paid-in capital = Common at par + Additional paid-in capital

The *additional* just means the portion of the paid-in capital above what is assigned to common at par. Usually, the only way to calculate additional paid-in capital is to take the total paid-in capital and subtract common at par. Additional paid-in capital is sometimes called *paid-in surplus*, *capital surplus*, or *capital paid-in above par*. The terms are synonymous, although the latter is the most accurate description. The word *surplus* is undesirable here, because it may imply there is surplus cash lying around the company. This, of course, is not true. The cash in this case, for example, will shortly be used to buy some land and construct a factory. All of these items— Paid-in capital, Common at par, and Additional paid-in capital—are just accounting entries reflecting the fact that sometime in the past some money was paid into the company in exchange for stock. If the cash is still there, it would be in the cash account on the left-hand side of the balance sheet. By looking at the accounting entries, there is no way to know when the cash was paid in or what has since been done with the cash.

If the par value had been declared at $2, then the ownership equity portion of the balance sheet would look like this:

Ownership Equity

Paid-in capital:
   Common stock (at par value $2 per share) ... $200
   (authorized 100 shares, issued 100 shares,
   outstanding 100 shares)
   Additional paid-in capital 250
Retained earnings 19

Total ownership equity $469

"Authorized 100 shares" simply means that the stockholders agreed that the company's ownership *may* be split into as many as 100 shares. In the case of JMC, the ownership has, in fact, been split into 100 shares, and therefore there are 100 shares authorized, issued, and outstanding. If the stockholders thought they might want to sell more shares later on, they would first have to vote to authorize—or *permit*—the president or officers of the company to sell more. Once the company has been authorized to sell more shares, it may sell such shares at any time in the future or it may never sell them. *Authorize* simply means permission. It does not require that such shares actually be sold.

"Issued 100 shares" means that at some time in the past the company issued 100 shares. *Issued* usually means *sold*, but a company may also issue shares of stock in exchange for assets, or may give shares away—perhaps to employees. Once a share has been issued, it is *outstanding*, and will remain outstanding unless the company buys it back.[1] When a company buys back its stock, those shares are called *Treasury shares*. Treasury shares do not represent ownership in the company and are not considered to be outstanding shares.

"Outstanding 100 shares" means that JMC's ownership is currently divided into 100 shares. If JMC bought back 10 of its shares, there would only be 90 shares outstanding, and JMC ownership would be divided into 90 shares. In this case, the *Common stock* account would

---

1 When a company buys back its own stock, those shares are no longer considered outstanding. But if a person who owns the stock sells his or her shares to another person, then those shares are still outstanding.

say "Authorized 100 shares, issued 100 shares, outstanding 90 shares." For most investment purposes, the number of shares outstanding is the relevant number, and that is what we will focus on in this book.

Let's assume that JMC did not repurchase any Treasury shares, so there are still 100 authorized, issued, and outstanding. Now let's see what happens if the shareholders authorize an additional 200 shares but JMC only issues 50 of them. Assume those 50 additional shares were sold for $6 each, and that the par value of JMC's stock is still $1. Then the Ownership Equity would look as follows:

Ownership Equity

Paid-in capital:
  Common stock (at par value $1 per share) ... $150
  (authorized 300 shares, issued 150 shares,
  outstanding 150 shares)
  Additional paid-in capital 600
Retained earnings 19
Total ownership equity $769

When a company wants to sell more shares, it could ask the shareholders to authorize them at the next annual stockholders' meeting. Or, in an emergency, a special stockholders' meeting could be called expressly for authorizing more shares. Of course, the stockholders might vote not to authorize more shares, in which case the company would not be permitted to sell any more shares.

DEFINITIONS

- **Paid-in capital**—The total amount of dollars paid into the company by stockholders for stock. This figure is made up of the sum of *Common stock at par value* and *Additional paid-in capital*. The total dollars in *Paid-in capital* almost never changes unless the company issues more stock.

- **Par value**—An arbitrary figure set by the company that distinguishes one of the two components of paid-in capital. Some companies use *stated value* in place of *par value*. There is a minor distinction that is irrelevant for most purposes. Par value is the same for all common shares. Additional paid-in capital probably is not.

- **Additional paid-in capital**—This can be calculated by taking Paid-in capital and subtracting Common stock at par value.

- **Retained earnings**—The total profits earned by the company for all years since its inception, less any losses in any years since inception, less all of the dividends paid since inception. Retained earnings is often called *earned surplus*, or *retained profits*. Again, the word *surplus* is undesirable, since it might imply that surplus cash is lying around in the company. It is likely that this cash has long since been spent.

Notice that the categories "Common stock at par" and "Additional paid-in capital" do not tell you how much was paid for each share or when the shares were sold. In fact, most companies have sold new shares on more than one occasion, and received a different price on each occasion. Again, the paid-in capital portion of the ownership equity account only tells you how much money was received in total for all those times when the company sold shares.

Do not confuse the company's selling *new* shares with individuals who already own shares selling their shares to another individual. This will be discussed in Chapter 5. For now, we are only interested in how to account for money that comes into the company when the company writes up new shares and sells them to someone for cash.

REVIEW: EQUITY IS NOT THE SAME AS CASH

The $300 that JMC raised from the sale of the new stock, as well as the $150 Jones had put in, is called *equity money*. That equity money was put into the company as cash. Eventually some or all of that cash will be spent, perhaps on new plant and equipment, or more inventory, or anything else. As the money is spent, the "Cash" account will go down, but the "Common at Par" and "Additional Paid-in Capital" accounts will not. These latter two equity accounts just reflect the fact that a certain amount of equity money was paid into the company for stock at some time or times in the past.

The equity is permanent. If the cash is spent on new plant and equipment, then that equity will be in the form of plant and equipment. If the cash is spent on inventory, then the equity will be in the form of inventory. When that inventory is sold, the equity will again be in the form of cash, until it is used to buy inventory again, and so on. The "Cash" account will go up and down every time there is a transaction involving cash, which would be many times each day. But the equity accounts, "Common at Par" and "Additional Paid-in Capital," only go up when the company issues new stock, and are unlikely to go down except under unusual circumstances.

3

Borrowing Money as the Company Grows

JMC has now raised $300 of the $500 it is seeking. Having improved its equity position (i.e., put more equity, or cash, permanently into the company), it is now possible that another $200 can be raised by borrowing. Note the difference between equity money and money borrowed. Equity money is money put permanently into the company in exchange for stock (ownership rights). The equity money itself will never be paid back, although the individual who paid it in did so with the idea that either (1) he will get more back in dividends later, or (2) the equity (stock) will increase in value so that it can be sold to another individual for more than he paid for it.

Money that is borrowed, or debt money, must be paid back in the exact amount and with interest according to a specified time schedule. Therefore, people who lend money to the company have the disadvantage of not having ownership rights, but instead have the advantage of a fixed time schedule and legal rights for getting their money back with interest.

Since $200 is more than the company expects to earn this year, it would not make much sense to borrow $200 on a short-term basis (i.e., to plan to pay it back within one year). Furthermore, since the factory to be constructed with the money should be usable for many years, there is no reason why it should not be paid for over many years.

Hence, JMC went to an insurance company and asked for a five-year term loan.[1] The insurance company said it would consider making a loan to JMC and assigned one of its investment officers to examine the books (financial records) of JMC and to study the mousetrap and its potential market. The insurance company decided that although the loan was risky, it would go ahead and loan JMC the $200 under the following stipulations:

1. JMC was to pay back the loan at the rate of $30/year for four years, and then pay the remaining $80 at the end of the fifth year. Each payment was due on December 31 of that year.

2. JMC must pay 8 percent interest annually on the outstanding balance, to be paid at the rate of 4 percent semiannually, on June 30 and December 31.[2]

3. In the event JMC could not meet any one of its interest or payback requirements, the insurance company could immediately declare the company "in default" and require the entire loan to be repaid immediately. In other words, the company could be forced to liquidate its assets (i.e., sell its factory and all its property and equipment) in order to raise money to meet the interest and payback obligations. In the event that the money raised from selling the company's assets was not enough to meet the insurance company's and other creditors' claims, the insurance company would be the first to be paid with whatever cash could be raised.

JMC had no objections to the first two requirements. The firm felt certain it could meet the annual $30 payback requirement, called a *sinking fund*, with little difficulty. It was also confident that it could meet the large $80 payment at the end of the fifth year. This large payment at the end is called a *balloon*. Both the $30 sinking fund payments and the $80 balloon payment are called *return of principal* (as distinguished from interest). In the language of finance, JMC borrowed $200 principal amount under a term loan agreement requiring a $30 annual sinker beginning in the first year.

---

1 A "term" loan typically implies a loan of three to seven years. Borrowing for longer than that is more often done by selling bonds (discussed in a later chapter).

2   To understand how the interest payment schedule works, assume the loan was made on January 1. In that case, the first interest payment would be $8 on June 30 of the first year. This is 4 percent of $200, the amount outstanding during that period. Similarly, the second interest payment on December 31 would also be $8 since the entire $200 was outstanding during the period. But on December 31, $30 of the loan would be paid back. This leaves an "outstanding balance" of $170. Thus the third and fourth interest payments, on June 30 and December 31 of the second year, would each be $6.80, which is 4 percent of $170. Similarly, the third-year payments would each be $5.60, and so on.

On the third requirement, JMC said it could not let the insurance company have the first, or senior, claim on assets in the event of forced liquidation because the bank had already been promised that. As it happens, the bank loan was due to be paid back within one week, but Jones knew the monthly cash problem might come up again; that is, JMC would have to go on buying raw materials and paying wages during the month even though JMC would not be paid for the sold traps until ten or more days after the end of the following month. In other words, Jones knew the company would need future bank loans to meet the late-month cash needs (pay its bills) while the company had large accounts receivable (i.e., money owed to it). JMC would be able to pay back the bank loan when accounts receivable are received. In the language of Wall Street, JMC would need bank loans *to finance receivables*.

The insurance company understood the problem because many of its loan customers had the same difficulty, and it waived that requirement. The loan was consummated.

DEFINITIONS

- **Short-term debt**—Loans that must be repaid within one year, whether payable to banks, suppliers, insurance companies, individuals, or whomever. On the balance sheet, however, this term frequently means just short-term bank debt.

- **Long-term debt**—Loans that will be paid back after one year.

- **Term loan**—A term loan is usually for a period of three to seven years and is therefore long term. It often has a sinking-fund requirement and may have a balloon payment.

- **Sinking fund**—Required partial repayment on a long-term loan. It can be payable annually, semiannually, or in any manner the borrower and lender agreed to at the time the loan is made. The sinking fund (or annual "sinker") is a return of principal.

- **Balloon**—A large payment to complete the repayment of a long-term loan. It is possible that a loan can have no sinking fund, and the balloon, when the loan is due, is therefore equal to the entire principal amount of the loan. It also happens frequently that the sinking fund pays out equal installments and there is no balloon at all.

On March 1, the loan and sale of stock to the four new investors had been completed. The new balance sheet appears as follows.

<table>
<tr><td colspan="2" align="center">JMC
Balance Sheet
3/1/91</td><td colspan="2"></td></tr>
<tr><td colspan="2" align="center">Assets</td><td colspan="2" align="center">Liabilities and
Stockholders' Equity</td></tr>
<tr><td colspan="2">Current assets:</td><td colspan="2">Current liabilities:</td></tr>
<tr><td>Cash ....</td><td>$575</td><td>Interest payable ....</td><td>$ 2</td></tr>
<tr><td>Accounts receivable ....</td><td>90</td><td>Short-term debt (bank)..</td><td>50</td></tr>
<tr><td>Inventory:</td><td></td><td>Tax payable ....</td><td>24</td></tr>
<tr><td>Finished goods.............</td><td>40</td><td rowspan="2">Total current liabilities .....</td><td rowspan="2">76</td></tr>
<tr><td>Raw materials ....</td><td>20</td></tr>
<tr><td>Total current assets ....</td><td>725</td><td>Long-term liabilities:</td><td></td></tr>
<tr><td></td><td></td><td>8% term loan ....</td><td>200</td></tr>
<tr><td></td><td></td><td>Ownership equity:</td><td></td></tr>
<tr><td></td><td></td><td>Paid-in capital</td><td></td></tr>
<tr><td></td><td></td><td>Common stock (par</td><td></td></tr>
<tr><td>Property, plant, and equipment:</td><td></td><td>value $1) (authorized</td><td></td></tr>
<tr><td>Equipment ....</td><td>20</td><td>100 shares, out-</td><td></td></tr>
<tr><td></td><td></td><td>standing 100 shares)</td><td>100</td></tr>
<tr><td></td><td></td><td>Additional paid-in cap.</td><td>350</td></tr>
<tr><td></td><td></td><td>Retained earnings..........</td><td>19</td></tr>
<tr><td></td><td></td><td>Total ownership equity .....</td><td>469</td></tr>
<tr><td>Total assets</td><td>$745</td><td>Total liabilities and equity</td><td>$745</td></tr>
</table>

Note that the right-hand side of the balance sheet is now called "Liabilities and *Stockholders'* Equity." We had previously used the term "Ownership Equity." Since the stockholders are the owners and have claim to the equity in the company, both terms mean the same thing and either is correct.

DERIVING AN EXPANDED BALANCE SHEET

In the month of March, JMC continued to make and sell mousetraps. From the following list of events that took place in March, it is possible to derive the income statement for March and a new balance sheet for March 31.

During the month of March, the following events occurred:

1. Raw materials costing $80 were purchased from a lumberyard. JMC could have paid the $80 with its now abundant cash, but it was still uncertain how much of that would be needed for the new land and factory, so JMC asked the lumberyard if it could delay the $80 payment for a while. Since JMC was now a good customer, the lumberyard agreed to extend credit for one month. Thus, instead of deducting the $80 from cash, JMC set up a new account under current liabilities, called *accounts payable*, for $80.

2. Raw materials costing $60 were converted into finished goods, of which two-thirds were sold.

3. At the end of the month, $10 worth of raw materials had been partially converted into mousetraps, but these traps had not yet been completed. Since this could no longer be called raw materials, and was not yet finished goods, it gave rise to a new inventory account— *work in progress*.

4. The store paid the $90 it owed to JMC for February sales.

5. The store sold the ten mousetraps it had left at the end of February, which included all of those that were in JMC's finished goods inventory as of March 1. The store also sold 20 more traps that it had received from JMC during March. For all of these traps, the store owed JMC $200. The store said it would pay JMC the $200, as usual, ten days after the end of the month.

6. Mr. Arbetter received $120 in wages, of which $80 was attributed to time spent building traps and $40 was considered general and administrative expense. Actually, some of Arbetter's time was spent talking to two new stores, which were considering carrying the line of mousetraps. Thus, the $40 might more properly be termed *selling, general, and administrative expense (SGA)*. Of the $80 of Arbetter's wages attributed to trap building, $60 was appointed to traps sold, $15 to traps finished but not yet sold, and $5 to the time spent on the traps that were partially completed at the end of the month.

7. Property on which to build the factory was purchased for $100. The factory was not yet started.

The following calculations were made to derive the March 31 financial statements.

Cash as of 3/1/91	$575
Add: Received from store	90
Subtotal	665
Less: Paid to Mr. Arbetter	120
Less: Property purchase..	100
Less: Bank loan paid back..	50
Less: Interest on loan	4
Total as of 3/31/91	$391
Accounts receivable as of 3/1/91	$ 90
Less: February's sales for which cash	
was paid to JMC during March..........................	90
Subtotal	0
Add: March sales to store, for which	
cash would be paid to JMC in April	200
Total as of 3/31/91	$200
Inventory: Finished goods as of 3/1/91	$ 40
Less: All finished goods as of 3/1/91 were	
sold during the month...	40
Subtotal	0
Add: Raw material converted but not yet sold....................	20
Add: Arbetter's wages attributable to traps	
finished but not yet sold	15
Total as of 3/31/91	$ 35
Inventory: Work in progress as of 3/1/91....................	$ 0
Add: Raw material converted but not-yet-completed	10
Add: Labor on raw material used in not yet	
completed traps	5
Total as of 3/31/91	$ 15
Inventory: Raw material as of 3/1/91	$ 20
Add: New purchases..	80
Subtotal	100
Less: Amount converted to finished goods	60
Less: Amount converted to work in progress	10
Total as of 3/31/91	$ 30

Property, plant, and equipment as of 3/1/91 .... $ 20
   Add: Purchase of property 100

Total as of 3/31/91 .... $120

Interest payable[3] as of 3/1/91 .... $ 2
   Less: This was paid when due on 3/15/91 (along
          with the other $2 of interest) 2

Total as of 3/31/91 .... $ 0

Short-term debt as of 3/1/91 .... $ 50
   Less: Paid off when due 3/15/91 50

Total as of 3/31/91 .... $ 0

Taxes payable as of 3/1/91 .... $ 24
   Add: Expected tax on income for March 9

Total as of 3/31/91 .... $ 33

Accounts payable as of 3/1/91 .... $ 0
   Add: Credit extended to JMC for raw material....................... 80

Total as of 3/31/91 .... $ 80

Retained earnings as of 3/1/91 .... $ 19
   Add: Profit for March 9

  Subtotal .... $ 28
   Less: Dividends paid .... $ 0

Total as of 3/31/91 .... $ 28

The *Cost of goods sold* for the month of March was calculated as follows:

Transferred from finished goods..............	$ 40
Transferred from raw materials[4]	40
Transferred from Arbetter's wages[4]	60
	$140

From these calculations, the income statement for March and the March 31 balance sheet on the following page are derived.

---

3 For simplicity, we have ignored the interest payable on the $200 term loan.
4 Actually, both these figures would have been first added to finished goods and then, when the product was sold, subtracted from finished goods and transferred to *Cost of goods sold*. We have ignored that step for simplicity.

JMC
Statement of Income
from 3/1/91 to 3/31/91

Sales		$200
Expenses......................................		
CGS	$140	
SGA	40	
Interest expense[5]	2	
	$182	182
Pretax profit		18
Income tax expense		9
Net profit after tax		$ 9

JMC
Balance Sheet
3/31/91

Assets		Liabilities and Stockholders' Equity	
Current assets:		Current liabilities:	
Cash	$391	Accounts payable	$ 80
Accounts receivable	200	Tax payable	33
Inventory:		Total current liabilities.......	113
Finished goods	35		
Work in progress	15	Long-term liabilities:	
Raw materials	30	8% term loan.................	200
Total current assets	671		
		Ownership equity:	
		Paid-in capital	
		Common stock	
		(par value $1) (authorized	
		100 shares, outstanding	
Property, plant, and equipment:		100 shares)	100
Property	100	Additional paid-in cap.	350
Equipment	20	Retained earnings	28
		Total ownership equity	478
Total assets	$791	Total liabilities and equity ..	$791

---

5 Note that although the entire $4 interest was paid in March, only $2 was taken as an expense. This is because the other $2 previously had been "expensed" in February. Again, we have ignored the interest on the $200 term loan for simplicity.

Although the derivation for the balance sheet is presented here, it is not necessary for the reader to follow each calculation. It is sufficient to come away with an understanding of the various terms on the financial statements, how they arise, and where they belong on the balance sheet or income statement.

It would be an interesting and worthwhile exercise to try to derive one income statement for the period from January 1 through March 31 to check your understanding of the material presented so far. An easy check to see if it has been done correctly is to see if the retained earnings and the taxes from the three-month income statement are equal to the retained earnings and taxes payable accounts on the balance sheet of March 31, 1991. (Don't forget the dividend.)

JUMPING AHEAD TO THE YEAR END

Through the end of the year the company continued to prosper. The new factory, designated Plant Number 1, had been completed by June and then expanded in September. Some automatic machinery for making mousetraps had been installed. The factory expansion and automatic machinery had been paid for by money coming from three sources: (1) profits from operations, (2) another term loan, and (3) more new stock that had been sold to some other friends.

At December 31, the financial statements of the company appeared as shown on page 32. Note the numbers have been expanded and modified considerably for clarity and realism.

Besides the changes in the numbers, the following changes should be noted:

1. The company had quite a bit of cash lying around. Rather than leave it in a checking account at the bank where it earns no interest, Jones thought it wiser to buy some government bonds, which pay interest and can always be sold for cash immediately, either through JMC's bank or through a broker. This is a common practice among corporations with large balances of cash. Besides U.S. Government securities, there are other means of investing cash that are safe and readily convertible into cash. Therefore, instead of *U.S. Government securities*, one often sees *marketable securities*. This does *not* refer to common stocks, whose prices are much less dependable and can be difficult to sell on short notice.

JMC
Balance sheet
12/31/91

Assets		Liabilities and Stockholders' Equity	
Current assets:		Current liabilities:	
Cash	$ 5,000	Accounts payable	$10,000
U.S. Govt. securities	25,000	Short-term debt	6,000
Accounts receivable	10,000	Taxes payable	2,000
Inventory:		Sinking-fund payments	
Finished goods	20,000	on long-term debt	
Work in progress	5,000	due within one year	2,000
Raw materials	15,000	Total current liabilities	20,000
Total current assets	80,000	**Capitalization:**	
		Long-term debt	
Fixed assets:		8% Term loan	10,000
		9% First mortgage bonds	20,000
Property	3,000	Stockholders' equity:	
Buildings	13,000	Common stock	
Equipment	44,000	(par value $1.00)	
Total fixed assets	60,000	(authorized 1,000 shares,	
		outstanding 500 shares)	500
		Capital surplus	4,500
		Retained earnings	85,000
		Total stockholders' equity	90,000
Total assets	$140,000	Total liabilities and equity	$140,000

JMC
Income Statement
for the Year Ending 12/31/91

Sales		$100,000
Expenses:		
CGS	$70,000	
SGA	18,000	
Interest charges	2,000	
Total expenses	90,000	90,000
Pretax profit		10,000
Income tax		5,000
Net profit after tax		$ 5,000

2. The *Property, buildings, and equipment* accounts were increased substantially.

3. The company once again went to the bank for short-term debt. This time it was for $16,000, of which $10,000 has already been paid back.

4. Note that the *Taxes payable* account is less than the full taxes for the year because, being a corporation, JMC had to begin estimating and paying taxes quarterly. Thus, only the estimated tax for the last three months remains on the balance sheet, as all the earlier quarters' taxes have been paid. When the final tax bill for the year is figured in early 1992, the taxes payable figure can be adjusted accordingly.

5. Recall that liabilities due within one year are classified as current liabilities. When JMC first took the 8% term loan, it was for $12,000.[6] But one of the stipulations was that a sinking-fund payment of $2,000 would be paid each year on December 30 beginning in 1992. Therefore, of the original $12,000 loan, $2,000 was due within a year and the remaining $10,000 was still classified as long-term debt.

6. The 9% First Mortgage Bonds were sold to a group of insurance companies in October 1991. They are called First Mortgage because if JMC should fail to make its payments to the insurance companies, they have the right to take possession of the building and sell it in order to get their money back.

7. The *Retained earnings* figure is obviously out of proportion. For a company that has been in business only one year, the retained earnings figure should be equal to the profits of the company that year, less the dividends paid by the company that year. The large figure presented would be more typical of a company that had been in business and making profits for many years. We use the large number for convenience.

8. *Capitalization* is a hard-to-define word. It comes up in many contexts within the business world. On the balance sheet, it usually refers to the combination of long-term debt plus stockholders' equity. In this sense, it refers to the money (or capital) used by the company to manufacture the products it sells. The machinery and equipment that were bought with this money can be thought of as

---

6 The term loan was actually for $200, of which $30 was due within one year, but again the numbers have been modified for realism.

capital. This, in fact, is the economist's definition of capital—goods (machinery) used to make other goods. Such machinery (or capital goods) can be paid for by (1) money put into the business by individuals who bought stock from the company (which may have happened on more than one occasion); (2) profits earned by the company; and/or (3) money raised by selling debt (bonds, term loans). Inventory, however, is not thought of as capital, but rather as the raw materials that are acted on by the capital (machinery) to make the company's products. Long-term debt and equity are usually thought of as financing capital equipment; short-term debt and other current liabilities are usually thought of as financing inventories or receivables until these can be converted into cash in what might be called the inventory cycle, or receivables cycle. Although we usually think of the balance sheet this way, it is not necessarily true. For example, there are many companies that use short-term debt to finance capital equipment or use long-term debt or equity to finance inventories.

RECAP ON THE STATUS OF JMC

JMC is still a private company. It now has 12 stockholders. According to the Securities and Exchange Acts (the laws that regulate purchases and sales of stocks and bonds), as long as there are only a small number of investors, a company will be deemed to be a *private company.* When a company is private, its owners have no obligation to publish financial statements, or to report to the Securities and Exchange Commission (SEC), and thus the profitability of the company does not have to be revealed to anyone except the Internal Revenue Service on the company's income tax return.

If JMC wished to sell shares of its stock to a large number of people, especially if they were unsophisticated investors, then according to the Securities and Exchange Acts, JMC might be deemed to be a *public company.* If JMC were a public company, it would have to register its stock with the SEC before it could be sold, and would have to file its balance sheet and income statement and other information with the SEC periodically. Why a private company might want to become a public company, and how it goes public, will be discussed in Chapter 5.

4

Ratios Investors Watch

When financial analysts first look at balance sheets or income statements, all they see is the same morass of numbers that the layman sees. To make sense of these figures, to evaluate a company's financial strength or weakness, and to get insights into possible stock market performance, a financial analyst must look at the relationships between the figures. The ratios discussed in this chapter are among those frequently used by analysts. The figures used are taken from JMC's financial statements of December 31, 1991, which are found at the end of Chapter 3.

STOCK EVALUATION RATIOS

Net Earnings per Common Share Outstanding

This ratio is one of the most important factors helping to determine what one should pay for a share of stock. The discussion here will set the stage for further discussion in later chapters. This ratio is usually called *earnings per share,* or abbreviated as EPS. It is simply the net earnings of the company for the year, $5,000, divided by the number of shares of common stock outstanding, 500. Therefore, JMC's earnings per share for 1991 were $10 per share.

$$\frac{\text{Net earnings}}{\text{Number of shares}} = \frac{\$5,000}{500 \text{ shares}} = \$10 / \text{share}$$

This ratio helps you to decide what to pay for a share of stock by telling you how much money that share can "earn." The earnings per share are not, of course, paid directly to the stockholder; they are kept in the company. The company may, however, declare a dividend from time to time, which *is* paid directly to the stockholder. The higher the earnings per share, the higher the dividend per share is likely to be. The astute reader should realize, then, that what someone should be willing to pay for a share of stock is not really related to what the share of stock is "earning" today, but *what it is expected to earn (and therefore potentially pay in dividends) over a period of time.* If a share of stock were earning $10 per share this year, expected to earn $20 next year, and $30 the following year, and the company was expected to pay out 50 percent of earnings as a dividend in each year, then you as the holder of one share of stock would expect to receive $5 + $10 + $15 = $30 over a period of three years. Thus, you would certainly be willing to buy the stock for more than the $10/share that the stock is earning today. How much more you would be willing to pay is related to two factors: (1) an evaluation of the risk that your estimates of the company's next three years' earnings and dividends are wrong; and (2) an evaluation of what the company can be earning, and therefore potentially be paying as dividends, beyond three years out. The exceptionally astute reader will now realize that what you should be willing to pay for a share of stock is not necessarily related to what you expect the company to earn and pay out as a dividend in the near future, but rather what you expect other investors will be expecting for potential earnings and dividends for the period beginning some time in the future. If this seems confusing, it is, but this is what stock prices are all about. Let's look at some examples.

Table 4.1 shows three hypothetical companies' expected dividends for six years, and the bank interest that can be had if one chooses to put one's money into a bank Certificate of Deposit earning 5 percent interest rather than buy any of three stocks. Presuming that $100 is put into the bank, the investor (certificate holder) would expect to get $5 a year in interest and get back the original investment of $100 at the end of six years.

Table 4.1   Expected Dividends of Three Companies

	Put in	Interest or dividend payment during year						Get back
		(1)	(2)	(3)	(4)	(5)	(6)	
Bank	$100	$ 5	$ 5	$ 5	$ 5	$ 5	$ 5	$100
Company A		5	6	7	8	9	10	
Company B..........		5	7	9	12	16	21	
Company C		0	0	0	20	30	40	

For Company A, dividends are expected to grow as shown for six years and then either go higher or stay at $10. If you had as much confidence in receiving these dividends as you had in receiving bank interest, you would presumably be willing to pay more than $100 for a share of stock of Company A. Again, how much more is related to the confidence that these estimated dividend payments will actually come to pass. The problem is that one almost always has less confidence in receiving dividends from a company than getting interest from a bank. Also, as one looks further out in time, confidence in earnings and dividend estimates gets lower and lower, whereas confidence in bank interest remains fairly high.

For the sake of the discussion, assume Company A will continue to pay a dividend of $10 for every year in the future after the sixth year and that investor confidence in Company A's dividend-paying ability is as high as confidence in a bank's interest-paying ability. In that case, Company A would be worth $200 per share at the end of six years. Why? Because a $10 return (dividend) per year on a $200 investment is identical to a $5 return per year on a $100 investment. Therefore, what would you be willing to pay now for a stock with Company A's dividend expectations and a "known" value of $200 at the end of six years? Obviously, more than $100. If the future amount and timing of dividends is known with 100 percent confidence, and assuming the interest rate stays at 5%, the value the stock is worth today can be figured out mathematically.[1] The math is beyond this book, but under these assumptions a share of stock in Company A works out to be worth $187. In the real world, however, there is never 100 percent certainty, so the stock would presumably sell for less than $187, given these best-guess dividend estimates.

Company B is expected to pay even higher dividends over six years and therefore a share of its stock should sell for more than a share of

---

1 We are ignoring tax consequences.

Company A's stock, provided there is similar confidence in the dividend estimates, and a similar expectation for receiving a steady dividend (in this case, $21 per year) in each year beyond the sixth year. Company C pays no dividend today and is not expected to for three years, but then its dividend-paying power will be much higher than Company A or B. Would you pay more today for a share of Company C or Company B? Once again, the answer depends to an important degree on your confidence that the dividends will actually be received, and, of course, the further out in the future, the lower your confidence.

In this example we talked about dividends, but we said earlier that the price of the stock is related to its expected earnings. Wall Streeters generally talk about earnings because it is presumed that what a company earns is a good measure of what it can pay as dividends. The more a company earns, the more it can presumably pay in dividends. In reality, dividends are not paid from earnings but are paid from cash. In a given year, a company may earn nothing—or even lose money—but choose to pay the dividend anyway, provided, of course, it has the cash available to do so. Thus, if a company is losing money in a given year and still pays the dividend, we might say (from an accounting point of view) that the dividend was paid out of retained earnings rather than current earnings. However, if a company is losing money over a period of years and sees no immediate expectation of a good profit, it is unlikely that it would continue to pay a dividend and deplete all its cash reserve. It is common practice today for a company to maintain a dividend for a few quarters, or even a year or more, if management believes that earnings will only be low, or a loss, for a short period. But over a period of years, it is generally presumed that if there is not a continuing flow of earnings, there cannot be a continuing flow of dividends.

Remember that when a dividend is declared and paid, it is deducted from *Cash* on the left side of the balance sheet and deducted from *Retained earnings* on the right. The cash account reflects the actual dollars belonging to the company, and the retained earnings account is just an accounting entry (see Chapter 2 for review).

Price-to-Earnings Ratio

There are no rules about how much one should pay for any given amount of earnings per share, or dividends per share. In the example from Table 4.1 it is not clear whether Company C or Company B is worth more today. Only by long experience of studying the relationship between the price of a stock per share and its expected earnings per share, called the *price-to-earnings ratio*, does one begin to develop a feeling for what a stock is really "worth."

$$\text{Price - to - earnings ratio} = \frac{\text{stock price}}{\text{earnings per share}}$$

If we assume the stock is selling at $100 per share and the earnings per share are $10, then the price-to-earnings ratio, often referred to as the price-earnings ratio, or just the P/E, would be "ten times," or just "ten."

$$P/E = \frac{\$100}{10} = 10\times$$

At this point, however, we are all well ahead of our story. We will return to this ratio in Chapter 18.

Book Value Per Common Share

This is simply the book value, defined in Chapter 1, divided by the number of shares outstanding.

$$\text{Book value} = \frac{\text{Total assets} - \text{Total liabilities}}{\text{Number of shares}}$$

$$= \frac{\$140,000 - \$50,000}{500 \text{ shs.}} = \frac{\$90,000}{500 \text{ shs.}} = \$180 \text{ / share}$$

This ratio tells you about how much money each share of common stock could be expected to receive if the company were liquidated. When a company is liquidated, it means all assets are sold and the money received is initially used to pay off the debts (liabilities). Then, if there is any money left over, it is split up among the common stockholders in proportion to how many shares of stock each owns. As a practical matter, in the case of a liquidation, after all the debts are paid off, it is unlikely that the stockholders would realize book value. The exact figure of $180/share assumes that each of the assets could be sold for exactly the value at which it is carried on the books (on the balance sheet.) Normally, however, when a company is liquidated, its inventories are sold for less than their value on the books. If the plant and equipment are well used and worn, they might be sold for much less than their book value. On the other hand, an efficiently operating plant might sell for more than its book value because another company buying the plant would be able to save all the costs of building it. Land is often worth more than what it originally cost.

When a company is liquidated, the amount of money raised selling off the assets is sometimes not enough to pay off all the liabilities. In this case it is usually known in advance which liabilities get paid off first. Recall that the bank and the insurance company who made loans to JMC both wanted to be paid first in the event of liquidation, but JMC told the insurance company that it had given the bank first priority. Similarly, the priority of all other liabilities is usually predetermined, either by negotiation, as with the bank and insurance company, or by law. The law in most states specifies that in the event of liquidation the first priorities are any back wages owed to employees and any taxes owed.

Liquidation can occur either voluntarily, because the board of directors decides to do it, or more likely because the company is bankrupt. Bankruptcy usually occurs when a company is unable to pay a debt or debts that are due. This debt can be a bank loan, an interest payment, an account payable to a supplier, or any other debt. The party owed the money can go to court and ask that the company be legally declared bankrupt, or as sometimes happens, the company voluntarily goes to court to declare bankruptcy. We will discuss bankruptcy briefly in Chapter 10.

Even ignoring the value in bankruptcy, it is important to understand book value per common share because some investors like to use this ratio as a benchmark against which to measure the price of stock. While most stocks sell for more than book value, some stocks sell at slightly below their book value, perhaps as much as 25% below. However, book value per share is often thought of as a price below which a stock will not fall for long, for the following reason: If the book value of a company were $10 per share and its stock was selling for $4, someone could attempt to buy all the stock and voluntarily liquidate the company, thereby realizing a $6 per share profit. In practice, this does not happen often to a public company with widely held stock (many stockholders), but it is a real enough possibility that many stocks do seem to stop going down when the stock is selling well below book value—say, 25 to 50 percent below. When a stock does go that far below book value, it often does not stay there long because the low price attracts buyers.

Yield

The yield on a common stock is defined as the dividend received by the investor divided by the price of the stock. The dividend received usually refers to the dollar amount of dividends expected to be received over the next 12 months. Since the yield also depends on the price, it is important to know what price you are talking about. If a stock pays a $5 dividend per year and the price of the stock is $100 today, the yield to the investor today is 5 percent.

$$\frac{\text{Dividend}}{\text{Stock price}} = \frac{\$5}{\$100} = 5\%$$

If the current price of the stock is $83, the yield is 6 percent.

$$\frac{\text{Dividend}}{\text{Stock price}} = \frac{\$5}{\$83} = 6\%$$

However, an investor who purchased the stock at $50 a few years ago might say his yield, based on his purchase price of $50, is 10 percent.

$$\frac{\text{Dividend}}{\text{Stock price}} = \frac{\$5}{\$50} = 10\%$$

When investors talk about the yield on a stock without otherwise specifying, they generally mean the dividend expected over the next 12 months divided by the price of the stock today. Since the price of the stock generally changes daily, the expected yield over the next 12 months also changes daily.

Yield usually refers to the return to an investor. The word occasionally has other uses, but you would know this by the context of the discussion. Bond yield, like stock yield, refers to the return to an investor but is more complicated and will be discussed in Chapter 9.

PROFITABILITY RATIOS

Return on Total Capital Employed in the Business (After Taxes)

Return, in this case, means net profit after taxes. *Capital employed in the business* means the total value of everything under Capitalization on the balance sheet, which for now means long-term debt plus equity. Recall that capitalization may be thought of as the sources of money that bought the capital assets (i.e., the machinery and equipment that the company uses to make its finished goods). Therefore, *return on capital* is a measure of how efficiently the company is able to use its assets to generate profit.

$$\frac{\text{Net profit after tax}}{\text{Total capitalization}} = \frac{\$5,000}{\$120,000} = 4.2\%$$

The return on capital is regarded by many analysts as one of the most important ratios in analyzing a company. By showing how efficiently a company is able to use its assets to generate profit, the analyst has an excellent basis for comparison of two or more companies. Such a comparison is particularly useful for comparing companies in the same industry. For example, if three shoe manufacturers had returns on capital of 12, 8, and 6 percent, respectively, regardless of the size of the companies it could be concluded that the company with the 12 percent return had the potential to be the fastest growing since, proportional to its capital assets, it will be generating the largest amount of cash to use to buy even more capital assets to enable it to keep growing.

The 4.2 percent return on capital just shown was calculated by dividing JMC's net profit for 1991 by the total capital on the balance sheet at the end of 1991. However, the profit earned in 1991 was really earned using the capital that was there at the beginning of the year. Thus the 1991 return-on-capital ratio would be better calculated by dividing the 1991 profit by the capital at the *beginning* of the year, rather than at the end of the year. In this example we were unable to do that because we did not know the total capital at the beginning of the year. If we had the information available, we would divide the 1991 net profit by the total capital on the December 31, 1990, balance sheet. (The total capital at the end of 1990 is, of course, the same as the total capital at the beginning of 1991.) This ratio would be considered more accurate than the 4.2% calculated. Some analysts prefer to use the *average total capital*, found by averaging the total capital at the beginning and end of the year.

Return on Common Shareholders' Equity

This ratio is very similar in meaning to return on total capital. In this case, it is presumed that part of the measure of the efficiency of a company is its ability to borrow money (long-term) to help make the company grow. A company usually cannot borrow money unless it has a good equity base to begin with (i.e., has a high proportion of equity relative to the amount of debt it wishes to borrow). Thus, the profits earned by the use of assets, whether these assets were bought with equity money or debt money, are really all a return to the fact that the equity money was there in the first place.

$$\frac{\text{Net profit after tax}}{\text{Stockholders' equity}} = \frac{\$5,000}{\$90,000} = 5.6\%$$

Like the return-on-capital ratio, the return on stockholders' equity ratio would be better calculated by dividing the return (the profit) by the equity at the beginning of the year rather than the equity at the end of the year.

Pretax Profit Margin

The pretax profit margin, also called the *pretax return on sales*, is the profit before taxes divided by the total sales for the same period.

$$\frac{\text{Pretax profit}}{\text{Sales}} = \frac{\$10,000}{\$100,000} = 10\%$$

Like the previous two ratios, profit margin is also a measure of the efficiency of a company. If two companies of roughly the same size, which sell the same products, have differing profit margins, the one with the greater margin is probably the more efficiently managed. Again, the company with the highest margin is likely to be the fastest growing since it is able to generate the most cash to plow back into the business.

Within a given industry, the company with the highest pretax profit margin is also likely to be the safest investment because, if sales or profitability were to decline, the company that started with the higher profit margin might only have its profit reduced; but the company that had a low profit margin to begin with could show a loss and eventually go out of business.

Return on Sales After Tax

This is also called the *profit margin after taxes* or just *net profit margin*. It has about the same meaning as the pretax profit margin. The only case where it would make a difference when comparing two companies is if the two companies had differing tax rates. When the companies being compared have approximately the same tax rate, the analyst can use either the pretax or after-tax profit margin with the same comparative results.

Tax Rate or Effective Tax Rate

The tax rate is the actual tax paid divided by the pretax profit.

$$\frac{\text{Tax paid}}{\text{Pretax profit}} = \frac{\$5,000}{\$10,000} = 50\%$$

The term arises because corporate tax laws are so complex that even though the ordinary tax rate on income might be 35 percent, by the time all the additions (e.g., surtaxes) and subtractions (e.g., deductions, credits) have been figured in, it is unlikely that any company will actually be paying precisely 35 percent.

FINANCIAL CONDITION RATIOS

The previous five ratios relate primarily to the profitability of the company (i.e., its ability to generate new cash). Another set of important ratios relates to the financial condition or solvency of the company. Even a company with high potential profitability is of little investment worth if it is about to run into debts greater than it can afford to pay. The financial ratios that follow help to assess the ability of the company to meet its cash needs in the future.

Current Ratio

This is defined as current assets divided by current liabilities.

$$\frac{\text{Current assets}}{\text{Current liabilities}} = \frac{\$80,000}{\$20,000} = 4{:}1$$

The current ratio is a measure of the company's ability to pay off its short-term liabilities. Recall that current assets are those expected to be converted into cash within a year. Current liabilities are those that must be paid within one year. Since, in the normal course of business, current assets are continually being added (inventory, accounts receivable) and current liabilities are continually being paid off, the current ratio can be regarded more generally as a measure of the company's ability to meet day-to-day needs. An old rule of thumb is that a current ratio of two to one (2:1) is a minimum safety margin, but that is not particularly meaningful today. The ratio varies a lot, depending on the nature of a given company's business. An electric utility, for example, has little day-to-day fluctuation in its costs. Since utility costs are so predictable in advance, there is little need to keep extra cash around beyond what is known to be needed. When a current ratio is very low, say 0.2:1, it could indicate that the company will need to go and borrow money in the near future. Again, this would vary from company to company.

Quick Ratio or Acid Test

The quick ratio is defined as current assets, less inventories, divided by current liabilities.

$$\frac{\text{Current assets} - \text{Inventory}}{\text{Current liabilities}} = \frac{\$80{,}000 - \$40{,}000}{\$20{,}000} = 2{:}1$$

The quick ratio, like the current ratio, is a measure of the company's ability to pay off debt in the short run. This assumes that, if the company were forced to pay off its debt in a hurry, it would not have time to sell inventory. The rule of thumb is that a quick ratio of 1:1 or better would be considered good. Again, this will vary from company to company, depending on individual circumstances. A company could have a quick ratio of well under 1:1 and be in good financial shape.

Cash Ratio

The cash ratio is cash plus marketable securities divided by current liabilities.

$$\frac{\text{Cash} + \text{Marketable securities}}{\text{Current liabilities}} = \frac{\$5{,}000 + \$25{,}000}{\$20{,}000} = 1.5{:}1$$

This is merely a more stringent version of the quick ratio, or acid test.

The significance of the last three ratios lies not so much in the actual ratios, since they vary widely from company to company, especially companies in different industries, but in the changes that occur over a period of time in the same company. If a financial analyst saw the figures in Table 4.2, she would immediately conclude that the financial status of the company was weakening, and it might need to raise some outside money, either by borrowing or by selling stock.

Table 4.2 Ratios of XYZ Company over Time		1991	1992	1993	1994
	Current ratio	$\frac{2.4}{1}$	$\frac{2.5}{1}$	$\frac{1.2}{1}$	$\frac{0.7}{1}$
	Quick ratio	$\frac{1.1}{1}$	$\frac{0.9}{1}$	$\frac{0.6}{1}$	$\frac{0.5}{1}$
	Cash ratio	$\frac{0.8}{1}$	$\frac{0.8}{1}$	$\frac{0.4}{1}$	$\frac{0.3}{1}$

This would be a flag telling her something is wrong in the company. She would try to confirm this by looking at the profitability ratios and seeing if they, too, were declining. She would also ask the company officers what has caused this deterioration in financial position. Often the company officers will explain things that the analyst cannot read from the financial statements.

Inventory-to-Sales Ratio

A company's inventory is always turning over. That is, old inventory is constantly being sold, and new inventory is constantly being added. A company likes to have enough inventory on hand so that it can fill all its customer's orders, but it does not like to have more than it needs because it costs money to carry the extra inventory. Companies learn over time about how much inventory they should carry to balance these needs. The actual inventory level in a company will vary around the desired level, as shipments to customers pick up and slow down, and as new inventory is manufactured or purchased. To be sure there is enough inventory, most companies need to schedule their manufacturing and inventory purchasing well in advance. As a result, if sales to customers suddenly slow down unexpectedly, a company can end up with far more inventory than it needs before it can stop the manufacturing process or purchasing of raw materials. Such a buildup of inventory can be an early warning to investors that there might be something wrong. On the other hand, a buildup of inventory would be expected if the company's sales were growing, and would not be an indication of a problem. So the best way to watch the inventory level is to look at it in relation to the company's *sales*. In the case of JMC, the inventory-to-sales ratio at the end of 1991 was as follows:

$$\frac{\text{Inventory}}{\text{Sales}} = \frac{\$40,000}{\$100,000} = 40\%$$

Like many other ratios, one year by itself is hard to interpret, but watching it over a period of time can reveal potential problems. Suppose, for example, JMC has inventory-to-sales ratios as follows:

	1990	1991	1992	1993	1994
Inventory-to-sales ratio	43%	40%	46%	41%	65%

A financial analyst looking at these ratios would want to know immediately if there was a good reason for the inventory buildup in 1994. An acceptable reason might be that JMC had announced a new line of improved mousetraps that was expected to lead to higher sales and profits in 1995 and beyond, but that announcement caused customers to cancel their orders for traps in 1994. With this explanation, the stock might be attractive to buy. Without a good explanation from the company, it is possible that investors will never know the real reason for the inventory buildup. But it might be that another company is making a better mouse-trap, or is selling traps cheaper than JMC, and JMC's business is being hurt. If this were the reason, JMC stock could be headed down and should be sold. Although we do not know if this is the reason, in the absence of a satisfying explanation, we as investors are better off assuming the worst and selling the stock.

Some analysts, instead of looking at the inventory-to-sales ratio, turn it upside down and look at the sales-to-inventory ratio. Looked at this way, it is called the *inventory turnover ratio*. Using the same inventory and sales numbers used to calculate the earlier percentages, the inventory turnover ratio for the same years would look as follows:

	1990	1991	1992	1993	1994
Sales-to-inventory ratio *or* Inventory turnover ratio	2.3x	2.5x	2.2x	2.4x	1.5x

In the language of Wall Street, we would say that JMC's *inventory turns* slowed sharply in 1994, indicating a potential problem.

When calculating either inventory-to-sales, or the inventory turnover ratio, some investors use *cost of goods sold* instead of *sales*. This is because the sales level can sometimes change just because the company's selling prices changed, and this could distort the ratio. Since the cost of goods sold comes from the inventory that was actually sold, it is a more accurate reflection of the amount of inventory that was sold, and therefore gives a more accurate ratio.

Accounts Receivable-to-Sales Ratio

Like the previous ratio, the ratio of accounts receivable to sales can be an indication that something is wrong at the company. This ratio is also best watched over a period of time. JMC's receivables-to-sales ratio at the end of 1991 was as follows:

$$\frac{\text{Accounts receivable}}{\text{Sales}} = \frac{\$10,000}{\$100,000} = 10\%$$

If this ratio stayed at about the same level over a period of time, it would not tell us anything. But if the ratio suddenly jumped to a much higher number, it might indicate that customers were not paying their bills, and that, in turn, could mean that JMC would be unable to pay its accounts payable, interest, and the like, and could be headed for bankruptcy. Thus, if you as an investor see the receivables-to-sales ratio getting too high, you should try to find out the reason for it, and if there is not a satisfying explanation, you should sell the stock.

DEBT AND INTEREST RATIOS

The next two financial ratios relate directly to the ability of the company to raise more money if needed.

Interest Coverage Ratio

The interest coverage ratio, sometimes called times-interest-earned or earnings coverage ratio, is a measure of the company's ability to meet its interest charges. If a company owing money were unable to meet its interest charges when due, the bank or person to whom the interest and loan was owed often has the right to demand that the company pay off not just the interest but the entire loan as well. If the company cannot meet this obligation, it risks being forced into bankruptcy. Thus, investors must watch a company's finances closely to make sure it will be able to meet all its interest and principal repayments on schedule.

The interest coverage ratio answers two questions: (1) How much money is available to pay interest? and (2) How many times larger is the available amount than it needs to be? In other words, how safely is the interest covered? Since interest is paid with cash, we could simply look at the cash on the balance sheet to see if it is enough to cover interest payable. But that really is not satisfactory because, if a company used all its cash to pay interest, the company would be unable to continue operating. What we are really interested in is the ability of the company to generate sufficient cash over a period of time to meet its interest payments over the same period. Thus, the way this ratio is usually calculated is to look at the income statement to see how much money came in and how much money had to go out before interest was paid. The difference is how much money was earned that is available to pay interest. The calculation is usually done using a full year's results, either the past year, or the expected results for the current year, or some future year.

Ratio calculation		
Sales	$100,000	(Came in)
Less: Cost of goods sold	−70,000	(This money had to be spent or there would be no products to sell)
Less: Selling, general and administrative expense	−18,000	(This money also had to be spent or the company could not function)
Money available to pay interest	$ 12,000	

Therefore, there is $12,000 *available* to pay interest, and interest is "covered" six times (6x).

$$\frac{\text{Money available to pay interest}}{\text{Total interest}} = \frac{\$12,000}{\$2,000} = 6\times$$

Note that *taxes* do not enter into the calculation. This is because interest charges are deducted *before* pretax profit and taxes are calculated. Thus, if interest charges were $12,000 in this example, there would be no pretax profit and therefore no taxes to be paid.

While the ratio calculation is perfectly correct and shows you exactly what you are calculating, it is usually presented differently in the financial press. Note that this statement says exactly the same thing in a different way:

$$\frac{\text{Earnings before interest and taxes}}{\text{Total interest}} = \frac{\$12,000}{\$2,000} = 6\times$$

In the language of Wall Street, interest coverage is 6 times (6x). This means pretax, pre-interest earnings ($12,000) would have to fall to one-sixth of its existing level before the company would be in jeopardy.

With interest covered 6 times, this company probably would be able to borrow a limited amount of additional money without too much difficulty. But if interest were covered 44 times (for example, earnings of $88,000 before interest and taxes, and interest charges of $2,000), the analyst would know that the company could borrow money very easily and would be able to do so at a lower interest rate than the company with earnings coverage of only 6 times. On the other hand, if interest were covered only 2 times, and if perhaps the current and quick ratios were weak or deteriorating, the analyst would suspect that this company might be in trouble and could have difficulty borrowing additional money.

In addition to interest coverage, many investors also use a similar ratio called the *fixed charge coverage ratio*. This ratio is calculated much like the interest coverage ratio; but, in addition to interest, it also takes into account certain other fixed charges, such as fixed lease payments and perhaps some other minor items. JMC is not leasing any assets so we will not do that calculation here.

Debt to Total Capitalization

This usually refers to long-term debt only, divided by total capitalization.

$$\frac{\text{Long-term debt}}{\text{Total capitalization}} = \frac{\$30,000}{\$120,000} = 25\%$$

The less debt already in the total capitalization, the more easily (i.e., at lower interest) the company will be able to borrow money. What constitutes a "safe" ratio depends, again, on the nature of the company and its industry. An electric utility, for example, where earnings are very predictable, can easily borrow money above a 50 percent debt/total capital ratio, even if interest coverage is low. However, a company in which earnings fluctuate widely may have trouble borrowing more than 30 percent of its total capitalization, primarily because the ability to cover interest or to meet sinking-fund payments might be seriously impaired in a year when earnings are low.

5

Going Public

A common difficulty of students trying to understand the stock market is the confusion between the company's stock and stock of the company that is owned by individuals (or mutual funds, trusts, or other financial institutions). The confusion is best cleared up by pointing out that both categories are identical. All of a company's stock is owned by someone.

Shares of stock merely represent percentages of ownership in a company. The company has no stock of its own. It cannot own itself. A company may buy back its stock from individuals (or financial institutions) with the company's money, but that stock, called *treasury stock*, no longer represents partial ownership of the company. These treasury shares may not be voted by the company at stockholders' meetings and they do not receive dividends. Such shares are without value unless reissued by the company.

The statement, "JMC, Inc., has 500 shares outstanding," doesn't mean JMC, Inc., has them. It means JMC ownership is divided into 500 equal parts, each share representing one five-hundredth. Individuals or other *persons*[1] own them. It would be clearer to say, "JMC, Inc., has 500 shares

---

1 *Person* is a more general term that includes individual people as well as organizations such as mutual funds, pension funds, insurance companies, trust companies, and the like. From here on, when we talk about a "person" buying or selling stock, we mean any such organization or individual person.

outstanding, which are owned by persons." If some of the persons who owned the stock sold their shares to other persons, it simply means that part of the ownership of the company has changed hands. Regardless of the price at which the stock changed hands, there is no change in any of the company's accounts. There are still only 500 shares outstanding. The Common stock at par value and Additional paid-in capital accounts do not change. Those figures only represent the total amount of money that was paid into the company when each share of stock was issued *by the company* to its *first* owner. By way of analogy, if I buy a new Oldsmobile, the money goes to General Motors. If I then sell my Oldsmobile to my neighbor, he pays me. General Motors never sees the money that my neighbor paid me. That car can change ownership every day and it has no effect on the financial statement of General Motors.

JMC is currently a private company. This means that none of its stock has yet been registered with the Securities and Exchange Commission. When a company is private, it is limited by law to having only a small number of shareholders (investors). The Securities and Exchange Acts require that before stock can be sold to the public (a lot of investors) it must first be registered with the SEC. Thus, prior to going through the registration process (discussed shortly), JMC is limited in its ability to sell new shares of stock, and JMC's 12 stockholders are also limited in their ability to sell their stock to other investors. By going public—that is, registering shares of stock with the SEC—it becomes much easier for both the company to sell new stock and for existing private shareholders to sell their stock.

Thus, there are two reasons why the company may want to go public:

1. The company wishes to raise more capital, and does not want to borrow or have another private stock offering. In this case, the company writes up new shares (provided they have been authorized by the stockholders) and sells them to new (or old) investors. All the money from this sale goes to the company.

2. Existing stockholders want to sell their stock and raise money for themselves. In this case, all the money from the sale of the stock goes directly to the stockholders who sold their stock.

In the latter case, we say it is the existing shareholders who are "bringing the company public." Of course, it is the company officers who must file the registration statements with the SEC, but the shareholders usually have specific rights to force the company officers to do so. Typically, when a new company is formed, the investors who are putting up their money in exchange for the initial "private" stock decide among themselves, right at the beginning, when and under what circumstances those stockholders can force the company to go public. For example, the initial stockholders may have agreed that "any time after the company has been profitable for at least two years, and if a majority of us are in favor, then we will have the right to have company officers take all the necessary steps for us to have a public offering." The agreement might also add something like, "Each of us may sell up to 30 percent of his or her shares at the time of this offering and up to another 30 percent of the shares at the time of the next offering, which cannot be forced for at least two years. In addition, however, if the company itself is offering new shares to the public *at any time*, then each of us may also join the offering and sell up to 20 percent of our already outstanding shares." Every company's agreement with its initial stockholders is different.

REGISTERING THE STOCK

For whichever of the above reasons the company is going public, the shares to be sold to the public must first be registered with the SEC. This means the company must send to the SEC a statement of (1) how many shares of stock will be sold, (2) whether it is new shares being sold by the company or already outstanding shares being sold by current stockholders to other individuals, or some of each, and (3) certain financial and other information about the company to help potential investors (buyers) make a proper evaluation of the risks involved in buying this stock. This information filing is called an "S-1." A summary of the most relevant information is put together in a small booklet called a *prospectus*. The SEC examines the S-1 and the prospectus. If it is not satisfied that enough information has been presented, it requests more. The SEC does not attest that the information presented is truthful, or even that it is adequate for investors to make an informed decision. But when the SEC gives its permission for the stock to be sold to the public, investors generally assume there is enough information presented that, if truthful, an investor should be able to make an informed decision about the worth of the stock. If the information is found to be fraudulent, however, the people who bought the stock based on the information contained in the prospectus may be able to return the stock to the company and have their money refunded. Furthermore, the perpetrators of the fraud are subject to criminal prosecution. While the prospectus is pending with the SEC, the company is allowed to print and distribute a *preliminary prospectus*, sometimes called a *red herring*. This name derives from the fact that the company is required to print in red ink on the front page that this is only a preliminary prospectus and is subject to change.

When the SEC is satisfied that the prospectus is sufficiently informative, it declares the registration to be "effective." Once the registration has been declared effective, both the company and the stockholders who are selling their shares are free to sell all or just some of the shares that were just registered. They may not sell any other shares. Recall that the prospectus had to state how many shares each stockholder or the company was registering. Once the registered shares have been sold, those shares are registered *forever* and may be sold from one investor to another every day without another prospectus.[2]

The newly registered shares do not have to be sold right away, although they most often are. A registration statement can remain effective for anywhere from 60 days to over a year, depending on circumstances. Often a company can amend a registration statement with updated information to keep it "effective," but eventually the effective time lapses and, at that point, any of the registered shares that were not sold are no longer deemed registered, and they cannot be sold until a new registration statement is filed and declared effective. The reason a registration lapses is that, with the passage of time, the old information becomes out of date and potential investors no longer have enough current information to make an informed decision.

There are some exceptions to the formal registration procedure. First, under Rule 144, almost any stockholder who has held unregistered stock for at least two years may sell some shares to the public without registering them—provided that the amount of shares being sold is under 1% of the outstanding shares of the company and that certain conditions are met. After three years, stockholders who are not officers or directors of the company can sell all their shares to the public without any restrictions. Once such unregistered stock is sold under Rule 144, it would then be free to trade forever, as if it had been registered. Second, under Regulation S, a company can sell unregistered stock to offshore (non-American) buyers, and that stock can be sold freely among offshore buyers. Under certain circumstances, that stock can eventually come back to the U.S. market and be treated as registered stock.

---

2 There are some unusual circumstances when already-registered shares must be registered again. These are discussed later in this chapter.

PRIMARY AND SECONDARY OFFERINGS, AND GOING PUBLIC

When a company sells new stock, either privately (unregistered stock) or publicly (registered stock), the sale of stock is called a *primary offering*. When existing shareholders sell their already-outstanding stock, either to other private individuals or to the public, it is called a *secondary offering*. Therefore, in a primary offering, the money from the sale of the stock goes to the company. In a secondary offering, the money from the sale of the stock goes to the stockholders who are selling their stock. If this distinction is clear, it should be apparent that there is no limit to the number of primary offerings a company can have. Similarly, there is no limit to the number of secondary offerings a "company" can have. "Company" is in quotes because it is not really the company having the secondary offering; rather, it is the stockholders. It would really be more accurate to say: "There is no limit to the number of secondary transactions that can take place in a company's stock."

The first time that registered shares of a company are sold to the public, whether as a primary or secondary offering, we say the company is "going public," or "having its initial public offering." The company may subsequently have many more public offerings, but none of those subsequent public offerings means the company is going public. The company is already "public" as a result of its initial (or first) public offering, sometimes called its IPO. When a company does a subsequent public offering (after its initial public offering), we could simply say the company is "doing another primary offering," or is "selling a new issue."

By the precise definition of *secondary*, every time a person sells one or more shares of stock to another person, he or she has made a secondary sale. Therefore, every purchase or sale of stock, on a stock exchange or over the counter, is technically a secondary sale. The word *secondary*, however, is not normally used that way. Shares that are sold from one person to another are just called *trades*.

In Wall Street jargon, a *secondary offering* most often refers to blocks of unregistered stock that are owned by individuals or financial institutions that are being registered and sold to the public. For example, if Mr. Jones or his original four investors in Jones Mousetrap Company decide to have their stock registered and sold to the public, that would be a secondary offering. If their stock was being sold under Rule 144 (without a registration), that would still be a secondary offering because the stock is already outstanding. Similarly, financial institutions also may have blocks of unregistered stock that they wish to register and sell to the public as a secondary offering. Such unregistered stock would have originally been purchased from the company as a *private placement* (discussed in the next section).

Less frequently, a secondary may refer to re-registering previously registered stock. For example, if a large fund or individual holds a major block of stock, usually more than 10 percent of the company's total outstanding shares, and wishes to sell it all at once to the public, the holder may first need to have the company file a prospectus with the SEC. This usually occurs when the holder of the stock is an *insider*, which means he or she has access to information about the company that the general public does not. While a prospectus obviously cannot reveal every bit of information that an insider knows, it is theoretically required to reveal at least "all material information" about the company that the prospective buyer would need to make an informed decision about whether or not to buy the stock. This "material disclosure" requirement applies to all prospectuses, whether for stock that is being reregistered or stock being registered for the first time.

Although the usage of *primary* and *secondary* as described here is generally accepted on Wall Street, the term *secondary* has also come to be used by some people to mean any public offering of new stock by a company that occurs after the initial public offering. Correct usage would refer to these subsequent public offerings as *new issues*, or as a second public offering, a third public offering, and so on. Each of these subsequent public offerings of new stock *by the company* would, of course, be a primary offering. Unfortunately, this misuse of the term *secondary* can create confusion, since it may not be clear from context whether a *secondary offering* is, in fact, correctly referring to already outstanding stock, or is incorrectly referring to a primary issue.

PRIVATE PLACEMENTS

A *private placement* occurs when a company sells new, *unregistered* stock to individuals or financial institutions. Such a sale would, of course, be a primary offering because the company is getting the money. A company may prefer to sell a private placement of unregistered stock because it wants to raise money quickly and avoid the time-consuming and costly process of filing a registration statement for a public offering. It is also possible that the company has some information that it does not wish to reveal that would have to be disclosed in a prospectus if the stock were to be registered and offered to the public.

Note that a company can sell a private placement of unregistered stock even though the company is already public. Again, being "public" just means that the company already has *some* public shares outstanding. It does not mean that *all* the company's shares have been registered and are free to trade among the public. While new, privately placed shares are not registered, they still must be authorized by the existing shareholders.

In a private placement of stock, the actual stock certificate usually has a statement stamped on it, called a *legend*, which says that those shares have not been registered and may not be resold unless a registration statement is in effect, or "unless an exemption from such registration is available," such as under Rule 144, previously discussed. Such stock is sometimes called *legend stock*, or *investment letter stock*, or just *letter stock*. The legend also says that the stock has been acquired "for investment." The laws governing the resale of this legend or investment letter stock are not precisely defined; in some cases the law means the stock may be held for a period of as little as four months, and in other cases means it must be held for a period of two or three years before it can be sold without a registration.

DEFINITIONS

- **Primary Offering**—When a company creates new shares and sells them, either publicly or privately, it is a primary offering. In a primary offering, the company receives the money from the sale of the shares.

- **Secondary Offering**—When investors who own shares of a company sell their already outstanding shares to other investors, it is a secondary offering. In a secondary offering, the individuals or institutions who sold the stock get the money, not the company. A secondary offering most often refers to unregistered stock held by investors that is being registered for the first time and sold to the public.

Unfortunately, in recent usage, the word *secondary* has come to also mean any public offering of new shares by the company *after* the initial public offering. These subsequent public offerings *by the company* should more properly be referred to as primary offerings or new issues.

- **Public Offering**—Any time registered stock is being sold, it is a public offering, whether it is a primary or a secondary offering.

- **Initial Public Offering**—The first time that any stock of a company is being sold to the public, it is the company's initial public offering, or IPO. An IPO can be a primary or a secondary, or a combination of both.

- **Private Placement**—Any time unregistered shares are being sold, it is called a private placement or private offering. A private offering will be a primary offering if it is being sold by the company. A private offering will be a secondary offering if already outstanding unregistered shares are being sold from one investor to another.

WHY A COMPANY GOES PUBLIC

Let us now return to why a company goes public. The first reason is that the company wants to raise money. This would lead to an initial public offering that is a primary offering. A second reason would be because some of the existing stockholders want to sell some of their shares to raise money for themselves. This would lead to a public offering that is a secondary offering. In fact, many stock offerings are *combined offerings*, meaning that some of the shares being offered are primary shares being offered by the company, and others are secondary shares being offered by existing shareholders. Let's look more closely at the latter.

Assume Ms. Smith owns 100 shares of JMC and JMC's earnings per share are $10. Assuming the company is paying out 50 percent of earnings as a dividend (i.e., $5 per share per year), Smith will receive a total of $500 per year in dividends. If Smith were to sell the stock, however, she could get more for it than the $5 per share it brings her this year. This is because the purchaser of the stock can look forward to a future stream of hopefully increasing earnings and dividends. The rationale for this was discussed at the beginning of Chapter 4. If it is not familiar to the reader, now would be a good time to review. Let us assume that experienced investors have told Smith that they would be willing to pay $100 per share for JMC stock. If the stock is earning $10 per share and investors are willing to pay $100 per share, we would say the price-to-earnings ratio, or P/E, of the stock is ten (10×).

$$P/E \text{ ratio} = \frac{\text{Price}/\text{share}}{\text{Earnings}/\text{share}} = \frac{\$100}{\$10} = 10\times$$

In other words, investors are willing to pay 10 times current earnings per share (or 20 times the current dividend) for a share of JMC stock. In Wall Street language one would say, "Investors are willing to pay 10 times earnings for JMC," or, "JMC's price-to-earnings ratio is 10×," or, "The investment community will capitalize JMC's earnings at 10 times." Note the use of the word *capitalize*. Again, this is a word with many meanings. In this case, it refers to what price-to-earnings ratio people are willing to pay for a stock.

If Smith sells her hundred shares at $100 a share, she will have a total amount of $10,000 in cash, compared with the $500 per year she might have expected to receive in dividends if she held the stock. This is the main reason why initial stockholders of a company want the company to go public—because the public's willingness to pay a high price-to-earnings ratio enables the original stockholders to receive in cash today what they would not otherwise get for years, if ever, in dividends.

An initial investor does not, of course, need to sell all of her shares to get rich. For that matter, she does not need to sell any. Suppose Ms. Smith chose to hold all of her stock. Instead, assume the company itself, or other individuals, sold stock to the public to raise money. If the public paid $100 per share to the company, and assuming the stock continued to trade at about that price, Smith would know that her stock was "worth" $10,000 because she could sell it for that (after registering it, of course). Knowing this, she could probably borrow money by putting up the stock for collateral.

It is this willingness of stock market investors to pay a high multiple of current earnings (some companies have gone public with P/E ratios of more than 40×) that provides incentive for people with good ideas to start their own companies. Similarly, this incentive causes people with capital to invest in new ventures, as did the four individuals who invested in Jones Mousetrap Company in Chapter 2.

This incentive is also one reason why companies sometimes lose their best people. An engineer with a new idea might get a bonus from his company for the idea, but it is far less than what he will make if he forms his own company and keeps a lot of the stock for himself, as did Jones in JMC. Recall that Jones had only put up one-third of the money but kept 60 percent ownership in the company.

One way that companies are able to prevent their key employees from leaving is to give them company stock options.[3] These options offer individuals a way to make a lot of money in a stock even if they did not put any money into the company at the beginning. Assume, for example, that Ms. Appel is a valued employee of XYZ Corporation, and management of XYZ has given her a stock option on 100 shares of XYZ stock. The stock option may say something like the following:

> Ms. *APPEL* has the right, anytime in the next three years, to purchase from the company 100 shares of stock at $100 per share.

What this says is that Ms. Appel is being offered the right to buy a given number of shares (100 in this case) of XYZ stock *anytime* within a specified period (up to three years in this case) for a price that is decided today ($100 per share). Say, for example, Ms. Appel was given this stock option on January 4, 1994, at which time XYZ's stock was selling at $100 per share. It is now May of 1996 and XYZ's stock has appreciated to $300 per share, which Ms. Appel thinks is as high as it is likely to go before January 4, 1997. Thus, she decides to *exercise* her option. So she calls whomever is administering the plan and says she wishes to exercise her option and buy 100 shares at $100 per share. She can now turn around and sell it the same day at $300, and make a $200 profit per share. Since her option was for 100 shares, she has made a gain of $20,000 on top of her regular salary.

If, however, the stock goes down while she is holding the option, she has lost nothing since she has not paid anything yet and does not have to. In most large companies, management can offer enough shares in options to keep most good employees happy without having to give away a significant portion of the company. Options also help to keep employees because, in most companies' stock option plans, if the employee leaves the company, he or she must forfeit options. Before management can offer any stock options to any employees, however, the company's whole stock option plan must be approved by the stockholders at their annual meeting.

---

3 These are options to buy shares of the company directly from the company, and are not the same thing as publicly traded options one can buy through a stockbroker.

6

JMC Goes Public

In March of 1992, JMC decided business was going so well that it was time to build a second mousetrap factory, to be designated Plant Number 2. Once again, the question arose as to where the money would come from to build the plant. In other words, how would the plant be financed.

With long-term debt comprising 25 percent of total capitalization and earnings coverage of 6 times (6×; see ratio calculations in Chapter 4), it is doubtful that JMC could borrow the $10,000 it needed for the new plant.

A bank or insurance company, which was considering making the loan, might have accepted the 25 percent debt-to-total capitalization ratio and even the 6× earnings coverage, but these figures were computed *before* the loan was to have been made. A potential lender obviously would want to know what the ratios would be *after* the loan had been made. Assuming JMC would have to pay 10 percent interest per year on a $10,000 loan, the annual interest would be $1,000. As a result, the interest coverage would be reduced to 4×.

$$\frac{\text{Annual earnings before interest and taxes}}{\text{Annual interest}} = \frac{\$12,000}{\$2,000 + \$1,000} = \frac{\$12,000}{\$3,000} = 4\times$$

Interest on existing debt ⬑   ⬐ Additional interest on presumed $10,000 debt increase

The debt-to-capitalization ratio would increase to 31 percent.

Old debt ⌐⌐   ⌐ New debt

$$\frac{\text{Debt}}{\text{Capitalization}} = \frac{\$30,000 + \$10,000}{\$120,000 + \$10,000} = \frac{\$40,000}{\$130,000} = 31\%$$

Old capitalization ⌐   ⌐New debt

With this lower earnings coverage and higher debt ratio, Mr. Jones realized that it was unlikely that his small company would be able to get a $10,000 loan. (For large, established companies such as General Motors, these ratios might be acceptable).

Thus, JMC decided it would have to raise more equity money, which is another way of saying, "sell new stock." Since none of the current 12 investors wanted to put any more money into the company (i.e., buy any more stock from the company), it was decided that the company would have to sell stock to the public. It also occurred to some of the 12 stock-holders that, as long as the company was going through the process of registering new stock to sell, they could take advantage of this registration to sell some of *their* stock, too. So, it was decided to register some new shares (primary) as well as some of the already outstanding shares (secondary).

Since neither Jones nor the others knew how to go about selling stock to the public, they consulted Mr. Greenshades, who suggested they contact an investment bank. An investment banking firm has nothing to do with banking in the usual sense of checking accounts and personal loans. Rather, an investment bank is a firm that helps businesses raise money by selling new stock or bonds to either the public or as private placements to financial institutions such as banks and insurance companies.

Jones contacted three investment bankers, all of whom visited the company within the next few weeks. Mr. Gaines, from the firm of Gaines & Wynn, Investment Bankers, Inc., explained to Jones that his firm had brought many companies like JMC public and was quite experienced. Mr. Gaines suggested Jones keep a number of considerations in mind. First, he explained that the price of a stock is at all times related to how well the company has been doing and is expected to do. But within that constraint, there is quite a bit of room for the price to move around.

From his years of experience, Mr. Gaines thought that in the current stock market environment, with JMC's expected growth rate of earnings per share of about 12 percent annually, the stock might be expected to sell at a price-earnings[1] (P/E) ratio of somewhere between 10x and 15x.

---

1 "Price-earnings" ratio, "price-to-earnings" ratio, and "P/E" mean the same thing. We will use them interchangeably.

Therefore, if JMC was expected to earn $2 per share this year, the stock might be expected to sell between $20 and $30 per share. Whether the stock would tend to sell at the low end of this range (or even lower), or at the high end of the range (or even higher) would be hard to predict, but would be related to a number of factors that determine how well the investment community regards JMC stock, including:

1. the company's earnings history—whether earnings growth has been slow or fast, steady, or erratic
2. the growth potential of the company, including the expected growth of the industry it serves
3. the state of the economy and the stock market
4. the market share of the company's products
5. the uniqueness of the company's products—whether it is the only company making these products, or one of several companies making similar products, and subject to price competition that might hurt earnings
6. the amount of debt in the company's capitalization
7. how well company management is regarded
8. whether the company's business is subject to government regulation
9. what price-earnings ratio similar companies sell at
10. the probability that something could go wrong—how likely it is that investors could be surprised by a downturn in earnings when continued earnings growth was expected

Factors such as these, and many others, will impact what price investors are willing to pay for a stock.

DILUTION

Mr. Gaines pointed out that JMC would obviously want to sell its shares for as much as possible, for two reasons: (1) so the selling stockholders could get the most possible money for their shares, and (2) so the company could raise its money selling as few shares as possible so as to give away the least possible percentage ownership of the company (i.e., have the current shareholders suffer the least *dilution*).

Dilution is an important concept in understanding the stock market. Dilution occurs when outstanding shares of stock in a company become worth less as a result of the company's issuing more shares. Look at the following example.

Currently, JMC has 500 shares outstanding and is earning $5,000; thus, it has earnings per share of $10.

$$\frac{\text{Earnings}}{\text{Shares outstanding}} = \frac{\$5,000}{500} = \$10 \,/\, \text{share}$$

Assume the company pays 50 percent of earnings as a dividend, so the dividend per share is $5. Assume also that JMC stock will sell at a price-earnings ratio of 10. Therefore, one share of stock will sell at $100.

EPS		P/E		Stock price
$10	×	10×	=	$100

At first glance, with the stock selling at $100, it appears that JMC would have to sell 100 shares to raise $10,000.

$$100 \text{ shares} \times \$100/\text{share} = \$10,000$$

But adding 100 new shares will lower EPS as follows:

$$\text{EPS} = \frac{\text{Earnings}}{\text{Shares outstanding}} = \frac{\$5,000}{500 + 100} = \frac{\$5,000}{600} = \$8.33\,/\,\text{share}$$

↑ Old shares   ↑ New shares

If the stock sells at a P/E ratio of 10, it would now only sell at $83.33. Therefore, we could say that issuing 100 new shares has *diluted* JMC's earnings from $10.00/share to $8.33, or about 17 percent dilution.

Note also that with the stock at $83, JMC cannot raise $10,000 by selling 100 shares as long as the P/E remains at 10.

EPS		P/E		Stock price		New shares		Money raised
$8.33	×	10×	=	$83	×	100 shares	=	$8,333

Thus, JMC still has to sell more stock to raise the $10,000. But that will lower EPS even further. It turns out that to raise $10,000, 125 new shares must be sold, which produces a 20 percent earnings dilution.

					EPS	P/E	Stock price	New shares	Money raised

$$\text{EPS} = \frac{\$5,000}{500 + 125} = \frac{\$5,000}{625} = \$8 \times 10\times = \$80 \times 125 = \$10,000$$

↑ Old shares   ↑ New shares

The 20 percent dilution reflects the fact that earnings would be $8/share after the new stock was issued, but were $10/share before the new stock was issued. Thus, each of the original 500 shares' earnings was diluted by 20 percent as a result of the issuing of new shares.

If the new stock were to sell at a price-earnings ratio of ten times earnings, it would sell at $80 per share after the new stock was issued, compared to $100 per share before the new stock was issued, a 20 percent decline. Similarly, if the dividend payout ratio remained at 50 percent, the dividend would now have to be reduced to $4 per share, also a 20 percent decline.

The dilution calculations were based on a P/E ratio of 10×. What if the stock were selling at a P/E of twenty times earnings? In that case, it works out that only 56 new shares need to be sold to raise $10,000, and earnings dilution is not as severe.

$$\text{EPS} = \frac{\$5,000}{\underset{\underset{\text{Old shares}}{\uparrow}}{500} + \underset{\underset{\text{New shares}}{\uparrow}}{56}} = \frac{\$5,000}{556} = \overset{\text{EPS}}{\$8.99} \times \overset{\text{P/E}}{20\times} = \overset{\substack{\text{Stock} \\ \text{price}}}{\$180} \times \overset{\substack{\text{New} \\ \text{shares}}}{56} = \overset{\substack{\text{Money} \\ \text{raised}}}{\$10,080}$$

Thus, with a higher price-to-earnings ratio the same amount of money can be raised selling fewer shares. This results in less dilution, only about 10 percent, which lowers earnings to $8.99. Also, if the dividend payout ratio remains at 50 percent, the dividend would be $4.50 per share, instead of the $4.00 per share in the case with the P/E of 10×. This is why current stockholders like to have the highest P/E possible when new shares are being sold (issued).

The dilution calculations here are correct as far as they go, but the calculations did not consider what JMC will do with the $10,000 it raised. The money is intended to be used to build a new mousetrap plant that is expected to generate more earnings. But since it takes time to build a new plant, let's assume that, until the money is needed, JMC invests the $10,000 in U.S. Treasury bills that pay 5 percent interest. If the $10,000 is invested for one year while the plant is being built, it will earn $500 interest. Thus, assuming a P/E of 10×, a more complete dilution calculation would be:

Earnings from mousetrap business ⌐   ⌐ Interest earned

$$\text{EPS} = \frac{\$5,000 + \$500}{\underset{\underset{\substack{\text{Old} \\ \text{shares}}}{\uparrow}}{500} + \underset{\underset{\substack{\text{New} \\ \text{shares}}}{\uparrow}}{125}} = \frac{\$5,500}{625} = \$8.80$$

Under these assumptions, EPS are only diluted from $10.00 to $8.80, or 12 percent, not the 20 percent shown previously. Similarly, the 10 percent dilution calculation, assuming a P/E of 20×, was not exactly correct, either.

In the real world, when a company announces an equity financing (intention to raise money by selling new stock), investment analysts immediately go through these calculations, making assumptions where necessary, to see what the dilution will be and try to judge how it will affect the stock price. If the offering was a total surprise to investors, the stock would be very likely to go down by at least as much as the dilution. If investors thought the financing was being done because the company was having serious problems, the P/E ratio would probably also decline and the stock would fall even further. If the new financing reflected a great new opportunity for the company, the P/E might expand and the stock would go down less than the earnings dilution.

Often, an announcement of an equity offering is not a surprise to investors. Investors who closely watch a company's financial statements can often see in advance that the company will need to raise new cash. Similarly, a company will sometimes tell investors that it would like to do an equity financing sometime in the next year or so. When a financing is expected, the stock price usually adjusts gradually in advance, and the market's reaction when the announcement of the new financing is made may be minor.

An interesting and unusual example of dilution in an equity financing occurred in a Polaroid equity offering a number of years ago. Since Polaroid did not need the money immediately, it invested the money at about 6 percent interest. At the time, Polaroid was selling at a very high P/E, over fifty times earnings. Thus, when analysts did the dilution calculation, it turned out that the interest on the money that Polaroid would receive added so much to earnings that, even with the increased number of shares outstanding, Polaroid actually showed an *increase* in EPS rather than a decrease. This is called *negative dilution*. It is very unusual and only happens when a stock is selling at a very high price-earnings ratio.

Polaroid's earnings per share as reported (before the new equity offering):

$$\frac{\text{Earnings}}{\text{Shares}} = \frac{\$58.9 \text{ Million}}{31.7 \text{ Million}} = \$1.86 / \text{share}$$

Polaroid's earnings per share, adjusting both earnings and shares for the equity offering:

Additional earnings from interest received after investing
the $100MM raised from the equity offering

$$\frac{\text{Earnings}}{\text{Shares}} = \frac{\$58.9 + \$2.7}{31.7 + 1.1} = \frac{\$61.6}{32.8} = \$1.88/\text{share}$$

New shares from the offering

Dilution points to a key concept in the relationship of the stock market to capitalism. We showed earlier that the stock market will pay a higher P/E for a company with faster earnings growth and, therefore, potential dividend growth. Thus, the greater the company's potential growth, the higher the P/E and, therefore, the less dilution that will be suffered in a new stock offering. In the language of Wall Street, a company with a high P/E can do an equity financing (sell new stock) much cheaper (at less dilution) than a company with a low P/E. This seems socially desirable because the high P/E, reflecting a high expected growth rate, implies the market's expectation that this company's products will be in great demand. If a company's products are in great demand, then it indeed seems desirable that the company be able to raise money cheaply in order to expand its ability to make its products and satisfy that demand.

Thus, we see the two sides of the capitalism "coin." On one side are the investors who wish to invest their capital (money) where they see the fastest growth. On the other side are the companies that wish to raise capital. The result is that the companies with successful products (i.e., what consumers want) have the easiest (cheapest) ability to raise money to increase production of those products. So the profit motive is not the *purpose* of capitalism, as some people erroneously believe; rather, the profit motive is a *mechanism* that causes capital to be invested in those areas of the economy that are growing rapidly, reflecting consumers' demands.

SELLING THE STOCK

When a company offers new stock, it can attempt to sell it for whatever price it wants. Obviously, if it is too high, nobody will buy it. If the price of the stock appears unreasonably low, the existing stockholders may try to prevent its sale because their stock is being diluted too much. In the real world, the company, usually with the help of its investment banker, decides on a price that appears likely to attract investors. Then the investment banker's sales team sends out prospectuses and calls customers to see what they are willing to pay for the stock. The actual price can be adjusted up or down as the date of effective registration approaches and market conditions indicate that it was priced too high or could have been priced higher.

Mr. Gaines had now explained why it is desirable from both the company's and current stockholders' points of view to sell the shares for as much as possible. However, Gaines recommended not pricing the stock too high because it might not all be sold, in which case the price would have to come down to sell the remaining shares. In that case, most of the initial buyers would have a loss right away, which is considered undesirable for establishing a good market for a new issue of stock. Conversely, if the stock came (was offered) at an attractive price (i.e., at slightly less than it was "worth"), there would probably be a great demand for the stock and not only would it be sure to be sold, but it would probably rise in price immediately after it was free to trade on the open market. That way, everyone who initially bought the stock would have a profit, and people would remember it favorably as a very successful offering—or as a "hot" issue. This can make it easier for the company to sell additional stock offerings in the future.

Next, Mr. Gaines explained that it was desirable to have an active, stable public market for the stock. This would also make it easier for either JMC or existing shareholders to sell more of their stock on another occasion.

Due to these considerations, Gaines said it was important that the stock be "widely held," or "widely distributed"; that is, there should be a large number of stockholders because, if a large number of people each owned a few shares of the stock rather than a small number of people each owning a large number of shares, it was more likely to produce an active market for the stock. Also, Gaines suggested placing some stock "in strong hands" (i.e., some stock should be sold to financial institutions or investors who have a reputation for holding stock for a while and not selling the minute they see a small profit, or panicking and selling if the stock falls a little). Mr. Gaines explained that his firm had many wealthy individual clients, as well as close contacts with major institutions, and was sure he would have no trouble selling the stock to a wide range of investors.

Jones then asked how much he could get for the stock. Gaines explained that he would first have to study JMC's books (financial records) and the potential growth rate of the company, but from his experience, he judged the public would probably be willing to pay a price-earnings ratio of between 10 and 12 times earnings. Mr. Gaines said he would want a commission of $.50 per share and that his firm would *underwrite* or guarantee to sell the issue. That means that Gaines & Wynn would actually buy the entire issue from JMC and then resell or distribute it to the buyers. This way, if for any reason some of the buyers backed out at the last minute, Gaines & Wynn would be stuck with the stock, and JMC would be paid for all the new shares. Jones liked that idea but thought it only reasonable to meet the other two investment bankers anyway.

Mr. Slick then arrived, representing the firm of New Ventures, Inc. New Ventures had a reputation for dealing with highly speculative stock issues. For example, many of the companies New Ventures had brought public had gone bankrupt within a year or two and the stockholders had lost all their money. Other issues, however, had made millions for New Ventures' clients. Jones was afraid, therefore, that the type of client Slick dealt with would be a very nervous stockholder, and the panic selling that Mr. Gaines had referred to might be more likely to occur if Slick's clients were the initial stockholders. Jones, of course, had every bit of confidence that JMC would not go bankrupt and, therefore, even if the stock did at some time go down, he presumed it would go back up as soon as the investment community realized there was nothing wrong with JMC. Nevertheless, it is this type of wild fluctuation in the price of a stock that may scare away some potential buyers of the stock who prefer more stable, steady prices.

Slick was quite aware of his company's reputation, and he explained to Jones that, besides the highly speculative companies New Ventures had brought public, it had also done offerings for many more stable companies such as JMC. Slick also pointed out that New Ventures had a large number of clients and for a company such as JMC it would place (sell) the stock with the more stable customers. Slick said he thought JMC could be brought public at about 14 times earnings and that New Ventures would ask a $.60 per share commission.

Jones stopped to think. "If Slick takes us public (sells the stock to the public) at 14 times earnings, rather than 10 times earnings as Gaines suggested, then we will get more money for each share and have less dilution, so it would certainly be worth paying the slightly higher commission." Slick also said that since JMC was a small company and did not make a particularly glamorous product, it might be hard to sell the stock. Thus, New Ventures would only take the deal on a "best-efforts" basis. This means New Ventures would sell as much of the stock as it could, but if it was unable to sell all the stock, it wanted to return the unsold shares to JMC (or the original owners) rather than buy it itself. Slick's reason was that New Ventures was a much smaller firm than Gaines & Wynn and had much less capital that it was willing to risk if it had to retain some JMC stock in the event the offering was not completely sold out (i.e., sold to the public).

Jones, being conservative, decided he would rather take slightly less money for his stock but have the offering *underwritten* or guaranteed. Thus, Slick was told the best-efforts basis was unsatisfactory and, after being thanked for his trouble, was shown the door.

The third investment banking firm was quite similar to Gaines & Wynn but would only underwrite or guarantee the offering at nine times earnings, less commission. Also, Gaines & Wynn not only had a better reputation and quality image but offered a number of financial consulting services that the other firms did not. Finally, Gaines & Wynn could do more to help JMC stock later on because of its stock brokerage and investment research contacts with a large number of institutional customers. So Jones called Mr. Gaines and asked him to handle the offering. Gaines immediately came out to JMC's office and examined the books.

SPLITTING THE STOCK

One of his first suggestions was a 10-for-1 stock split in order to get wider distribution. If the stock were split 10 for 1, that means each stockholder who had one share would be given nine additional shares, so he or she would now have 10 shares. Each of the ten shares after the split, however, would only be worth one-tenth as much as the shares before the split. Instead of having 500 shares outstanding, JMC would now have 5,000. There would be no change in any of the company's accounts. The only difference would be that, instead of having 500 shares outstanding, each representing one five-hundredth of ownership in the company, there would now be 5,000 shares outstanding and each would represent one five-thousandth of ownership in the company. Actually, there would be two minor changes on the balance sheet as follows: first, the stockholders (in this case the current 12) would have to vote to authorize at least 5,000 shares; second, if the stock is being split 10 for 1, the par value would have to be divided by 10. Thus, the stockholders' equity portion of the balance sheet would now look like this:

Stockholders' Equity	
Paid-in capital	
Common stock at par value ($.10)	
(authorized 5,000 shares,	
outstanding 5,000 shares)	$ 500
Capital surplus	4,500
Retained earnings	85,000
Total stockholders' equity	$90,000

Compare this to the stockholders' equity section of JMC's balance sheet at the end of Chapter 3. The reason for the change in par value is this: The number of shares outstanding multiplied by the par value must always equal the dollar figure in the *Common stock at par value* account. Since no new money comes in because of a stock split, the $500 figure remains the same. Thus, with 5,000 shares now outstanding and $500 in the *Common stock* account, the par value must be reduced to $.10 to make the figures balance.

The reason for the stock split, Gaines explained, was to get wider distribution. JMC currently had 500 shares outstanding. If JMC sold an additional 125 shares, it would raise the desired $10,000, *but only 125 shares would be in the hands of the public.* This would be a very thin market, exactly opposite the wide distribution Gaines had recommended. However, if the stock split 10 for 1 before the public offering, the $10,000 could be raised just as easily, but there would be 1,250 shares in public hands rather than 125 shares; hence more stockholders, hence wider distribution.[2]

After a 10-for-1 split, but before the new issue, the earnings per share would be reduced to $1.

$$\frac{\text{Earnings}}{\text{Shares}} = \frac{\$5,000}{500 \text{ shares} \times 10} = \frac{\$5,000}{5,000 \text{ shares}} = \$1.00 / \text{share}$$

After both the stock split and the new issue of 1,250 shares, the EPS would be $.80 per share.

$$\frac{\text{Earnings}}{\text{Shares}} = \frac{\$5,000}{500 \text{ shares} + 1,250 \text{ shares}} = \frac{\$5,000}{6,250 \text{ shares}} = \$.80 / \text{share}$$

Note that although the existing stockholders were diluted by the new offering, they were not diluted by the stock split. If there had been just a

2 Actually, 1,250 shares is still too thin for a real-world example; 100,000 shares might be considered a minimum, but dealing with such large numbers would make the example hard to follow.

new offering and no split, one share of stock would be diluted from 1/500th of ownership in the company to 1/625th ownership. Conversely, if there had been a split but no new offering, then a person who owned one share of stock worth 1/500th of the company would, after the split, now own 10 shares out of 5,000, which is the same percentage ownership as 1 out of 500.

Let's also look at how this impacted the 100 shares that Ms. Smith (one of the original investors in the company) wanted to sell. After the new issue, but if the stock had *not* been split, Smith could expect to sell her 100 shares at $80 per share for a total of $8,000. After the new issue, but now assuming the stock *was* split, she would have 1,000 shares that she could now expect to sell at $8 per share, still totaling $8,000. She was no better or worse off after the split.

She was, however, worse off as a result of the dilution from the new issue. Had there not been a new issue, her 100 shares were worth $10,000 (assuming earnings-per-share of $10 and a price-to-earnings ratio of 10). But as a result of the dilution from the new issue, her 100 shares were now only worth $8,000.

Despite this immediate decline in value from the dilution resulting from the new issue, the new issue can still be good for stockholders. This is because the money raised from the stock offering is presumably going to be used in a way that raises company earnings enough in the future to more than offset the decline due to dilution. This was what Jones anticipated when he decided to sell the new stock to finance the new plant.

Jones saw the logic of the split and the other 11 owners (stockholders) of JMC agreed. So they voted to increase the authorized shares to 6,250. This authorized enough shares for both the stock split and the new offering.

Since some of the 12 investors wanted to sell some of their shares to the public, it was decided to have a "combined" offering. This means that some of the shares being offered are from the company—a primary offering—and some of the shares are being offered by selling stockholders—a secondary offering. All the shares will be sold at the same price, and Gaines & Wynn will keep the same commission per share.

The selling stockholders, who now owned 5,000 shares after the split, decided to sell a total of 1,000 of *their* shares to the public. Thus, the combined offering was 2,250 shares, 1,250 being primary (the proceeds of which would go to the company) and 1,000 being secondary (the proceeds going to the selling stockholders). *After the offering there would be 6,250 shares outstanding, not 7,250. The 1,000 shares being sold by selling stockholders were already outstanding, they are merely changing ownership. Only the new shares being sold by the company add to the number outstanding.*

With Mr. Gaines' help, JMC put together a prospectus and registered with the SEC to sell 2,250 shares. Even though the company was selling only 1,250, the entire 2,250 being offered had to be registered. After about three months of letters back and forth between the SEC and JMC, the SEC was satisfied that the prospectus contained enough information for potential buyers to make an informed decision. On September 1, 1992, the SEC declared JMC's registration to be effective.

Gaines & Wynn could have placed (sold) the entire 2,250 shares itself, but as is customary, it only placed some of the stock, in this case 800 shares, and distributed the rest to other investment bankers and stockbrokers to distribute to their clients. Gaines & Wynn and all the other dealers (investment bankers and stockbrokers) participating in the offering are called the *selling group*. Gaines & Wynn, of course, splits the commission with the other dealers. There are two reasons Gaines is willing to give some of the offering to other dealers. First, other investment bankers give Gaines some of their business, so everybody has a more even flow of business. Second, most investment bankers have only a limited number of clients. By having many dealers selling the stock, it gets better publicized among all potential investors. Thus, there is more demand for the stock and less risk that the issue will not be able to be sold. Also, if the issue cannot all be sold, rather than have to buy all the remaining stock itself, and risk its going down, Gaines & Wynn will split the risk with the other members of the underwriting syndicate.

The underwriting syndicate is usually composed of some, but not all, of the dealers in the *selling group*. Again, the underwriting syndicate consists of those dealers who have agreed to participate in the purchase of any shares of stock that were not able to be sold to the public. Those dealers who are in the selling group but who are not in the underwriting syndicate simply sell as many shares as they can and return the rest to the syndicate. The syndicate then either sells them directly to the public or redistributes the shares to other members of the selling group who have more demand for the stock. Those members of the selling group who are part of the underwriting syndicate get a higher commission than those who are not because they are taking some risk if all the shares cannot be sold. Those dealers in the selling group who are not in the underwriting syndicate are taking no risk and therefore get a smaller commission.

   With the wide exposure the selling group provides, it hopes there will
be excess demand for the stock (i.e., there will be people who wanted
some of the stock but were unable to get any on the offering). Some of
these people, it is hoped, will still want the stock and will then try to
buy in on the open market after the offering is completed. This is called
the *after market*. The after market literally refers to any trade made
between members of the public after the investment banker or underwriter has completed the offering. In common usage, however, *after
market* refers to the hour or two, or even day or two, immediately following the offering when there is a lot of trading between investors who
were unable to get any stock in the offering and those who did get stock
in the offering but are selling it immediately either to make a quick
profit (if the stock went up) or cut their losses (if the price went down).
   By the time the JMC registration had become effective, the selling
group had already called its clients to see who was interested in buying
the JMC stock. Since there was a lot of interest in JMC stock, the issue
was "fully subscribed" when the registration became effective, which
meant each dealer (underwriter or not) had enough customers who wanted
to buy the stock and it could all be sold.
   Shortly after the registration became effective at 10:00 A.M., September 1, 1992, the stockbrokers and underwriters immediately called the
clients to whom they were selling the shares and told them the stock was
"free to trade." This meant that as of that moment those individuals
who had subscribed to the stock were now the owners of registered,
freely tradable stock and could sell it if they wished. Where could they
sell it?

7

Over-the-Counter and NASDAQ Trading

Most stocks, when they initially come public, are traded either on the NASDAQ Stock Market or on what is called the *over-the-counter* market, where smaller companies' stocks are traded. A few bigger companies doing an initial public offering will qualify for and choose to become immediately listed on the New York Stock Exchange (NYSE) or the American Stock Exchange (ASE), but these are the exceptions.

The over-the-counter market most precisely refers to the market where those stocks that are too small to qualify for trading on the NASDAQ market are traded. But more broadly defined, over-the-counter, or OTC, trading refers to almost all trading that is not done on the New York or American Stock Exchanges. This would include (1) the NASDAQ Stock Market, the largest, whose trading mechanism is much more like over-the-counter trading than NYSE or ASE trading, (2) the over-the-counter market for smaller stocks, (3) some over-the-counter trading done in the trading rooms of many brokerage firms when they have both buy and sell orders for the same stock, and (4) the *Instinet*® computer-based trading system run by Reuters PLC. In the Instinet system, buyers and sellers place orders and execute trades directly through the Instinet computers, without ever talking to each other or to stockbrokers. The Instinet system now constitutes perhaps 15 to 20 percent of over-the-counter trading. However, the NASDAQ Stock Market accounts for more than 75 percent of the broadly defined over-the-counter trading, and since its trading mechanism is typical of most over-the-counter trading, we will limit our discussion here to the NASDAQ trading mechanism.

THE NASDAQ STOCK MARKET

NASDAQ stands for National Association of Securities Dealers Automated Quotations system. The NASD, or National Association of Securities Dealers, is an organization composed of virtually all dealers who trade securities. Currently, more than 5,400 firms are members of the NASD.

The NASDAQ Stock Market is not an exchange like the NYSE or the ASE, where essentially all the trading is done in single place. Rather, the NASDAQ Stock Market is a computer network connecting close to 500 of the largest NASD member firms who have chosen to act as "market makers." Each market maker member of this network has a computer display screen, called a NASDAQ workstation, which can provide up-to-the-minute information about the prices of all stocks. Since all of these display screens are connected to a central computer, all market makers generally have access to the same information at the same time. We will discuss shortly what a market maker is and how the firm, or its market makers, "make" a market.

The NASDAQ network of market makers trades stocks of over 4,900 different public companies. Stocks, of course, are bought and sold, not traded, but the term *trade* is still commonly used. Each of the 500 or so dealers who act as market makers will choose to make markets (that is, buy and sell the stock) in some, but not all, of the public companies that are listed on the NASDAQ Stock Market. In fact, on average, only about ten NASD member firms will be making a market in the stock on any particular company. As might be expected, companies that have relatively little publicly traded stock will have fewer market makers, perhaps only two or three, and larger companies whose stock is very actively traded might have 50 or more market makers. Any member of the NASD who qualifies as a market maker can choose to make a market in any number of NASDAQ listed stocks, and any market maker who is currently making a market in such stocks can stop making a market in one or more of those stocks. NASD member firms will only choose to make markets in those issues where they see enough stock being traded for them to believe their firm can make a profit by "making a market."

When a company first comes public, the investment banking firm that brought the company public almost always chooses to make a market in the stock. Other NASDAQ members will also try to make a profit by making a market in the new stock. When a stock initially comes public there is usually a high volume of early trading because some people who bought stock on the offering wish to take a quick profit (assuming it went up) and others who did not get any stock in the offering, or did not get as much as they wanted, begin to buy. Thus, a relatively large number of market makers initially make a market in a new stock. Typically, however, after a few weeks or months, the volume of stock trading declines, and many of the market makers will drop out. Conversely, if the stock proves to be an active trader—that is, the stock continues to trade a large number of shares every day—then other market makers will come in.

MARKET MAKERS

To understand what it means to make a market, let's first look at the role of the market maker and then look at an example of how a trade is done. In our example, the investment banking firm of Gaines & Wynn brought JMC public, so the market making department of Gaines & Wynn has chosen to make a market in JMC stock. That means that the person at Gaines & Wynn who will be making the market will be willing to buy JMC stock at a price of her choosing (if someone wants to sell it to her), and she (the market maker) will be willing to sell JMC stock at a slightly higher price to any trader who wants to buy from her (at her higher price.) Each market maker sets his or her own selling price and buying price. Let's say the Gaines & Wynn market maker thinks the stock is worth about $13 a share. She might declare her market to be $12³/₄ bid, $13¹/₄ offered. Her *bid* is the price she is willing to pay to buy JMC stock. Her *offered*, or *asked*, is the price at which she is willing to sell the stock. So if a trader at another firm wants to sell JMC stock, Gaines & Wynn (notice that we typically use the name of the firm making the market, not the name of the person who is actually making the market) will be willing to pay $12³/₄ for that stock, and if someone wants to buy JMC stock, the Gaines & Wynn market maker will sell it to the buyer at $13¹/₄. The difference between the bid and the offered, in this case $0.50 (or ¹/₂ point), is called the *spread*. Note that investors sometimes say "¹/₂ point" and other times say "$0.50." The two mean exactly the same thing and are used interchangeably.

The Gaines & Wynn market maker hopes to "make the spread" of $0.50 by buying stock at $12¾ and selling it a half point higher at $13¼. To do this, she types her market onto her computer display screen, "JMCC $12¾ bid – $13¼ offered." "JMCC" is the call letters, or *symbol*, assigned by the NASD to JMC, Inc.[1] Now, her $12¾ – $13¼ market, or really the Gaines & Wynn market, will appear on the display screen at any of the desks of any the NASD member firms who call it up by pressing JMCC.

How wide the spread is between the bid and the asked depends on how actively a stock is traded. For a stock that trades very actively, such as Microsoft or Intel, a market maker's spread would typically be ⅛ of a point. For less actively traded stocks, the spread might be ¼ or ½ point. Infrequently traded stocks might have a spread of ¾ of a point or more. The less actively a stock is traded, the wider the market maker spreads will usually be. This is because a market maker is less certain of being able to buy or sell the stock whenever she wants to, and thus needs a wider spread to reduce her risk. She cannot make her market too wide—say $12¼ bid – $13¾ offered—because, if she does, she will not do any trades; other market makers will come in and make a narrower market (perhaps $12¾ bid – $13¼ offered), and traders who want to buy or sell the stock will go to the other market makers rather than to Gaines & Wynn. Thus, the Gaines & Wynn market maker must keep her market narrow and competitive or she will not do any business and will not make any money; but she also cannot make her market too narrow or she is likely to lose money and won't be able to stay in business.

A TRADE IN JMC STOCK

Now let's watch a trade. Assume Mr. Green bought 1,000 shares of JMC on the initial public offering and decides he would like to sell it at $14. He calls his stockbroker at StockUp Brokerage firm and asks him to sell the 1,000 shares at $14. The broker then writes the ticket to sell the 1,000 shares at $14 and gives the ticket to his trader. The StockUp trader presses "JMCC" on his computer to call up the market on JMC and sees something like this:

Gaines & Wynn:	$12¾ bid	$13¼ offered	10 × 10
XYZ Brokerage:	$12½	13⅜	10 × 30
ABC Brokerage:	$12½	13⅛	10 × 10

---

1 NASDAQ-traded securities typically have 4 or 5 letters in their symbols, whereas NYSE- and ASE-listed stocks usually have 3-letter symbols.

From left to right, we see first the name of the market making firm followed by that firm's bid price, offered price, and the market maker's *market size*. Market size means how many shares the firm will buy or sell at its posted bid and offered prices. The "10×10" is read "one thousand by one thousand" and means the Gaines & Wynn market maker will buy 1,000 shares at her posted bid price of $12^3/_4$ and will sell 1,000 shares at her posted offered price of $13^1/_4$. Note that market size is expressed in hundreds of shares. So the second market maker is willing to buy up to 1,000 shares at his bid price and will sell up to 3,000 shares at his offered price of $13^3/_8$. A market maker can show any size she wants, but she is obligated to buy or sell up to that many shares at her posted price if someone wishes to sell to her or buy from her. For this reason, most market makers just "make" their market at 10×10, so they are only obligated to buy or sell up to 1,000 shares. In fact, the market maker may buy or sell many more shares that she posted, and often does, but it is safer to only commit yourself to a small number.

When the StockUp trader saw the JMCC markets on his screen, he saw that the Gaines & Wynn market maker had the highest bid, but that no one was bidding (that is, willing to pay) $14 per share. If any of the other market makers were bidding $14 for JMC, then the StockUp trader could type onto his screen that he is selling 1,000 shares at $14 to that market maker, and the trade would be done (or *executed*), and the computer would notify the other market maker that he had bought 1,000 shares of JMC at $14. However, since none of the bids were anywhere near $14, the StockUp trader reported that back to the broker who called Mr. Green and told him that the best bid for his stock at the time was $12^3/_4$. Mr. Green was anxious to sell as he needed the money to pay for a new car, but he didn't want to sell at $12^3/_4$. So he told his broker to try to sell it at $13^1/_4$ but not to take any price lower than $13. The broker relayed this information back to his trader. The StockUp trader once again called up the JMCC market on his screen. At this point he noticed that Gaines & Wynn had raised its bid to $13 bid, and was now offering the stock (was willing to sell the stock) at $13^1/_2$. The StockUp trader also noticed that Gaines & Wynn still had the highest bid. At this point the StockUp trader had three choices. First, he could *hit the bid*. That is, he could type in that he is selling 1,000 shares of JMC at $13 and have the computer send that message to Gaines & Wynn. At that point the trade would be done and the computer would notify Gaines & Wynn that it had just bought 1,000 shares at $13. Second, the StockUp trader could make a counteroffer. He could type in an offer of 1,000 shares at $13¼ and wait to see if Gaines & Wynn (or any other market maker) was willing to pay the $13¼. The Gaines & Wynn market maker might say yes, she would pay the $13¼, or she might counteroffer by typing in that she would pay $13⅛ for 1,000 shares of JMC. Thus, the StockUp trader (representing the seller) and the Gaines & Wynn market maker (representing herself, or more accurately her firm, Gaines & Wynn), could negotiate through the computers and see if they could come to a price agreement. As a third alternative, the StockUp trader, seeing that Gaines & Wynn was the best bid, could call the Gaines & Wynn market maker on the phone and try to negotiate a price.

The StockUp trader noticed that Gaines & Wynn had raised its bid price by ½ point. This told him that Gaines & Wynn might be anxious to buy the stock and thus might be willing to pay more than its posted bid price of $13. So he typed in his offer of $13¼ and sent it through the computer to Gaines & Wynn. The Gaines & Wynn trader was, in fact, anxious to buy some stock because she had sold quite a bit at her original offering price of $13¼ and, as yet, did not have enough shares of stock to deliver to the people to whom she had sold it. So the Gaines & Wynn market maker, seeing the 1,000 shares of JMC offered to her at $13¼, decided to call the StockUp trader on the phone and see if she could negotiate a better price. On the phone they agreed that StockUp would sell 1,000 shares of JMC to Gaines & Wynn at $13⅛. This was then typed into the computer so the trade could be processed by both firms, and so the notice of the trade would appear on the *ticker* or the screens in all the trading rooms that subscribed to the NASDAQ service. It is a NASDAQ rule that all trades must be reported to the central computer, usually within 90 seconds of the trade, for dissemination to the public. It has been deemed that the public's interest in a fair and efficient market is best served by requiring the price and volume of all trades to be public information. This is true of all stocks that are listed on the NYSE, ASE, and NASDAQ. Very small stocks, however, those that are too small to qualify to be traded on NASDAQ, are still traded over-the-counter, where there is currently no requirement that any information about trades be made public.

This example explains the basic trading mechanism on both the NASDAQ and OTC markets. In practice, for most NASDAQ traded stocks, there will be more than one market maker who has the same bid or offered price. In this case traders are free to negotiate with any or all of the market makers to obtain a better price, or a trader may have a market maker he prefers to use. Some market makers compete for the trades by offering traders what is called "payment for order flow." This is a practice whereby the trader for the brokerage firm, StockUp in our example, agrees to direct most or all of its orders for a given stock or stocks to a particular market maker, in exchange for which the market maker pays a small amount, perhaps two cents per share traded, back to the brokerage firm trader. In these cases, however, it is understood that the market maker receiving the payment for order flow must execute the trade at the best posted bid or offer, even if that better price was posted by a different market maker. This practice has generated controversy, as some people question whether this system always results in the customer receiving the best available price for the trade.

THE NASDAQ MARKETS

The NASDAQ Stock Market actually consists of two different markets. The larger is called the *NASDAQ National Market* (NASDAQ NM) and includes primarily the larger, more actively traded companies. The smaller or less actively traded issues are traded on the *NASDAQ SmallCap Market*. The NASDAQ SmallCap Market is not the over-the-counter market for smaller stocks mentioned earlier. That OTC market is primarily for companies that are too small to qualify for either of the two NASDAQ markets.

NASDAQ National Market

Prices of issues on the NASDAQ National Market appear in *The Wall Street Journal* under the heading "NASDAQ NATIONAL MARKET ISSUES." There are about 3,600 companies whose stock is currently traded on the NASDAQ NM. To qualify to be listed on the NASDAQ NM, a company must meet the requirements of either of two alternatives. Table 7.1 lists the primary requirements of each of the alternatives.

Alternative 1 is generally the easiest to meet for companies that meet the net and pretax income requirements. For companies that do not meet these income levels, the requirements of Alternative 2 may still be met. Alternative 2 requires that the company be larger in terms of net tangible assets, have at least a three-year operating history, and have a larger public float.

Table 7.1   Listing Requirements for the NASDAQ National Market

	Alternative 1	Alternative 2
Net income (in latest fiscal year or 2 of the last 3 fiscal years)	$400,000	no requirement
Pretax income (in latest fiscal year or 2 of the last 3 fiscal years)	$750,000	no requirement
Net tangible assets	$4 million	$12 million
Public float (shares)	500,000	1 million
Market value of float	$3 million	15 million
Operating history	no requirement	3 years
Minimum bid price for stock	$5	$3
Number of market makers	2	2
Number of shareholders	400*	400
*800 under certain circumstances		

The *float* is the number of shares that are publicly traded that are not owned by any officer or director of the company, and are not owned by anyone who owns more than 10 percent of the company's total shares outstanding. Remember that, when a company first comes public, not all of the shares are registered and publicly tradable—usually just a portion. The shares that are not yet registered are not part of the float. Thus, the number of shares in the float is almost always less than the number of shares outstanding. The float will be increased each time there is an additional offering of registered stock, whether primary or secondary. The float can also increase with the addition of shares sold under Rule 144. Rule 144 says that shareholders of unregistered stock are allowed, in certain circumstances, to sell small amounts of their stock to the public without registration. Such Rule 144 stock, as it is called, although never actually registered, is treated as if it were registered, and becomes part of the float. Thus, over many years, the float of a company's stock generally becomes an increasing portion of the total number of shares outstanding, and approaches 100 percent for older, established companies. The *market value of the float* refers to the number of shares in the float multiplied by the current price of the stock. So while the size of the float changes only occasionally, the market value of the float changes every time the stock price changes.

Companies that are listed on the NASDAQ National Market are not automatically removed from the list if they fall below the requirements. Companies are permitted to fall below the initial listing requirements for specified periods of time before they are taken off the list, and even then the NASD may decide to let the company retain its listing.

NASDAQ SmallCap Market

Companies that do not meet either of the alternatives for the NASDAQ National Market may still qualify to be traded in the NASDAQ SmallCap Market. These stocks appear in *The Wall Street Journal* under "NASDAQ SMALL-CAP ISSUES." "Cap" is short for *capitalization*, which in this context means the market value of all stock of the company, registered or unregistered. So "small-cap" is just another way of saying smaller companies.

To qualify to be traded on the SmallCap Market, a company must meet the requirements given in Table 7.2.

Table 7.2 Listing Requirements for NASDAQ SmallCap Market		
Total assets	$4 million
Total stockholders' equity	$2 million
Public float	100,000 shares
Market value of float	$1 million
Shareholders	300
Minimum bid price	$3
Number of market makers	2

There are about 1,900 different stocks that qualify for the NASDAQ SmallCap Issues list. You won't see that many issues priced in the newspaper on any given day because the paper only lists those that actually traded the previous day.

As with the NASDAQ National Market, if a company, once listed, falls below these initial listing requirements, it is not automatically delisted unless it falls down to certain lower levels for certain periods of time.

OVER THE COUNTER: THE PINK SHEETS

Finally, we say that stocks that do not qualify for either the NASDAQ NM or the SmallCap Issues list are traded *over the counter* or *in the pink sheets*. The pink sheets, so called because they are printed on pink paper, are a compilation of bids and offers submitted every day by market makers to the National Quotation Bureau, which publishes and distributes them. These bids and offers, however, are only quotes and market makers are not obligated to buy or sell any stock at these prices, as they are on posted prices on the NASDAQ NM and NASDAQ

SmallCap markets. Traders wishing to buy or sell stocks listed in the pink sheets must call one or more of the listed market makers and negotiate a price. Most pink sheet stocks are very small companies, but there are some exceptions, notably certain foreign companies that do not want to be listed on either NASDAQ or the exchanges because they do not want to comply with the SEC's disclosure requirements.

For some of the pink-sheet stocks, market makers will post prices on what the NASD calls its OTC Bulletin Board. The Bulletin Board can be seen on any NASD trader's or market maker's screen, and its purpose is to let others know who is making a market in a particular issue, and give an indication of about what their price might be. All negotiation and trading is done over the phones.

Trading on a stock exchange, such as the New York Stock Exchange or the American Stock Exchange, is slightly different in terms of how the price of the purchase or sale is reached. The difference is that instead of many market makers, as in the NASDAQ or OTC markets, stocks that are listed on an exchange are traded primarily in one place (at the stock exchange) with only one market maker, called a *specialist*, executing or overseeing most of the trading in that stock. We will return to this in Chapter 17.

PART 2

Securities Other than Common Stock: Bonds and Preferred Stock

8

Financing Growth: Selling New Stock versus Selling New Bonds

In early 1994, JMC decided to build another new mousetrap plant. The bigger, more efficient plant that JMC management had in mind, to be designated Plant Number 3, was estimated to cost $20,000 to build and equip. There are four common ways a company can obtain enough money to finance (pay for) a new plant. First, the company can sell new stock, called an equity financing. Second, the company can borrow the money, called a debt financing. These are called external or outside financings. Third, the company can use cash that has built up as a result of profits earned from operations in past years. In this case, we say the company is "financing the plant from retained earnings." This is called an internal financing. Investors use the phrase "financing from retained earnings," even though it is really financing from cash. This is to distinguish it from cash that was raised by selling new stock or bonds. The phrase "financing from retained earnings," then, is specifically telling you that the cash being used for the financing is cash that was earned by the company in prior years that was not used to pay for something else.

A fourth and less common way to finance a plant would be to sell off existing assets to raise cash. For instance, a company that made both furniture and clothing might decide the clothing business was by far the most attractive and should be expanded, and the company might sell off its furniture business to raise cash for a new clothing goods plant.

JMC did not have enough extra cash (unused retained earnings) available to build the new plant. Cash and U.S. Government securities at December 31, 1993, were only $15,000, and much of that was needed for the day-to-day operations of the company. JMC could have waited until enough cash was saved up from future retained earnings, but management anticipated it would take three or four years to do that and they were eager to get started on the plant now because they wanted to reach new markets for their mousetraps before a competitor did. Thus, an external or outside financing was needed. Management decided it was preferable to finance this plant with borrowed money rather than by selling new stock. The reason for this decision will be shown shortly.

The company felt safe borrowing the money because even if the net profit level did not increase as a result of the new plant, they knew they would be able to repay the loan over time just from the profit earned from already existing plants. As it happens, management's projections showed that, as a result of the newer and more efficient plant, earnings should go up substantially when the new plant was completed.

The $20,000 might have been borrowed from a bank, but the company did not want to go to a bank, primarily because it liked to use bank borrowings for short-term needs, such as receivables financing and unexpected needs, which occur from time to time. If JMC used a major bank borrowing to build the new plant now, banks might be reluctant to lend the company more for receivables financing or in an emergency later on. Also, loan agreements with banks are usually very restrictive in terms of financial ratios the company is required to maintain. Management wished to borrow in a way that left them freer than under the typically tight bank agreements. Selling bonds in the public market usually provides such an opportunity for a company in good financial condition. While this kind of borrowing also places restrictions and obligations on the company, these are typically less burdensome than bank arrangements. The debt financing (bond sale) was planned for early spring 1994.

WHY JMC DECIDED TO SELL BONDS

Let us now catch up with the changes at JMC, look at its latest financial statements, and see why management chose to sell bonds rather than new equity (stock). The factors affecting the decision between selling new bonds and selling new stock reveal a lot about the way corporations think; and understanding this can help investors predict in advance whether a company is more likely to do an equity financing or a debt financing when new cash is needed. Similarly, it can help investors determine the impact of a new stock or bond offering on the existing stock. Understanding this, however, is not necessary in order to understand what bonds are. Thus, the reader can skip ahead to Chapter 9 without missing any necessary information, if desired.

On September 1, 1992, JMC's stock issue was sold and $10,000 was received (ignoring commissions). That $10,000 was quickly put to use to build the then-new Plant Number 2, which was completed by December 31, 1992. Thus, in 1993, JMC had the benefit of Plant Number 2 for the whole year, in addition to the old Plant Number 1. As a result of this expanded capacity and an increase in the price for which the traps were sold, JMC's sales in 1993 moved up to $125,000. The full-year 1993 income statement looked like this:

JMC		
Income Statement		
For Year Ending 12/31/93		
Sales		$125,000
Expenses:		
CGS	$ 86,000	
SGA	22,000	
Interest Charges	3,000	
	111,000	111,000
Pretax profit		14,000
Taxes for the year		7,000
Net profit after tax		7,000

The balance sheet at the end of 1993 was as follows:

JMC
Balance Sheet
12/31/93

Assets			Liabilities		
Current assets:			Current liabilities:		
Cash .... $	7,000		Accounts payable .... $		8,000
U.S. Govt. securities....	8,000		Short-term debt		2,000
Accounts receivable	14,000		Taxes payable		2,000
Inventory:			Sinking-fund payments		
Finished goods.........	25,000		on long-term debt		
Work in progress	7,000		due within one year ..		2,000
Raw materials	21,000		Total current liabilities ...		14,000
Total current assets	82,000		Capitalization:		
			Long-term debt:		
Fixed assets:			8% Term loan		6,000
Property	4,000		9% First mortgage		
Plant...........................	15,000		bonds.......................		20,000
Equipment	51,000		**Stockholders' Equity**		
Total fixed assets	70,000				
			Common stock (par		
			value $.10) (authorized		
			6,250 shares, outstanding		
			6,250 shares)		625
			Additional paid-in capital		14,375
			Retained earnings		97,000
			Total stockholders'		
			equity		112,000
			Total liabilities		
Total assets	$152,000		and equity		$152,000

Compare this with the balance sheet of 12/31/91 at the end of Chapter 3. The following changes have occurred:

1. *Common at par* and *Additional paid-in capital* were increased when JMC sold new stock in September 1992. Cash went up at that time too, but the cash was since spent on new property, plant, and equipment.

2. *Property, plant, and equipment* are up by $1,000, $2,000, and $7,000 respectively, reflecting Plant Number 2 that was built with the money

raised on the stock offering. Note that the old Plant Number 1 is still in place and operating. At this point we are assuming that the old plant has not yet begun to wear out or deteriorate, so it is still carried at its original cost.

3. *Accounts receivable* and each of the *inventory* categories are up. This results from the increased sales level due to the new plant. Obviously, additional *raw material* is needed to feed the new plant, which in turn results in more *work in progress* and a higher level of *finished goods* awaiting sale to the expanded customer list. Since the sales level is higher, the *accounts receivable* level is also higher.

4. *Cash* is down. This reflects the following: *(a)* money spent to increase the level of inventory; *(b)* money used to reduce accounts payable and short-term debt; and *(c)* money spent to meet the sinking-fund obligations under the 8% term loan agreement. The latter declined $2,000 in each of the years 1992 and 1993.

5. *Retained earnings* is up, reflecting both the $5,000 earned in 1992 and the $7,000 earned in 1993.

SELLING BONDS VERSUS SELLING STOCKS

JMC management wanted $20,000 to build the new plant. To decide whether it would be preferable to sell new stock or bonds, it is necessary to project the income statement and balance sheet into the future to see what they would look like under the different assumptions of either a new stock sale or a new bond sale.

Since both plants were operating at full capacity in 1993, we start by assuming that the income statement for 1994 would look the same as 1993 if business continued to be good but no new plant capacity was added. This is shown in the lefthand column in Table 8.1.

Assumption A—no external financing (wait a few years) results in an income statement that looks like the 1993 income statement. Actually, future earnings under Assumption A would enable JMC to repay some debt, which would result in lower interest payments and therefore produce slightly higher earnings; but this difference is minor, compared to the potential changes resulting from a new stock or bond sale, so we will ignore it.

Assumption B—the sale of $20,000 worth of bonds. Under this assumption, the following factors went into JMC management's income statement projections. First, after discussions with Gaines &

Wynn (investment bankers), JMC concluded that it would have to pay
about 10 percent interest per year. Second, management was now quite
experienced in the manufacture of mousetraps and knew how to build
a plant that would be more efficient (i.e., produce traps for a lower
cost per trap). Finally, management knew that with the JMC sales
force and management already in place, selling, general, and administrative expense would not go up as much as sales. As a result of
detailed calculations, including these factors, management projected
that the income statement would look like the Assumption B column
in Table 8.1 once the new plant was operating.

Table 8.1   JMC's Income Statement under Two Assumptions

	Assumption A —no external financing	Additional yearly sales and expenses from new plant	Assumption B —sell bonds
Sales	$125,000	$ 40,000	$165,000
CGS	86,000	25,000	111,000
SGA	22,000	5,000	27,000
Interest	3,000	2,000	5,000
Pretax profit	14,000	8,000	22,000
Tax (assume 50%)	7,000	4,000	11,000
Net income	$ 7,000	4,000	$ 11,000
Shares outstanding	6,250		6,250
EPS	$ 1.12		$ 1.76

Assumptions A and B also produce the following changes on the
balance sheet and in certain ratios shown in Table 8.2. Again, under
Assumption A—no external financing, we simply use the current balance sheet as indicative of the future.

Table 8.2   Interest Coverage and Debt Ratio under Assumptions A & B

	Assumption A —no external financing	Assumption B —sell bonds
Long-term debt	$26,000	$46,000
Equity	112,000	$112,000
Long-term debt / Total capital	18.8%	29.1%
Interest coverage	5.7×	5.4×

By selling bonds to build the new plant, we see that earnings per share, once the plant is up and running, should rise dramatically. On the other hand, interest coverage declines and long-term debt as a percentage of total capital moves much higher (i.e., both these ratios deteriorate). Thus, selling bonds will change the ratios so that it might be more difficult for JMC to borrow any additional money should the need arise. The effect on earnings, however, is so favorable as to make the bond sale worthwhile despite this potential problem. Furthermore, the higher earnings will enable JMC to pay back its debt faster, which will, in turn, cause a reduction in interest expense. Therefore, the debt-to-total capital ratio could again decline and the interest coverage improve (go higher). Review these ratios in Chapter 4.

Assumption C—the $20,000 is raised by having another offering of new stock. This, of course, may result in earnings dilution (i.e., although the new plant will produce more earnings, the increased number of common shares outstanding may result in a net decline in earnings per share). But it is also possible that the increase in earnings, as a result of the new plant, will be so big that, despite the increased number of common shares outstanding, the EPS figure will increase. This is called negative dilution. In order to find our which is the case, one must go through the dilution calculation like that shown in Chapter 6.

Table 8.3 JMC's Earnings with New Plant Financed by Stock		Assumption C —sell new stock
	Sales	$165,000
	CGS	111,000
	SGA	27,000
	Interest	3,000
	Pretax profit	24,000
	Tax	12,000
	Net income	$ 12,000
	Shares outstanding	?
	EPS	?

JMC stock is currently selling at a price-earnings ratio of 6 times (6×). Thus, it turns out that to raise $20,000, JMC would have to sell 2,425 new shares.

$$\text{EPS} = \frac{\$12,000}{6,250 + 2,425} = \frac{\$12,000}{8,675} = \$1.38 \times 6\times = \$8.28 \times 2,425 = \$20,079$$

Old shares ⤴   ⤴ New shares

| | | EPS | P/E | Stock price | New shares | Money raised |

If JMC did the stock offering but had not yet built the plant, then earnings would be diluted as shown in Table 8.4 under Assumption C. Assume that the cash from the offering is not earning any interest while it is waiting to be used to build the plant.

Table 8.4   JMC's Income Statements under Two Assumptions

	Assumption A —no external financing	Assumption C —sell new stock —new plant not yet running
Sales	$125,000	$125,000
CGS	86,000	86,000
SGA	22,000	22,000
Interest	3,000	3,000
Pretax profit	14,000	14,000
Tax	7,000	7,000
Net income	$ 7,000	$ 7,000
Shares outstanding	6,250	8,675
EPS	$ 1.12	$ .81

Thus, the stock offering alone would result in earnings being diluted from $1.12 to $0.81 per share, a big decline, and the announcement of such an offering could cause the stock to go down. But JMC management also did the dilution calculation assuming what they expected sales and earnings would look like *after* the new plant was up and running. That calculation is *Assumption D* shown in Table 8.5.

Assumption D shows that the projected profit from the new plant is so great that it will more than compensate for the increased number of shares outstanding, and earnings should rise from $1.12 to $1.38.

Although earnings would be diluted initially from the stock sale, the expected sales and earnings growth resulting from the new plant would more than offset the dilution and result in EPS increasing, if all went as planned. Thus, management might be willing to do the stock offering, even knowing that the stock may go down in the short run. However, the resulting increase in EPS from the stock sale is much lower than the increase in EPS from a bond sale. Therefore, since higher earnings should produce a higher stock price in the long run, it is in the best interests of the current shareholders for the money to be raised by selling bonds rather than by selling stock. This is true even though the bond sale results in a weakening of the balance sheet, while the stock sale results in improvement of the balance sheet, as shown in Table 8.6. Thus, the company decided to go ahead with the bond sale.

Table 8.5   Comparing JMC's Income Statements under Three Assumptions

	Assumption A —no external financing	Assumption B —sell bonds —new plant operating	Assumption D —sell new stock —new plant operating
Sales	$125,000	$165,000	$165,000
CGS	86,000	111,000	111,000
SGA	22,000	27,000	27,000
Interest	3,000	5,000	3,000
Pretax profit	14,000	22,000	24,000
Tax (assume 50%)	7,000	11,000	12,000
Net income	$ 7,000	$ 11,000	$ 12,000
Shares outstanding..........	6,250	6,250	8,675
EPS	$ 1.12	$1.76	$ 1.38

Compare the interest coverage and debt ratios shown in Table 8.6.

Table 8.6   Interest Coverage and Debt Ratios for Three Options

	Assumption A —no external financing	Assumption B —sell bonds	Assumption D —sell new stock
		—new plant up and running—	
Long-term debt........	$ 26,000	$ 46,000	$ 26,000
Equity	112,000	112,000	132,000
Long-term debt / Total capital	18.8%	29.1%	16.5%
Interest coverage......	5.7×	5.4×	9.0×

An interesting exercise is to work through the numbers and see what would be the effect of equity financing (selling new stock) if the price-earnings ratio were 15× or 30×. Answer: If the P/E were 15×, the money could be raised by selling 780 new shares. This would result in EPS of $1.71 after the new plant was up and running. This is only slightly below the $1.76 resulting from a bond sale. In this case, it would probably be preferable to raise the money selling stock, because the minor shortfall in EPS (compared to selling bonds) is more than made up for by the stronger balance sheet (i.e., less debt and better interest-coverage protection). If the P/E were 30×, the $20,000 could be raised selling 370 new shares, which would result in EPS of $1.81. This is even higher than the EPS resulting from the bond sale and, therefore, it would certainly be preferable to sell new stock at thirty times earnings rather than bonds, because it results not only in higher EPS but also leaves a better balance sheet.

However, with JMC stock selling at six times earnings, a bond issue seemed preferable to a new stock issue. Mr. Jones decided that it was time for his entire management team to learn more about bonds, so Mr. Gaines was asked to come in. He made the presentation reported in Chapter 9.

9

Bonds

A bond is a contract between a company that is borrowing money and the people and institutions who are lending the money. The borrower is called the bond *issuer*. The lenders are the *bondholders*. A bond *certificate* is the piece of paper that says that the bondholder is the lender and has the right to be paid back by the issuer on a certain date or dates, and to receive interest from the issuer on certain dates. The certificate gives little other information. Rather, it refers to an *indenture*, which is the complete detailed agreement between the lender(s) and the borrower. The indenture states all the obligations of the borrower and all the rights of the lender in the event that the borrower fails to live up to the agreement. The *trustee* under the indenture is a person (typically a bank) who looks out for the rights of the bondholders. If, for example, you are a bondholder of Company XYZ and have not received your interest payment, you would call the trustee, not Company XYZ which owes you the interest. In fact, most typically, the borrowing company makes the interest payment to the trustee who, in turn, distributes it to the bondholders. If the company fails to make the interest payment, the trustee is obligated to take legal action against the company or to invoke some other right stated in the indenture. The trustee also watches the borrowing company's financial statements to make sure they are maintaining certain financial ratios agreed to in the indenture. Should the company fail to meet these agreements, the trustee is again obligated to act to help the bondholders invoke their rights (discussed later).

The term *bond* usually refers to a loan that is backed by a specific asset or group of assets. *Backed by*, or *secured by*, means that if the company issuing the bond cannot meet its interest or repayment obligations, then the bondholders may be entitled to take possession of the assets securing, or backing, their loan and sell them to get their money back. Or, if the company is being liquidated, the money raised from selling those particular assets must be used to repay the bondholders.

The term *debenture* refers to a loan that is very much like a bond except it is not backed by any specific assets. Rather, debentures are a *general obligation* of the company, which means that if the company is liquidated, debenture holders are only repaid if there is enough money after all other lenders with a higher priority, such as bondholders, are paid off. Despite this clear difference, the word *bond* is often used when referring to a debenture. We will sometimes adopt that convention in this book when referring to things that apply equally to bonds or debentures. The term *note* is also sometimes used interchangeably with *bond* or *debenture*, although notes usually are loans of less than 10 years, while bonds or debentures typically have lives of 10 years or more.

A company can have more than one issue of bonds or debentures outstanding at one time. In this case, each issue would have its own indenture and its own trustee. The obligations under the various indentures could be similar or they could be different. An indenture sometimes precludes the company from having any further bond issues without permission of the existing bondholders under that indenture.

The bond features covered in this chapter concern both nonconvertible bonds and convertible bonds. Convertible bonds, however, also have additional important features, which are covered in Chapter 11. The current discussion refers primarily to corporate bonds (i.e., bonds issued by a corporation). Bonds issued by a government agency or a city or state have many similar features but are not covered here.

Issuing bonds is similar to issuing new stock. If a company wishes to issue new bonds and sell them to the public, the bonds must first be registered with the Securities and Exchange Commission and a prospectus must be distributed to buyers. The actual selling process through an underwriter or investment banking group is also similar to a new stock sale, as discussed in Chapter 6. When bonds are initially registered and sold by a company, it is a primary offering and the money goes to the company. Once registered and initially sold, the bonds can be bought and sold on the secondary market at any time, just like stocks, at whatever price the buyer and seller agree upon.

BOND FEATURES

Maturity

Maturity is the date the bond must be paid back by the borrower. *Final maturity* is the last date the borrower must pay back any of the bonds of a particular issue that are still outstanding. Some of the bonds of an issue may have matured ahead of final maturity under a sinking-fund provision or may have been paid back earlier under a call provision (discussed in Chapter 10).

Face Value

Face value, also called *face amount* or *par value*,[1] is the amount of money the company must pay back if the bond is redeemed at final maturity. If the bond matures ahead of final maturity under a call provision (discussed later), the amount that must be paid to the bondholder may be slightly more than the face value.

Face value for most bonds is $1,000 (i.e., each bond represents a loan of $1,000). Occasionally, a particularly large issue may include some bonds with face values of $5,000 or $10,000. Similarly, one occasionally sees an issue that has bonds with a face value of less than $1,000. These are called *baby bonds*. In this chapter we will always be referring to $1,000 face amount bonds.

Redemption and Retirement

These words do not mean exactly the same thing. *Redemption* usually refers to returning the bond certificate to the company or trustee in exchange for the amount of money due. When a bond is redeemed, it is automatically retired forever. It cannot be reissued, like treasury stock. *Retirement* can happen either because the bond was redeemed, or because the issuing company bought the bond in the secondary market. When a bond is repurchased in a secondary market by the issuing company, it is automatically retired forever.

Suppose a company bought one of its bonds in the secondary market for $984, or $1,072, or any other price. Once the issuing company has bought back one of its bonds, the interest and debt repayment obligations on that bond cease to exist. The company cannot owe itself money or interest anymore than you or I can owe ourselves interest. Of course, if a company has bought back some, but not all, of the bonds of a

---

1 Do not confuse par value of a bond with par value of a common stock. They are unrelated.

particular issue, it still has its obligations to the remaining outstanding bondholders. Also, the company usually remains under the restrictions of the indenture until all the bonds under that indenture are retired.[2] A company may buy back its bonds simply because it has extra cash lying around or because it is obligated to do so under a sinking-fund provision.

Sinking Fund

A *sinking fund* is an obligation to retire a certain amount of bonds on or before a specified date ahead of final maturity. A bond issue may or may not have a sinking-fund provision. To illustrate, suppose ABC Company issued $100,000 worth of bonds (100 bonds) on January 1, 1990. The indenture has a sinking-fund provision, which says the following:

> The bonds final maturity is December 31, 2008, except that at least $5,000 face value (5 bonds) must be retired each year by December 31, beginning in the year 2000.

Thus, the sinking fund is $5,000 a year in each of the years 2000 to 2007, for a total of $40,000. The remaining outstanding $60,000 would then be redeemed for face value at the final maturity date, December 31, 2008. The repayment at final maturity, if it is larger than the annual sinking-fund requirement, is called a *balloon* payment. A bond issue that has no sinking-fund payment and is completely redeemed at final maturity is called a *term bond* or a *bullet*. While term bonds need not be retired before final maturity, there is no reason why the company cannot buy back some (or all) of the issue earlier in the secondary market, if they are available. A bond may have no balloon and, rather, be redeemed in equal sinking-fund installments. For example, the indenture for a $100,000 issue may specify a $10,000 sinking fund for each of the last ten years up to and including the final maturity.

A company may meet its sinking-fund obligations in a number of ways. One way is simply to buy the necessary amount of bonds on the secondary market prior to the specified date and retire them. Although ABC Company in this example is required to retire at least $5,000 face value prior to December 31, 2000, it is allowed to retire more. It is common to see a company try to get one or two years ahead of the required sinking-fund schedule, so if, in a given year, it is unable to buy any bonds back, it will have already met its contractual obligation.

---

2 Indenture restrictions can be changed by a vote of the bondholders. When a company wants to change its indenture restrictions, it will usually offer bondholders a small increase in the coupon, perhaps $1/2\%$, in exchange for voting for the indenture change.

The purpose of the sinking fund is to help assure that the bond issue will be retired at final maturity. If there were no sinking fund, ABC Company would have to come up with $100,000 at final maturity. By having a sinking fund, there is less to retire at final maturity, and also it forces the company to start planning its finances early to meet these obligations. If the company gets ahead of the sinking-fund schedule, it makes it that much easier to meet the remaining redemption obligation at final maturity.

Of course, a company's desire to buy back bonds ahead of schedule, or even according to schedule, does not obligate anyone to sell them. In the event that the company is unable to buy back any bonds in the market, the indenture usually provides an alternative mechanism for the company to meet its sinking-fund obligation by a random selection, called a *lottery*. Since each bond has a serial number, the trustee will draw numbers at random to select bonds for the required sinking-fund redemption. The bonds that have been selected will then mature perhaps one month later—to allow time to notify the bondholders and for the bondholders to deliver their bonds to the trustee. Since the bonds have now matured early under the sinking-fund lottery selection procedure, they will no longer earn interest after their sinking fund redemption date, and thus the bondholders would have nothing to gain by not surrendering them.

Whether the company meets sinking-fund obligations by buying bonds in the secondary market or by using the lottery procedure is usually up to the company. For example, if the company can buy a $1,000 face value bond for $940 in the market, that is obviously preferable to redeeming it at the full $1,000 under the lottery procedure because the company saves $60. If the bonds are selling at more than face value, or if there are none available to be purchased in the market, then the company invokes the lottery procedure.

A third way sinking-fund obligations are met is through serial redemption. When serial bonds are initially issued, it is specified that certain serial numbers will be retired in certain years, thereby constituting the sinking fund. Serial bonds are common today with state and local agencies, but are rare in corporate bonds, except in equipment trusts. An *equipment trust* is a bond issued for a particular purpose, such as an airline borrowing money to buy an airplane or a railroad buying railroad cars. Equipment trust bonds always specify that, if the company fails to meet its obligations under the indenture, the equipment trust bondholders get to take possession of the specified equipment, which they can then sell in order to get their money back.

Interest Payment

Most bonds require the company to pay interest semiannually, although there are a few bonds that specify that interest will be paid annually, quarterly, or even monthly. There are *registered* bonds and *bearer* bonds. If a bond is registered in your name, you will get a check in the mail for each interest payment. A registered bond belongs to the person in whose name it is registered and there is no risk if it is lost. On the other hand, a bearer bond belongs to the person who possesses it. It is not registered. Bearer bonds have attached coupons for each interest payment. When a given payment date is approaching, the bearer (bondholder) simply clips off the coupon with that date on it and presents it or mails it to the trustee for an interest payment.

The interest payment required by a bond is called its *coupon*. For the vast majority of bonds, the coupon is fixed; that is, it stays the same for the life of the bond. Some exceptions, called *variable rate notes* and *resets*, are discussed in Chapter 10. With that exception, we will assume for the remainder of the book that the coupon rate is fixed.

Let's look at a bond with a face amount of $1,000 and a coupon of $50 semiannually, for a total of $100 a year. In this case we would say the annual coupon is $100, and the *coupon rate* is $100 divided by $1,000, or 10%:

$$\text{Coupon rate} = \frac{\text{Coupon}}{\text{Face amount}} = \frac{\$100}{\$1,000} = 10\%$$

The coupon rate (a percent figure) is always stated as an annual rate, although the dollar coupon may be stated either as $50 semiannually or $100 annually.

Note that since the coupon is fixed, and the face amount is also fixed, the coupon rate must also be fixed. The price the bond sells for in the secondary market may vary above or below $1,000, but the coupon rate is always a fixed percentage *of the face value*, which does not vary. So the coupon rate for this bond will always be 10%.

Current Yield and Coupon Yield

The coupon rate is sometimes called the *coupon yield*. Coupon yield (which is fixed) should not be confused with current yield (which varies with price). The *current yield* is the dollar coupon (fixed) divided by the current price of the bond in the secondary market (which varies). The coupon yield and the current yield are annual yields because the bondholder receives one full coupon each year.

Table 9.1 compares coupon yield and current yield. Notice what happens to the current yield when the price of the bond goes up or down.

Table 9.1   Comparison of Coupon Yield and Current Yield

			Current yield (percent)	Coupon yield (percent)
A.	Coupon	$ 100	? %	10%
	Face amount	$1,000		
B.	Coupon	$ 100	12	10
	Current price	$ 833		
C.	Coupon	$ 100	10.6	10
	Current price	$ 943		
D.	Coupon	$ 100	10	10
	Current price	$1,000		
E.	Coupon	$ 100	9.2	10
	Current price	$1,086		

When a $1,000 par value or face value bond is selling at more than par (i.e., more than $1,000, as in case E), we say it is selling at a *premium* (to par). In this case, its current yield will always be less than the coupon yield. When a bond is selling below par, as in Cases B and C, we say it is selling at a *discount* (from par). In this case, its current yield will always be greater than the coupon yield.

Notice in cases B, C, D, and E that, as the bond price increases, current yield decreases. Conversely, as price decreases, current yield increases. From the other point of view, a declining yield implies a rising price. A rising yield implies a declining price. This inverse relationship between current yield and bond price is always initially confusing. If you become confused thinking about it, you can always refer back to this example, or, if you have a calculator handy, make up your own example.

Coupon yield and current yield are not to be confused with *yield to maturity*. This is discussed later in this chapter.

BOND RATINGS

Bondholders are always concerned with safety. Safety means the probability that all future interest payments, sinking-fund payments, and the final maturity payment will be met on time. Many investors do their own analysis of a company's financial statements and outlook and make their own judgments about the safety of their bonds, but other investors rely on one or more of four well-known independent rating agencies that establish and publish ratings on a wide variety of bonds. The four agencies are Moody's Investors Service, Standard & Poor's Corporation, Fitch Investors Service, and Duff & Phelps Inc.

The bonds or companies deemed by these agencies to be the most safe (i.e., have the highest probability of meeting all future payments on time) get the highest rating. We say these are the *most creditworthy*, or the *best credits*. The bonds that are deemed to have the most risk as to eventual payment of all obligations are called the *least creditworthy*, or *speculative credits*. It is common for bondholders to refer to a company as a *credit*. The ratings for each of the services are shown in Table 9.2.

Table 9.2   Comparison of Credit Ratings

	Moody's	S&P	Fitch	Duff & Phelps	
Safest	Aaa	AAA	AAA	AAA	High-grade bonds that are considered very safe.
	Aa	AA	AA	AA	
	A	A	A	A	Medium-grade bonds that are considered somewhat safe.
	Baa	BBB	BBB	BBB	
	Ba	BB	BB	BB	Lower grade—may contain some degree of speculation as to eventual payment of future interest and principal repayment obligations.
	B	B	B	B	
	Caa	CCC	CCC	CCC	Highly speculative as to payment of interest and principal; lowest ratings may include bonds already in default.
Least safe	Ca	CC	CC		
	C	C	C		

The ratings are based on a number of financial ratios as well as subjective factors. Standard & Poor's recently published certain three-year median financial ratios for industrial companies in each of their rating categories, including those shown in Table 9.3.

**Table 9.3   Examples of Median Financial Ratios[3]
              under Various Credit Ratings**

	AAA	AA	A	BBB	BB	B
Pretax interest coverage	16.66×	8.81×	4.63×	2.51×	1.59×	.69×
Long-term debt .... capitalization	11.7%	19.1%	29.4%	39.6%	51.1%	61.8%

If a company has good ratios but the trend has been deteriorating, or is expected to deteriorate, the rating agencies may rate its bonds lower than the ratios might suggest. We would say the creditworthiness of this company is declining. Similarly, if a company's ratios are improving, or are expected to improve, the agencies may rate the bonds higher than the ratios suggest, and we would say this is an *improving credit*.

Standard & Poor's and Moody generally give the same level of rating to a company's bonds. Sometimes one agency rates a particular bond one notch higher or lower than the other agency. This is called a *split rating*. On rare occasions, the ratings from these two agencies will be more than one notch apart. When a company has more than one bond issue outstanding, both or all of the issues of that company may be rated the same, or they may have different ratings. The bond issue with the higher rating will usually be the one that has the highest priority (gets paid back first in the event of bankruptcy) or has the best assets backing it.

A BOND'S YIELD IS RELATED TO ITS RATING

The lower a company's bond rating, the greater the risk that the company will default on some future interest, sinking fund, or final maturity payment, according to the judgment of the rating agency. When people buy lower-rated bonds, they demand a higher yield to compensate them for the higher risk of default. Bond yields, in fact, are directly related to the market's perception of the bond's risk, and a bond's price in the market will rise or fall to adjust its yield to changing perceptions of risk.[4] Similarly, when a company is issuing new bonds, it usually has to offer an interest rate comparable to the interest rates of similarly rated bonds already on the market. In fact, a company selling new bonds usually has

---

3 These figures taken from *S & P's Corporate Finance Criteria*, 1994 edition, with permission.
4 Bond prices also will rise or fall in the market to adjust the yield to changes in interest rates caused by economic or government policy factors.

to offer an interest rate slightly higher than similar bonds already in the market in order to induce potential investors to sell their old bonds and buy the new ones with which they are less familiar.

Investors do not always agree with the ratings agencies. Investors may evaluate a bond's risk, or creditworthiness, as being greater than or less than the ratings suggest. For instance, a bond may be rated AA, but the market (i.e., most investors) may feel it is more risky and should only be rated A. In this case the bond would be likely to sell at a yield closer to other A-rated bonds, rather than AA-rated bonds. In fact, it sometimes happens that the rating agencies only raise or lower their ratings after the market has already begun to reflect such a change. For the majority of bonds, however, the market usually agrees with the ratings agencies; thus, for these bonds, yields at any given time are related to their ratings.

In mid-March 1995, newly issued 10-year maturity bonds of industrial companies with the following ratings typically had the accompanying yields:[5]

AAA	7.46%
AA	7.54%
A	7.64%
BBB	7.84%

It is harder to identify a typical rate for lower-rated bonds because they vary more widely, but BB-rated bonds at the same time were generally yielding more than 9%, and B-rated bond yields were yielding 10%–12% or higher. This does not mean that all A-rated bonds had exactly a 7.64% yield. Other factors—such as sinking-fund provisions, call features, time to maturity, and individual investors' judgments about risk—would cause the yields to vary around the 7.64% level.

THE YIELD SPREAD BETWEEN RATINGS

Changes in interest rates and yields are often quoted in terms of *basis points*. A basis point is 0.01 percent, or one one-hundredth of a percentage point. For example, if interest rates went from 7% to 8%, we would say they went up by 100 basis points, or one full percentage point. If the rate then declined from 8% to 7.9%, we would say the rate declined by 10 basis points. Since interest rate changes are often small and gradual,

---

5 These figures taken from Salomon Brothers Inc "Bond Market Roundup: Abstract" March 17, 1995, with permission.

investors who work with these numbers every day find it easier to talk about changes in interest rates in terms of basis points. It is easier to say "The rate was down 20 basis points," rather than saying, "The rate was down by 20 one-hundredths of a percent, or one-fifth of a percent."

If interest rates in the economy in general moved upward, yields on bonds at each rating level would move up; but the yields at each rating level would most likely move up by slightly different amounts. As a result, the yield difference between two ratings levels, called the *yield spread*, will vary. Table 9.4 gives an example of how yield spreads can change when interest levels in general change.

Table 9.4 Examples of Yield Spreads

	January	% Spread	Basis point spread	November	% Spread	Basis point spread
AAA	8.10%			8.50%		
		.05%	5		.10%	10
AA	8.15%			8.60%		
		.10%	10		.13%	13
A	8.25%			8.73%		
		.15%	15		.30%	30
BBB	8.40%			9.03%		

Table 9.4 shows that yields rose in all ratings categories from January to November, but it also shows that the spreads between the ratings categories changed and became wider. The market factors causing such spread changes are numerous. Here it is sufficient to say that the relative positions will always remain the same: a AAA-rated bond will always yield less than a AA-rated bond, which will always yield less than an A-rated bond, and so on, except where the market disagrees with the ratings, or possibly when comparing different kinds of bonds. Bonds of industrial companies, for example, may have somewhat different yields than bonds of utilities, such as electric power companies.

Many bond investors watch yield spread changes closely and make buy and sell decisions on this basis. For example, when the spread between A-rated bonds and BBB-rated bonds is narrow, such as the 15 basis point difference in January, an investor might prefer to buy an A-rated bond. In this case he would only be getting an extra .15% yield if he took the greater risk with the BBB-rated bond. So he might prefer the safer bond. On the other hand, in November when the spread between A-rated bonds and BBB-rated bonds had widened to 30 basis points, the same investor might decide he would rather have the BBB-rated bond because he was now getting a lot more extra yield, .30%, to compensate him for the increased risk.

INTEREST RATES

There are many different interest rates in the economy. The most commonly watched interest rates include bank borrowing rates (what banks pay depositors for passbook accounts, certificates of deposit, and checking accounts) and bank lending rates (what banks charge customers who borrow for mortgages, personal loans, or business loans). The *prime rate* is usually the rate that banks charge their safest business borrowers. Higher-risk borrowers are charged a higher interest rate for loans. Investors also watch: (1) bond rates—the yield on U.S. Treasury bonds, corporate bonds, and municipal bonds issued by towns, states, and state agencies; (2) the *discount rate*—what the Federal Reserve charges when it lends money to banks; and (3) the *federal funds rate*—the rate banks charge when they lend money for a day or two to other banks to help them meet reserve requirements. There are other interest rates too numerous to mention: the rate on government treasury bills, government agency bonds, and commercial paper (loans from one corporation to another) are but a few.

When interest rates are rising, it is normally the case that each of these rates is rising, although perhaps by different amounts. The same holds true when interest rates are falling. Interest rates rise and fall for reasons too numerous to discuss here. Even if we listed, discussed, and became experts on all the apparently influencing factors, it would still be very difficult to predict whether interest rates would be rising or falling in the near and distant future. Even experts disagree on what are the key factors causing interest rates to change, and how. In sum, interest rates reflect in some complicated and perhaps unknowable way the entire economic outlook of the marketplace; that is, the anonymous result of each person's decision to borrow or lend at a particular time and interest rate. Because interest rates have a powerful effect on the economy,[6] certain rates, such

---

6 The question of whether interest rates determine the level and direction of economic activity, or whether the economy determines the level and direction of interest rates, is like asking which came first, the chicken or the egg.

as the *discount rate*, are fixed by the Federal Reserve at what it feels is best for the economy. Changes in the rates set by the Federal Reserve tend to have an effect on most of the other interest rates in the economy.

YIELD TO MATURITY

When a $1,000 face value bond is selling at $1,000 and has a coupon of $100, its coupon yield and current yield are obviously both 10 percent. However, if the bond price falls to $943, for example, the yield is not so obvious. The coupon yield is still 10 percent and the current yield is easy to calculate: the coupon, $100, divided by the price, $943, equals 10.6%. But a person buying the bond at $943 not only gets a $100 coupon each year, for a current yield of 10.6%, but also a capital gain of $57 when the bond matures at a $1,000.[7] Thus, the actual yield to the investor is higher than the current yield. The current yield reflects only the $100 coupon payment the bondholder receives each year, but ignores the capital gain. The yield to maturity figure includes both the annual coupon and the capital gain. The yield to maturity takes the capital gain into account as if it were coming in a little each year (rather than all at the end), so the yield to maturity figure, like the current yield, can be thought of as an annual return to the bondholder. Unfortunately, the calculation that gives the yield to maturity is more complex than it looks and cannot be done on a simple calculator. You need a special financial calculator, such as the Hewlett Packard 12C, in order to calculate an accurate yield to maturity. Here, we can only say with certainty the following:

- If a bond is selling at a *discount* to par (below $1,000), its yield-to-maturity will be *greater* than its current yield (because of the capital gain at maturity).

- If the bond is selling at a *premium* to par (more than $1,000), the yield-to-maturity will be *less* than the current yield because, in addition to the annual coupon payments received, the buyer of the bond will incur a capital *loss* when the bond is redeemed at par maturity.

Table 9.5 shows the coupon yield, current yield, and yield to maturity for a bond with a $70 annual coupon ($35 coupon semiannually) and 12 years to maturity.

---

7 In some circumstances this gain will be treated as a capital gain for tax purposes, and be subject to a lower tax rate, and in other cases it will be treated as ordinary income. In either case we will refer to it as a capital gain to distinguish it from the interest income that a bondholder also receives.

Table 9.5   Yield Comparisons on a $1,000 Bond at Different Prices

Price	Coupon yield	Current yield	Yield to maturity
$1,150	7.0%	6.1%	5.3%
1,100	7.0	6.4	5.8
1,050	7.0	6.7	6.4
1,000	7.0	7.0	7.0
950	7.0	7.4	7.6
850	7.0	8.2	9.1

For most investors the yield to maturity is most meaningful because it takes everything into account. However, individual investors have different investment requirements. Look, for example, at the bonds of three similarly rated companies shown in Table 9.6. Each matures 12 years from now, but because they were issued at different times they have different coupons. Bond A was issued at a time when AAs were yielding 4 percent, so its coupon payment is $40. Bond B was issued when AAs were yielding 7 percent, so its coupon is $70. Bond C was issued when AAs were yielding 10 percent, so its coupon is $100. Assume that AA rated issues today are yielding 7 percent.

Table 9.6   Comparing Bonds with the Same Yield-to-Maturity, but Other Differences

	Annual coupon	Coupon yield	Today's price	Current yield	Yield to maturity	Yearly interest	Capital gain (or loss) at maturity
Bond A ...	$ 40	4%	$ 759	5.3%	7.0%	$ 40	$241
Bond B....	70	7	1,000	7.0	7.0	70	none
Bond C ...	100	10	1,241	8.1	7.0	100	(241)

Notice that the price of each of the three bonds is such that they all have the same yield-to-maturity. Thus, a bond buyer who has no tax to worry about, and does not need the money until after 12 years, might be indifferent as to which bond is bought. If the bond buyer was a retired person who needed current income to live on, and was in a low tax bracket, the buyer would most likely prefer Bond C because of the higher current income. A wealthy person in a high tax bracket might prefer Bond A because Bond A pays relatively little interest, which would be taxed at a high rate now, but gives a big capital gain at maturity. So, that investor prefers Bond A because most of the tax can be deferred until maturity, and may possibly be taxed at a lower capital gains rate. Thus, individual tax considerations and financial needs may make one bond more attractive than another. For the person with no tax considerations, and not needing much money before the bond matures, the yield to maturity of 7% for each bond makes that buyer indifferent as to which bond to own.

HOW BOND YIELDS CHANGE

Bonds prices generally move up and down for two reasons. First, bond prices will move up or down to reflect changes in interest rates in the economy in general. How this happens is discussed shortly. Second, bond prices will move up or down to reflect an improvement or deterioration in the creditworthiness of a particular company. Price changes for this latter reason will be independent of how interest rates are moving in the economy in general. For example, even if interest rates in general are declining, and most bond prices are moving up, the prices of some bonds may decline because those bonds are becoming more risky. This makes sense because, as the risk increases, bond buyers would want a higher yield now to compensate them for the increased risk that a future interest or principal repayment might not be made.

To see how bond yields change, let's look at BLT Co. bonds that were issued on December 31, 1993. The bonds have a 6% coupon and mature on December 31, 2008. They are rated AA and have no sinking fund or call provision. Their annual coupon is $60 ($30 semiannually), or 6% of their face value of $1,000 per bond. When these bonds were initially issued to their first owners (a primary offering) in December 1993, AA-rated bonds were yielding 6%, so the BLT bonds were issued exactly at par. Mr. Wood purchased one of the bonds by paying $1,000 to the company (through his broker). Thus, his coupon yield was 6%, his current yield was 6%, and his yield to maturity was 6%. Mr. Wood intended to hold the bond until maturity.

In January 1994, the general level of interest rates began to rise. This meant bond prices began to fall. In January 1994, Mr. Wood looked in the newspaper and saw that his bonds were selling at $980. At $980, the current yield is 6.1% and the yield to maturity is 6.2%.

$$\text{Current yield} = \frac{\text{Coupon}}{\text{Current price}} = \frac{\$60}{\$980} = 6.1\%$$

$$\text{Yield to maturity (from calculator)} = 6.2\%$$

Notice that the current yield and yield to maturity always relate to the current price. From Wood's point of view, however, nothing has changed, since he does not intend to sell the bond. He still gets $60 in interest payments each year and $1,000 at maturity. He is still getting a 6% yield *on his original investment of $1,000.* But when we talk about bond yields we are usually not talking about some individual's yield based on a price he paid sometime in the past. We usually talk about the yield you would get beginning today if you bought the bond at today's price.

Why did the bond price fall? Or the interest rate rise? It did *not* do so because some government agency said that all AA bonds would now sell at $980 or would have a yield to maturity of 6.2%. Rather, what happened is this. Ms. D., Mr. E., and Mr. F were all holders of BLT Co. bonds and were sophisticated students of the bond market and interest rates. In early January 1994 they observed upward changes in other interest rates, such as the prime rate, and had been watching Federal Reserve moves in the markets. Each of them, independently, concluded that interest rates were about to go up. If interest rates went up on AA-rated bonds to, say 6.4%, that would mean that another company about to issue new bonds, Company XYZ for instance, would have to pay a coupon of $64 per $1,000 bond. If BLT Co. and XYZ had the same rating and other features of the bond were similar, and if BLT Co. bonds were still selling at $1,000 and yielding 6% exactly, it would obviously be preferable to buy the bonds of XYZ and get the higher coupon. Anticipating this, Ms. D decided to sell her BLT Co. bonds in early January and use the money to buy the bonds of XYZ. Because the bonds she was selling were just one of many AA issues on the market, she had to lower her price a little to make her bond more attractive to a buyer. Thus, the price was forced downward, say to $997. Mr. E and Mr. F were bond speculators and did not particularly care whether they bought the XYZ bonds or not; but because they expected interest rates to go up, they necessarily expected bond prices to go down, and wanted to sell their bonds, too. In the process of selling, they forced the price down even further. By January

20, the price had fallen to $980. Since each sale has a buyer and a seller, the $980 price and 6.1% current yield and 6.2% yield to maturity obviously reflected the balance that day of those who wanted to sell because they thought the bond was going lower, and those who wanted to buy because they thought the price had reached bottom and would stay there or move higher. Thus, yield to maturity on AA-rated bonds has now moved up to 6.2%.

The price moved down and the yield moved up, responding to many investors' individual decisions to buy and sell, which in turn reflected their anticipation of market changes and how best to invest their money. Markets always anticipate the future. The price of a bond or a stock (or many other items for that matter) on a given day always represents the "market opinion" (i.e., the balance of myriad investors' transactions that reflect differing opinions on whether the price is going up or down in the future).

In the example of BLT Co. we saw how bond prices fall and yields rise. Now let's look at the bonds of DZF Co. and see why bonds can sell at a premium to par (i.e., at over $1,000). DZF bonds were initially issued when interest rates were higher than today and thus had a 10% coupon. As interest rates fell, new, similarly rated bonds were issued that yielded only 9%, or $90 per annual coupon. DZF bonds suddenly became very attractive with their $100 coupon, and investors began to buy them. Investors were willing to pay a premium (more than par) for them because, even though they would ultimately incur a capital loss at maturity, the extra current income each year ($100 compared to $90 they could get on new bonds) would make up for the capital loss. Up to what price would investors pay for DZF bonds? The answer is, up to a price where its yield to maturity is the same as the yield to maturity of a new, similarly rated bond being issued today. That yield to maturity tells you exactly the price where you will be as well off buying either DZF bonds or the newly issued bonds with the $90 coupon.

If new AA-rated bonds being issued today were yielding 9%, and DZF bonds were selling at $1,057 for a yield to maturity of 9.2%, the yield to maturity of 9.2% is telling you that the DZF bonds are more attractive than the newly issued 9% bonds, because the extra income from the DZF coupons more than offsets the capital loss of $57 at maturity. In fact, investors would be willing to pay up to $1,073 for DZF bonds, at which point their yield to maturity would be exactly 9%, just in line with newly issued AA-rated bonds.

BOND TITLES

When you look at the balance sheet in the annual report of a company you will usually see each of the bond issues listed separately. A balance sheet with many bond issues may look like this:

Bonds:	
5.60%	Mortgage bonds due 2008
7.00	Equipment Trust Certificates due 2003
8.10	Sinking-fund debentures due 2002
6.25	Notes due 1999
9.40	Subordinated debentures due 2006
10 ½	Senior subordinated debentures due 2001
14.25	Junior subordinated debentures due 2007
5.00	Convertible subordinated debentures due 2003

Each of these issues is a separate contract with a separate indenture. The order in which they appear on the balance sheet is usually their priority in being paid off in the event of liquidation. The order of priority in liquidation is usually not the order in which they were issued nor the order in which they mature.

A company is not obligated to list debt issues in any particular order; one often has to refer to the footnotes or directly to the indentures to determine the priorities. *Moody's Industrial Manual* or *Standard & Poor's Corporation Records* are also helpful in this regard. These books are published by Moody's Investors Services and by Standard & Poor's, Inc. They provide a lot of basic data on almost all publicly traded stock and bond issues.

Bond titles usually indicate the issue's priority in liquidation. Let's look at each of the bonds in the previous balance sheet example to see what the words mean.

- **5.6% Mortgage bonds due 2008**—This bond has a coupon rate of 5.60 percent and final maturity is in 2008. There may or may not be a sinking-fund provision. The bond title does not tell us. The title, *mortgage bonds*, means that one or more specific pieces of property, usually buildings and equipment, are "pledged" to the bondholders.[8] Thus, in the event that the company cannot meet its obligations to the bondholders, the pledged property becomes the property of the bondholders, who can then sell it to get their money back.

---

[8] This is the same as saying the bonds are "backed by," or "secured by," the specified pieces of property.

- **7.00% Equipment Trust Certificates due 2003**—These are much like mortgage bonds except that the pledged property is usually a piece of transportation equipment, such as an airplane or a railroad car.

- **8.10% Sinking-Fund Debentures due 2002**—As discussed at the beginning of this chapter, not all bonds have a specific piece of property pledged to them. Bonds that do not are usually called debentures. If the company is unable to meet its obligations to the debenture holders (pay interest on time, for example) the debenture holders do not get to take possession of assets. They can, however, go to court and ask that the company be declared bankrupt. If that occurs and the company is liquidated, the debenture holders only get paid off after all debt holders with higher priority rights get paid off. The words *sinking fund* in the title give you the additional information that there is a sinking fund. Even if the title does not say sinking fund, there may be one. If there were not a sinking fund, the title of these bonds would simply have been "8.10% Debentures due 2002." Since there is a sinking fund and those words are included in the title, the title might be abbreviated "8.10% SFDs."

- **6.25% Notes due 1999**—Notes usually mean the same thing as bonds or debentures, but are issued with shorter maturity dates, ranging from 1 to 10 years. Longer maturities are normally called bonds or debentures.

- **9.40% Subordinated Debentures due 2006**—This title gives the information that the rights of the holders of these debentures are in some way subordinated to the rights of other debenture holders. "Subordinated" means lower ranking or lower priority. Most probably, it means that some other debenture holders get paid off ahead of the 9.40% subordinated debenture holders in the event of bankruptcy. Subordinated debentures can arise in two ways. First, suppose the 8.10% Sinking-Fund Debentures (SFD) were issued in 1986. The indenture for the 8.10% SFD said that if the company issued any new debt, the new debt would have to have lower priority in bankruptcy than the 8.10% SFDs. Thus, when the company wanted to issue some more debt in 1988, it had to be subordinated to the 8.10% SFDs. Thus, the 9.40s of 2006 get the title "9.40% Subordinate Debentures due 2006." They are often abbreviated "9.40% Sub. Debs. of '06." Subordination can also arise another way, described under the 10½% senior subordinated debentures.

- **10¹/₂% Senior Subordinated Debentures due 2001**—This title tells you that these 10¹/₂% debentures are subordinated to *some* debt issues, but are *senior* to others. *Senior* means "comes ahead of," or higher ranking; the opposite of subordinated. The title does not tell you which issues the 10¹/₂s are subordinated to, or senior to, but it appears that they are subordinated to the 8.10% SFDs, the Notes and the Bonds; and are senior to, or ranked ahead of, the 9.40% Subordinated Debentures, the Junior Subordinated Debentures, and the Convertible Subordinated Debentures. The ranking almost certainly relates to the issue's priority in being repaid if the company liquidates.

Let's look at why the 10¹/₂%s became "senior subordinated" even though they were issued after the 9.40% subordinated debentures.

When the 9.40%s were issued in 1988, the company had a lot of debt outstanding; and in order to make the issue attractive enough to be sold, the company not only had to pay a high 9.4% interest rate but also had to agree in the indenture not to issue any further bonds or debentures. However, in the 1991 recession, things got so bad that the company was faced with bankruptcy if it could not raise some more money quickly. It was almost impossible to sell new stock, and banks refused to make any further loans to the company. Thus, the company knew it would have to issue more bonds even though it had agreed not to in the indenture under 9.40% Sub. Debs. So the company's management wrote a letter to the holders of the 9.40% debentures explaining how bad the situation was and asked the bondholders to *waive* this agreement (make an exception) and allow the company to issue some new bonds or debentures. The letter further explained that if the company did not raise new money, bankruptcy was inevitable.

The letter also pointed out that, in the event of bankruptcy, the holders of the 9.40%s were the last people to be paid off, and that it was unlikely that they would get all, if any, of their money back. Further, the case might be in the bankruptcy court for years, and during that time they would not even get interest. Thus, it became apparent to the 9.40% debenture holders that it was in their best interests to waive their right and allow the company to issue new bonds, and then hope that the company could pull out of trouble and could continue to make good its interest and eventual redemption obligations.

The company's investment bankers said that it would be very difficult to sell a new debt issue since it would be so risky. In order to make the new debentures attractive enough to sell, the investment bankers not only suggested a $10^{1}/_{2}\%$ interest rate, but also suggested that the issue be given priority over the 9.40%s in the event of bankruptcy. Once again, the 9.40% debenture holders were approached and told that if they did not subordinate their rights in liquidation to the new debentures, that it was unlikely that the new debentures could be sold and, again, bankruptcy was inevitable.

The 9.40% debenture holders said they would give permission for the company to issue new debt (bonds or debentures) and would allow the new debt to be senior to them, but also said that although they made an exception this time, they still retained all their rights under the indenture and would refuse any further requests for additional new debt.

Thus the $10^{1}/_{2}$ Senior Subordinated Debentures were issued in 1991 and were senior to the 9.40% Sub. Debs. in liquidation rights, although they were still junior, or subordinated, to the 8.10% SFDs and all other debt issues already discussed.

- **14.25% Junior Subordinated Debentures due 2007**—In 1993 the company once again needed to borrow money to avoid bankruptcy. Again, the holders of the 9.40% Sub. Debs. (as well as the other debt holders whose indentures prohibited the company from further borrowing) were asked for their permission to allow the company to issue new debt. The 9.40% Sub. Deb. holders again granted their permission for the new debt, but this time they refused to subordinate their rights in the event of liquidation or bankruptcy. Thus, the company's new debt issue had to be junior to even the 9.40%s of 2006. As a result of this lowest priority, the new debentures were titled "Junior Subordinated Debentures." Also, because of this low priority in a company that was in poor financial shape, the company had to offer a very high coupon rate of 14.25% to induce people to buy them. Had the company been permitted to give this issue a higher priority in liquidation, say senior to the 9.40% Sub. Debs., then perhaps this issue could have been sold with a 12% or 13% coupon. Had this issue been even more senior, it might have been sold with an even lower coupon.

- **5.00% Convertible Subordinated Debentures due 2003**—Convertibles are usually the most junior debt issue in a company, although one occasionally sees a convertible bond that is backed by a specific piece of property, like a mortgage bond. In the case of these 5.00% Convertible Subordinated Debentures due 2003 (abbreviated 5% CSDs of '03), although we are not specifically told that they are junior to the 14.25%s, that is a good assumption, and we could find out for certain by checking the indenture.

Note also that convertibles usually pay a lower coupon rate because the opportunity to make a big profit from the convertible feature makes them very attractive to investors. This is discussed in Chapter 11.

10

Bonds: Advanced Topics

ORIGINAL ISSUE DISCOUNT AND ZERO COUPON BONDS

Most companies issue bonds at face (or par value) of $1,000 per bond and pay a cash coupon twice a year at whatever interest rate is appropriate for that company's rating at the time the bond was issued. Thus, a company wishing to borrow $60,000 would issue 60 bonds, and if 8% was the appropriate yield, the company would pay $40 semiannually for an annual or *full coupon* of $80 per bond a year. Its annual interest payment on the whole issue would be $4,800 (60 bonds × $80 coupon per bond = $4,800).

In recent years, however, some companies have chosen to sell bonds at less than the face amount. In this case we say the company has issued bonds at a *discount from par*. Such bonds are sometimes called *original issue discounts* and abbreviated OIDs. As an example, a company might issue a $1,000 face amount bond for $800. Although the company would have only borrowed $800, it would still have to pay back $1,000 when the bond matured. If this company wished to raise $60,000, it would have to sell 75 bonds instead of 60 bonds (75 bonds × $800 received per bond = $60,000). At maturity, however, the company would have to pay back $75,000 (75 bonds × $1,000 face value).

The reason a company would issue bonds for $800 when it knows it will have to pay back $1,000 later is that, because the bondholder has a built-in gain of $200 when the bond matures, the bondholder would be willing to take a lower annual interest rate than she would otherwise require in order to be willing to buy the bond. A company that needs to borrow money but that has a limited ability to pay interest might want to issue bonds at a discount to save on current interest payments. A company with an even more limited ability to pay a current coupon might wish to sell $1,000 face-amount bonds at an even deeper discount, say $600. This deeper discount (from face or par) would build in a $400 gain for the bondholder, who would thus be willing to take an even smaller annual coupon interest. At the extreme, a company that could not afford to pay any interest now might issue 0% coupon bonds, called *zero coupons* or *zeros*. With no coupon, the bond would need to be issued at a very deep discount, such that all of the return to the bondholder comes at maturity when the bond is redeemed at $1,000. Table 10.1 shows four different ways the company could borrow $60,000 and give the bond buyer an 8% yield to maturity.

Table 10.1   Alternative Bond Issues Priced to Give Same Yield to Maturity

Issue price per bond	Number of bonds sold	Repayment or face amount of total issue (at $1,000 per bond)	Coupon	Total annual cash coupon paid by company	Yield to maturity
$1,000	60	$ 60,000	8%	$4,800	8%
$ 800	75	$ 75,000	$5\frac{3}{8}$%	$4,031	8%
$ 600	100	$100,000	$2\frac{3}{4}$%	$2,750	8%
$ 390	154	$154,000	0%	$ 0	8%

Notice that the deeper the discount at which the bonds are originally issued (first column), the less interest that must be paid each year (fifth column). But this annual interest savings by the company is offset by an increasingly large repayment obligation at maturity (third column).

Notice also that in each case the yield to maturity is 8%. In practice, however, a company that might be able to issue bonds *at par* with an 8% yield to maturity would probably have to offer a higher yield to maturity on zeros, perhaps 10%. This is because the much higher repayment obligation at maturity (third column) makes full repayment more risky.

In summary, from the issuing company's point of view, the advantage of *deep discount* or *zero coupon bonds* is that the company has little or no interest payments for a number of years. The disadvantage is that there will be a much bigger repayment obligation at maturity than if the company had been paying a coupon all along. For these reasons, it makes sense for a company to issue zero coupon bonds when the company is currently cash short but expects that by borrowing money now the company will survive and prosper and be able to generate enough profit in the future to pay back the bonds.

From the bond buyer's point of view, zero coupon bonds may be preferable to full cash coupon bonds when saving for retirement or some other far-off event. This is because, with zero coupon bonds, the bondholder does not need to be concerned with reinvesting the coupons. Remember that since most bonds pay cash coupons twice a year, the bondholder will have to decide how to reinvest the coupon twice each year. If interest rates were to decline in the future, then each time a coupon payment is received, the bondholder would have to reinvest it at a declining interest rate—perhaps 7% or 6% in the previous example. By buying a zero coupon bond, the 8% yield to maturity is "locked in" and there is no risk of having to reinvest a cash coupon at a lower interest rate. An 8% "reinvestment" rate is built into the appreciation from the $390 issue price to the $1,000 maturity price.

If, on the other hand, interest rates were expected to rise, then the bondholder would prefer the bond that paid an 8% cash coupon. This is because as each coupon is received, it could be reinvested at a higher rate, perhaps 9% or 10%, with the result that the total amount of money available to the investor at maturity would be greater than what she would get with the locked in 8% rate of the 0% coupon bond.

RESETS AND VARIABLE RATE NOTES

Most bonds have a fixed coupon. That is, every coupon payment is the same. However, some issues have variable coupon payments. For these issues, called *variable rate notes* or *floating rate notes*, the coupon will vary with some other specified market interest rate. For example, a variable rate note may specify that the initial interest rate will be at 7%, but future coupons will always be at an interest rate that is 1.5 percentage points above the most recently issued 5-year U.S. Treasury (UST) note. So if the interest rate on the newest 5-year UST note is 4.5%, then the next interest payment on the variable rate note would be at a 6% rate. This would mean a coupon payment of $30 per bond, since coupons are paid semiannually. Since the interest rate on UST notes is always changing, it is likely that the coupon on the variable rate note will be different at each payment.

Another type of bond is called a *reset*. Reset bonds usually specify that the coupon rate will change only once or twice, and that the change will occur at a specified time, perhaps one or two years after the bond was issued. The amount of the change is usually also specified when the bond is issued, so buyers know exactly what their coupon will be both before and after the change, or reset. This, of course, is different from variable rate bonds, where bondholders may try to forecast future changes in the coupon rate, but cannot know for certain. A typical reset bond might be the "7%/10%s of 6-1-1999/2004." This title tells you that the coupon rate will be 7% of face value from the time the bond is issued until the reset date, which is June 1, 1999. At that time, the coupon rate will reset to 10% and stay there until maturity on June 1, 2004. Another reset might be the "0%/9%s of 9-1-1997/2007." These are 0% coupon bonds until September 1, 1997 and then become 9% cash-paying coupon bonds until maturity.

Some bonds can also have their coupons reset if some other event occurs, such as if the company gets a change in rating from the rating agencies, or if the price of oil or gold changes to a level specified in the bond's indenture. Reset and variable rate bonds are far less common than fixed coupon bonds, and will not be discussed further. For the remainder of the book it will be assumed that all bonds, notes, or debentures have a fixed coupon rate from the time they are issued until they are retired, unless otherwise clearly stated.

CALLS AND REFUNDING

When a company wants to raise money by selling bonds, it obviously wants to issue them at the lowest possible interest rate (given its rating). It also wants to have maximum flexibility on how and when it pays back the loan, and have the fewest possible restrictions of any sort in the indenture. Conversely, the buyer of a bond wants the highest possible interest and the greatest possible protection. The features and restrictions discussed in this section and the section on Covenants later in this chapter will have a bearing on what interest rate is actually necessary to sell the bonds.

A bond indenture may say that the bond is *callable* after a specified date. This means that the company that issued the bond has the right, at its option, to redeem the bond early, rather than wait until a sinking fund date or final maturity; and the bondholders have no choice. When a company *calls* a bond, the bondholder is notified by mail that the bond has been called (for redemption) as of a certain date. The bondholder, or the brokerage firm that holds the bond, will then return the bond to the trustee and the holder either gets a check in the mail, or the money is credited to the person's brokerage account. A bondholder who does not deliver the bond to the trustee will not get his or her money back, but the bond stops earning interest as of the call date, so the holder has no reason not to return the bond.

A company wants the right to call its bonds for a number of reasons. First, the company may have accumulated extra cash and wants to pay off the bonds so it will not have to make interest payments. Second, suppose the bonds were issued with an 11% coupon ($110 interest per year on a $1,000 face value bond) and yields on similarly rated bonds have now fallen to 8%. In that case, the company would like to issue new bonds with an 8% ($80) coupon and use the money raised from the new bonds to redeem the old bonds with the 11% ($110) coupon, and thereby save $30 interest per bond per year. The third reason the company might want to call its bonds is that the bond's indenture may have restrictions that are preventing the company from doing something it wants, such as issuing new debt or acquiring another company. By calling and redeeming a bond issue, its restrictive indenture ceases to exist and the company will once again have its flexibility.

From the bondholder's point of view, the call feature is undesirable. Bondholders who bought the bond with an 11% coupon would certainly not want to give it up when they could only reinvest the money at 8%. Therefore, other things being equal, if a bond were *callable*, prospective buyers of the bond would demand a higher coupon on the bond to compensate them for the risk that the bond might be called away just when it was most attractive. For example, if there were no call feature, the bond may be able to be sold when initially issued with a 10% coupon. On the other hand, if the company wants the right to call the bond at any time, it might have to pay an 11% coupon in order to get investors to buy the bond. If the company is willing to settle for a somewhat restricted call feature, it may be able to sell the bonds with a 10.5% coupon. This is typical of the factors that go into determining whether a bond will be attractive to a buyer at a given interest rate.

Given the company's desire to have the flexibility of calling the bond, and the bondholder's aversion to it, the call feature usually represents a compromise. Using as an example an 8% bond issued at par on June 1, 1992, and maturing on June 1, 2006, a typical call feature might begin as follows:

CALL FEATURE

"These bonds are callable at the option of the company *but not before* 6-1-97. If they are called on or after 6-1-97 but before 6-1-98, the company will pay the bondholders the face amount ($1,000) plus an 8% premium ($80). If they are called on or after 6-1-98 but before 6-1-99, the company will pay a 7% premium. If they are called on or after 6-1-99 but before 6-1-2000, the company will pay a 6% premium" . . . and so on down to no premium between 6-1-05 and maturity on 6-1-06.

With this call provision the bondholders are protected against having the bonds called away for the first five years after issue, and if the bonds are called by the company in the sixth through thirteenth year, the bondholders will get some extra money, referred to as a *call premium*, to compensate them. With this call feature, the bonds would still look attractive to buyers at the time of issue, but would add some flexibility for the company in the later years.

In the language of Wall Street, we would say, "This bond is noncallable five years and then callable at an 8% premium declining evenly to par in 2005," or, "This bond is NC 5 and then at $108 declining ratably to par in 2005." Both ways say the same thing. NC is the standard abbreviation for noncallable, and *ratably* means an equal amount each year. Including the call premium, the initial call price is $1,080. Bond investors, however, usually talk in terms of $100 when they mean $1,000, so we would say that the bond's *first call* is at $108. Similarly, the *second call* is at $107 (really $1,070), and so on. Before June 1, 1997, this bond was noncallable. After that first call date we would say the bond is *currently callable*, meaning it can now be called by the company at any time.

The call feature in the indenture also frequently says, "Although these bonds are callable from (date) to maturity, and with a (specified) premium, they may not be *refunded*." This means that it is okay for the company to call the bonds if it is because the company has sufficient cash available, *but it is not permitted to call the bonds if the money used to redeem them is obtained by issuing new bonds at a lower interest rate.*

DEFINITION

- **Refunding**—Refunding occurs when a company issues new bonds at a lower interest rate to pay back old bonds that have a higher interest rate. The term *refunding* does not refer to the process whereby the bondholder returns the bond to the company to get his money back. That is *redemption.*

An example of a refunding would be that given earlier in this section where the company wanted to call its 11% bonds in order to *refund* them by issuing new 8% bonds, saving $30 interest per bond.

To review, a bond indenture states whether the bond may be *called,* and if so at what price premiums at which dates. The indenture also states whether the bond may *refunded.* It is possible that the indenture for a given bond may state that the bond is "callable but not refundable." This means that the bond may be called if the company has enough cash generated from retained earnings, or if the company raised new cash from an equity offering (new stock), but the company may not call the bonds with money raised from selling a new issue of bonds that carry a lower interest rate.

From the point of view of the person who buys the bond and hopes to hold it to maturity to get the interest payments, a bond that is "callable but not refundable" would be more desirable than a bond that is callable for any reason. Obviously, it would be even better from the bondholder's point of view if the bond were not callable for any reason. If a bond is callable, the bondholder would prefer that the call provision have a limited number of years, a high call premium, and limitations on the reasons for which it may be called, such as nonrefundability. Any or all of these features are called *call protection.* If a potential buyer does not like the call features, he does not have to buy the bond. Many bonds issued today are callable at any time but are nonrefundable for a number of years. Others are noncallable and nonrefundable for the life of the bond. The call features can vary substantially from bond to bond and should be checked carefully by potential buyers.

YIELD TO CALL AND YIELD TO WORST

In Chapter 9 we learned that the yield to maturity is a yield number that considers both the coupon that the bondholder receives each year and the gain (or loss) that the bondholder realizes at maturity (the difference between the price she paid and the $1,000 face amount she receives at maturity). When a bond is *callable*, an interesting question arises as to what the bond's yield is. If the bond is not redeemed until final maturity, then the yield to maturity would be the yield the bondholder actually receives. But if the bond is *called* earlier, ahead of final maturity, then the bondholder's yield would be different, for two reasons: first, because she may have received a call premium (and therefore received more than the face value of the bond), and second, because she received the money earlier than final maturity. Thus, bond investors must do another yield calculation, called the *yield to call*. The yield to call is calculated the same way as the yield to maturity except that the yield to call uses the *call price* (including premium) instead of the face value of the bond, and uses the *call date* instead of the final maturity date of the bond. Looking at the 8% bonds due on June 1, 2006, described under "Call Feature" on page 124, notice that the bond was first callable on June 1, 1997 at a price of $1,080. The yield to call calculated using this June 1, 1997 call date and the $1,080 call price would be referred to as the *yield to first call*. The second call date for these bonds was June 1, 1998, and the call price at that time became $1,070. The yield to call using these numbers is referred to as the *yield to second call*, and so on. Since it is not possible to know in advance whether a bond will be called, bond investors calculate all of these yield figures—the yield to maturity and the yield to call for each call date—and generally use the lowest of these yields in determining whether they wish to buy, hold, or sell the bond. The lowest of these yields, whichever it turns out to be, is called the *yield to worst*, and is the minimum yield the bondbuyer will realize if she holds the bonds either until they mature or are called.

COVENANTS

When someone buys a bond, that person is lending money to a company for perhaps 10 or 20 years. Although the company may be very profitable and the bonds appear safe at the time they were issued, a lot can change over a number of years. If a bondholder perceived that the company's creditworthiness was deteriorating; that is, the company's financial condition was weakening and there was an increasing risk that the company would be unable to meet an interest payment or a principal repayment on time, the bondholder would ideally like to sell the bond. Unfortunately, people who might be buyers of the bond probably see the same information and also realize that the bond is becoming more risky. Thus, it would be hard to find a buyer for the bond except at a much lower price. To protect themselves as much as possible from deteriorating creditworthiness, bond investors require bond issuers to make a number of binding agreements that are designed to keep the company focused on maintaining its financial health. These agreements are called *covenants*, and are a major part of the bond (or debenture) indenture.

These covenants are not really very different from promises or agreements you would want if you were lending money to a friend to start a business. But because these covenants have been worked on by lawyers over many years, they are usually written in language that is difficult for the average person to understand. Many basic covenants are similar from company to company, and others are written specifically to fit individual company and lender needs. Financial institutions, such as mutual funds, insurance companies, and the like, usually read them carefully and would not buy the bonds if the covenants did not give them adequate protection. This is important because where covenants are weak, company owners (stockholders) have been known to take advantage of these weaknesses to benefit themselves at the expense of the bondholders. This was seen particularly in the 1980s in a number of lower rated bonds, where owners were able to take a lot of money out of the company and then let the company go bankrupt, leaving the bondholders with little or nothing. A number of basic covenants are discussed here. Covenants similar to these are found in almost every indenture.

1. *Maintenance covenants.* These covenants typically say the company must maintain certain financial ratios. A typical covenant might require the company to maintain interest coverage of at least 4 times (review the interest coverage ratio in Chapter 4). Another might require the company to maintain a net worth (same as book value) above some specified level.

2. *Limitation on additional debt.* This covenant might say that if the company wants to issue additional debt, it can only do so if its interest coverage ratio and long-term debt-to-total capital ratio would be above specified levels *after the new debt was issued*. This covenant might also specify that any newly issued debt must have a later maturity date than the issue covered by this indenture.

3. *Restricted payments*. These covenants are designed to limit or prohibit the company's ability to spend its money in certain ways that might hurt the bondholders. These restrictions typically include:

   a. *A limit on dividends*. This limits how much the company can pay as dividends to its stockholders. If the company paid too much as dividends, the business could suffer and it might be unable to repay the bonds when they are due. Worse, if the company saw itself getting into financial trouble and did not have the dividend limitation covenant, the company could sell all its assets or the entire business, pay all the cash as a dividend to the stockholders, and leave nothing for the bondholders.

   b. *A stock repurchase limitation*. For the same reasons, this covenant also puts a limit on how much money the company can use to buy back its stock.

   c. *A limit on junior debt repurchases*. This limits or prohibits the company's ability to buy back issues of the company's bonds or debentures that otherwise would not mature until after the bonds covered by this indenture. All of these *restricted payments covenants*, and others as well, are designed to keep the company's funds focused on the business and prevent the company from doing things that might unnecessarily weaken its financial condition.

Other covenants will limit the company's ability to sell its assets or merge with another company, and will require the company to maintain insurance on its property. The covenants may not seem important at the time the bonds are initially issued, but if the company begins to have problems a few years later, these protections can be critical to preventing the company from taking steps that could hurt the bondholders.

It must be remembered that the company directors' obligation is to look out for the best interests of the stockholders, not the bondholders. The covenants in the indenture are the bondholders' only safeguard. Covenant protection makes sure the bondholders do not suffer at the expense of the stockholders. If a company is willing to live with very restrictive covenants (which make the bondholders feel safer), the company will be able to issue bonds at a lower interest rate than if it were only willing to agree to weaker covenants.

Sometimes, despite management's best efforts, the company's fortunes decline and creditworthiness deteriorates anyway. The company may even go bankrupt. Even in these circumstances, the covenants work to protect the bondholder in many ways.

DEFAULT AND ACCELERATION

If a company fails to make an interest payment, a sinking fund payment, or the final maturity payment when it is due, the failure to make such a payment is called a *default*. Violating a covenant, such as those just listed, is also a default. Usually the indenture gives the company a 30-day "grace period" to *correct the default*; that is, to make the payment or get a financial ratio back in compliance with the covenant. If the company does not correct the default, then the bondholders must look at the indenture to see what their rights are, and what obligations the company has. Typically, the bondholder's rights include *making the entire principal amount of the bond or debenture issue due and payable immediately*. This process of making the entire loan due for redemption immediately (ahead of the final maturity date or sinking fund schedule) is called *acceleration*. In the language of Wall Street, one might say, "Bondholders forced acceleration of Company XYZ's bonds after XYZ failed to make an interest payment in time or within the grace period."

When a company is in financial trouble, forcing acceleration will often require the company to pay back more bonds than it is able. And that, in turn, can result in the company having to file for bankruptcy. In bankruptcy, the stockholders' investment may become worthless, or nearly so. It is this threat of acceleration and its consequences that forces companies to work hard to comply with the covenant requirements.

Bankruptcy can also sometimes leave the bondholders worse off, especially holders of lower priority debt, for whom there may not be enough money after all higher priority debt has been paid off in the event of liquidation. Thus, even though the company may be *in default*, debtholders sometimes choose not to exercise their right of acceleration, hoping that the company will be able to work its way out of trouble and eventually repay all its back interest and debt obligations.

BANKRUPTCY

When a court declares a company bankrupt, one of two procedures are usually followed. First, the company can try to do a *reorganization* under Chapter 11 of the Bankruptcy Act or, second, the company can liquidate under Chapter 7 of the Bankruptcy Act.

In a reorganization, the company and all the parties who are owed money try to make a plan agreeable to all, whereby debtholders usually agree to take less interest on their debt, perhaps forgoing interest for a few years, and to reduce the amount of principal that the company owes them. If everyone can agree on how much principal and interest each will give up, the court will usually approve the plan. Sometimes, if all but one or two parties can agree on a reorganization plan, the court may approve it anyway. This is known as a "cram down" on Wall Street. When this happens, the lower priority debtholders will usually have to give up more than higher priority debtholders, although the court has a lot of leeway in imposing a reorganization plan.

Sometimes, if the parties cannot agree on a reorganization plan, the company will liquidate. In a bankruptcy liquidation, the court oversees the selling of all the company's assets and then pays off the debtholders. In this case, the court usually follows the established debt priorities very carefully, so that lower priority debt may get paid nothing unless the higher priority debt is completely paid off. Before any debtholders are paid off, however, most states' laws specify that back wages owed to employees and certain taxes must be paid first, along with, of course, the bankruptcy lawyers' fees. The bankruptcy laws are complex and not especially relevant here. We are more concerned with successful companies.

11

Convertible Bonds

Convertible bonds[1] are just like straight bonds discussed in the last two chapters, except they have one additional important feature: They can be converted into stock. To demonstrate, suppose BCD Corporation issued $100,000 worth of convertible bonds on January 2, 1990. The bonds have a 14-year life and therefore mature in 2004. The *conversion feature* of these convertible bonds may say something like this:

> Each bond may be converted into 20 shares of common stock of the company at the option of the bondholder anytime after January 1, 1995.

This means that if you as the bondholder decide to convert, you mail your bond certificate to the company (or trustee) and by return mail you will receive a certificate for 20 shares of common stock of BCD Corp. Notice that this bond cannot be converted during the first five years of its life. Sometimes the indenture specifies that the bond is only convertible after a specified period (like this one). Sometimes the indenture may

---

1 The term *convertible bond* will be used in this chapter to mean either convertible bonds or convertible debentures. In fact, the vast majority of such convertible issues are debentures, but Wall Streeters often refer to both loosely as convertible bonds.

also specify that the bond cannot be convertible *after* a specified time. For example, a convertible bond may be convertible only for the first 10 years of its life and not thereafter. Most convertible bonds, however, are convertible any time before maturity.

Another more common way to write the conversion feature is as follows:

> This bond may be converted into common stock of the company at $50 per share.

This does *not* mean that the bondholder has to pay $50 per share. Although it is not clear from the wording, it means that *$50 worth of face value* of the bond may be exchanged for one share of common stock. Since the bond has a face value of $1,000, it therefore converts into 20 shares of common stock:

$$\frac{\text{Face value}}{\text{Conversion "price"}} = \frac{\$1,000}{\$50} = 20 \text{ shares}$$

Again, no cash is paid when a convertible bond is converted. The owner of the bond is giving up the bond, not cash, in exchange for the stock. When you mail the bond in (or have your broker deliver it) to exchange it for stock, you are giving up the right to receive future interest payments and the right to receive the face value of the bond at maturity. When the company receives the bond in exchange for stock, the bond is retired forever. There are no more coupon payments and the face amount of the bond is never paid in cash to anyone. The bond ceases to exist.

You cannot partially convert a bond. If you decide to convert a bond, you convert it entirely, in this case into 20 shares of common. However, if you own more than one bond you may convert only some, but not all, of your bonds.

Note that this bond converts into 20 shares regardless of the price you paid for the bond, or the price it happens to be selling for at the time you decide to convert it into stock. The *conversion rate* (the number of shares of stock the bond converts into) *is based on face value, not the current price*. The face value of the bond does not change. So even if the bond's price falls to $894, or rises to $1,150, or any other price, it still converts into exactly 20 shares, because the face value is always $1,000.

Although the conversion rate is fixed for the vast majority of convertible bonds, one occasionally sees a bond that has a variable conversion rate. The conversion feature of such a bond might say:

> This bond converts into 25 shares of common stock anytime before December 31, 1994; into 30 shares of common stock between January 1, 1995 and December 31, 1998; and into 40 shares of common stock thereafter.

Actually, the same variable conversion feature would more likely be written as follows:

> This bond converts into common stock at $40 per share anytime before December 31, 1994; into common stock at $33.33 per share between January 1, 1995 and December 31, 1998; and into common stock at $25 per share thereafter.

This means exactly the same conversion rates at the same times as written the other way above.

Some bonds with variable conversion rates state that the conversion rate changes when certain dates are reached, as in the previous example. Other convertible bonds have a conversion rate that varies depending on how much money the company is earning in future years. Variable conversion rate bonds are unusual, and for the remainder of the book it is assumed that a convertible bond's conversion rate is fixed.

PRICE OF A CONVERTIBLE BOND

The price of a convertible bond sometimes behaves differently from a nonconvertible bond. We saw in Chapter 9 that the price of a nonconvertible bond moves up or down due to changes in both interest rates in the overall economy and changes in the creditworthiness of the company issuing the bond. The prices of convertible bonds will also fluctuate for these reasons, but in addition, the price of a convertible bond can move higher than a similar nonconvertible bond if the market price of the underlying common stock (the stock into which the bond converts) moves high enough.

To illustrate, let's look at the convertible bonds of BCD Corporation. The bonds have a 5% coupon, are rated A, have eight years left to maturity, and convert into 20 shares of common stock (at $50 of face value of bond per common share). Suppose the underlying common stock is selling at $60/share. What would the bond sell for? Since each bond converts into 20 shares of stock, and each share is worth $60, the bond is therefore worth $1,200, because anyone owning the bond could convert it into 20 shares and sell them on the market for $60 each, for a total of $1,200.

Number of common shares per bond		Market price per common share		Value to bondholder if converted
20	×	$60	=	$1,200

With the stock price at $60, we would say the *converted value* of the bond is $1,200.

If the bond were selling for anything less than $1,200, say $1,000, someone could buy it, convert it, and sell the stock for $1,200 and keep the profit, $200 in this case. Thus, the price of a convertible bond will usually move up in line with the underlying common stock. For example, suppose the stock moved up to $70/share. Then the bond price would move up to $1,400.

Number of shares		Market value per share		Converted value
20	×	$70	=	$1,400

As long as the market price of the stock is above the conversion price of the bond (conversion price is $50 in this example) the bond price will move up in line with the stock price, as shown in Table 11.1.

Table 11.1   Convertible Bond Price in Relation to Stock Price

Common stock price	Bond price	Yields for a 5 % coupon with 8 years to maturity		
		Coupon yield	Current yield	Yield to maturity
$70	$1,400	5.0%	3.6%	Negative
65	1,300	5.0	3.8	1.08%
60	1,200	5.0	4.2	2.25
55	1,100	5.0	4.5	3.55
50	1,000	5.0	5.0	5.00

Notice that as the stock price moves higher, and therefore the bond price moves higher, the bond's current yield and yield to maturity move lower, and have little influence on the decision to buy or not buy the bond. At this point the decision to buy or sell the bond is based on its relationship to the stock price and the investor's outlook for changes in the stock price.

Suppose the price of the stock falls to $30 per share. The converted value of the bond then falls to $600.

Number of shares		Market value per share		Converted value
20	×	$30	=	$600

Does the bond price then fall to $600? Not likely. The price of this bond will only fall to the price where its yield to maturity is equal or close to that of similar 8-year, A-rated, nonconvertible bonds. Assume that similar 8-year, A-rated, nonconvertible bonds are currently selling at a yield to maturity of about 6.6%. For an 8-year bond with a 5% coupon to sell at a yield to maturity 6.6%, its price would be about $900. Thus, the price of the BCD bonds would be unlikely to fall below $900.

Suppose the price of the stock now rose to $45. At that price the converted value of the bond is exactly $900 (20 shares × $45/share = $900). So, for any stock price under $45, the bond will sell for about $900. As the stock price rises above $45, the bond price will begin to move up with it. In reality, even if the stock price were slightly under $45, it is probable that the bond would sell for slightly more than $900. This is because the conversion feature, which gives the bond the possibility of unlimited gains in the future, would cause some investors to be willing to pay a little more for the convertible bond than they would for an otherwise similar nonconvertible bond.

ADVANTAGE OF A CONVERTIBLE BOND FROM THE BONDHOLDER'S POINT OF VIEW

We can now see the advantage of a convertible bond from the bondholders point of view: It has the best features of both bonds and stock. If the stock price is low (relative to the conversion price) the bond has "downside protection" in that its price will behave like any other similar nonconvertible bond, and won't go below a level reflecting the appropriate yield. But if the stock price moves above the conversion price, the bond price will behave like the stock price, and there is no limit to how high it can go. For nonconvertible bonds, the bond price will always reflect only the appropriate yield. Nonconvertible bonds will not "participate" in the movement of the stock price (see Table 11.2).

Note that common stock alone does not have the downside protection of a convertible bond. If things look bad for a company, its stock can keep going lower even if there is a dividend, because there is always the possibility that the dividend will be cut, whereas the bond interest is a contractual obligation and must be paid as long as the company is able.

Table 11.2   Convertible Bond Price Stabilizing as Stock Price Falls

Stock price	Bond price	Coupon yield	Current yield	Yield to maturity*
$80	$1,600	5.0%	3.1%	Negative
70	1,400	5.0	3.6	Negative
60	1,200	5.0	4.2	2.3%
55	1,100	5.0	4.5	3.6
50	1,000	5.0	5.0	5.0
45	900	5.0	5.6	6.6
40	900	5.0	5.6	6.6
30	900	5.0	5.6	6.6
20	900	5.0	5.6	6.6

* Based on 8-year maturity

ADVANTAGE OF CONVERTIBLE BONDS
FROM ISSUING COMPANY'S POINT OF VIEW

Since the conversion feature adds the possibility of unlimited price appreciation (which nonconvertible bonds do not have), a convertible bond is obviously more attractive to the bondholder, other things being equal. Thus, if a company is willing to sell convertible bonds, it may be able to sell them with a lower interest rate than if it were selling nonconvertible bonds. How much lower the coupon would be is related to how attractive the conversion feature is. Suppose, for example, CDE Company has an A rating and its stock is selling at $40. If CDE sells nonconvertible bonds it would have to pay the current interest rate on similar A-rated bonds, which is 8%, or an $80 annual coupon for each $1,000 bond. If instead, CDE sells convertible bonds that convert at $40 per share (i.e., into 25 shares) the bonds would be very attractive because any upward movement in the stock would immediately cause an upward movement in the price of the bonds. Thus, investors might be willing to buy these convertible bonds with only a 3% yield, or a $30 coupon instead of the $80 coupon for straight (nonconvertible) bonds.

On the other hand, if CDE's convertible bonds only converted into 20 shares (at $50 per share) they would not be quite as attractive. In this case, the converted value of the bond today is 20 shares × $40/share stock price = $800, and the stock would have to move up from $40 to about $50 before the bonds began to move with it. In this latter case, the conversion feature is less attractive, although it still could be quite rewarding at some time in the future. With the less attractive conversion feature, the coupon necessary to interest investors in buying the bonds would be greater that the 3% that was necessary with the more attractive conversion feature, but would still be less than the 8% that would be necessary without a conversion feature. Perhaps the coupon would need to be 5% or 6%. In sum, the more attractive the conversion feature, the lower the interest the company will have to pay to get investors to buy their bonds. While paying a lower interest rate is an obvious advantage to the company, the related disadvantage is that if the bonds are converted, the more shares they convert into, the more earnings per share will be diluted.

Another advantage to a company is that sometimes, if a company is in trouble and needs to borrow money badly, it is possible that nobody would want to buy its bonds except at an interest rate that is so high that the company could not afford to pay it. In this case, a convertible bond with an attractive conversion feature might enable the company to sell bonds with a coupon rate it could afford to pay.

PREMIUM AND DISCOUNT TO CONVERSION

Let us look again at the bonds of BCD Corporation (see Table 11.1). Assuming BCD's stock is selling at $60, it is possible—in fact, it is probable—that the bond will not sell at exactly its converted value of $1,200. Suppose the bond is selling at $1,224. In that case, we would say it is selling at a $24 *premium to conversion* (i.e., $24 above its converted value). Normally, however, the premium is expressed as a percent of the converted value, and we would say it is "selling at a 2 percent premium to conversion." In other words, it is selling for a price 2 percent higher than its converted value.

$$\frac{\text{Premium above converted value}}{\text{Converted value}} = \frac{\$24}{\$1,200}$$

$$= .02 \text{ (i.e., 2\% Premium to \$1,200)}$$

Similarly, if the bond is selling at less than its converted value, it is selling at a *discount to conversion*. Suppose the bond is selling at $1,182. That represents an $18 discount from converted value, or a $1\frac{1}{2}$ percent discount.

$$\frac{\substack{\text{Dollar discount} \\ \text{from converted value}}}{\text{Converted value}} = \frac{\$1,200 - 1,182}{\$1,200} = \frac{\$18}{\$1,200}$$

$$= .015 = 1^1/_2 \text{ \% Discount to conversion}$$

One reason a bond sells at a discount to conversion is that if you wanted to buy the bond, convert it, and sell the common stock to keep the difference, you would have to pay commissions for buying the bond and selling the stock; and thus the bond is actually "worth" slightly less than its converted value. One reason a bond may sell at a premium to conversion is as follows. Suppose you expect a stock to go up, but very little of that stock is traded in a day. If you try to buy a lot of that stock, you might force the price up past what you want to pay for it. So you might want to buy the convertible bond instead of the stock. But if other investors are thinking the same thing, you may have to bid up the bond price to a *premium to conversion* in order to acquire all the bonds you want. You can do this and still, in effect, be "buying the stock" at an attractive price.

Another reason a bond may sell at a premium is that the bond's interest would make the bond more attractive than the stock if the stock paid no dividend or only a small dividend. You might have the same capital gain from either the stock or the convertible bond if the stock goes up, so why not buy the bond and also get the higher yield while you are waiting? Furthermore, suppose you are wrong and the stock goes down. By buying the bond instead of the stock, you at least have some protection against an extreme decline.

Do not confuse premium and discount to conversion (converted value) with premium and discount to par. When we say a bond is selling at a premium or a discount, one usually knows by the context whether the statement is referring to par or conversion. Assume the bonds of BCD Corporation are selling at $927 and its stock is selling at $45. The converted value of the bond is $900 (20 shares × $45/share = $900). With the bond priced at $927, it is selling at a 3 percent premium to conversion and a 7.3 percent discount to par. If the bond were selling at $990, it would be selling at a 10 percent premium to conversion and a 1 percent discount from par.

Investors look at a convertible bond's premium to conversion as a measure of the bond's risk. The larger the premium to conversion, the greater the downside risk. For example, a convertible bond with a 10 percent premium to conversion would have a greater risk than the same bond with a 2 percent premium to conversion. A bond selling at a discount from conversion would have relatively less risk unless the stock declined.

CALL RIGHTS AND SINKING FUND

A convertible bond may be callable or have a sinking fund, or both, the same as a nonconvertible bond. If the company calls the bond, or if it is about to be redeemed under a sinking-fund provision, the bondholder almost always has the opportunity to convert it first if he so chooses. By calling the bond, the company can sometimes "force" people to convert if the bond is selling above par. For example, suppose BCD's bonds are selling at $1,200, reflecting the underlying stock price of $60 a share, and the bond's call feature says that if the bond is called this year, the company must pay a call premium of 4% (review call premiums in Chapter 10). If the company wants to "force" conversion, it simply exercises its right to call the bonds and the bondholders are faced with a choice. They can either let the bond be called and receive $1,040 (par plus the 4% call premium), or they can convert the bond and receive $1,200 worth of stock. Obviously they would choose the latter. If the bond were selling at less than par plus the call premium, then holders would probably not convert. Rather, they would let the bond be called away and take the $1,040.

EFFECT OF CONVERTIBLE BONDS ON EARNINGS PER SHARE

We saw in Chapter 4 that the price one should be willing to pay for a share of stock is related to its current and expected future earnings per share (EPS) because that is an indication of possible future dividends. Forecasting future earnings is always a difficult task, and the presence of a convertible bond further complicates it, because if some or all of the bonds are converted, it will result in (1) more shares outstanding (which would lower EPS) and (2) less interest expense (which would raise EPS). The change in EPS as a result of conversion of a convertible bond can be large and is always considered by professional investors when estimating future EPS.

In this section we discuss the effects on earnings per share of converting a convertible bond, but we will not go through the actual calculations of converting. It is, however, a very instructive process and you are encouraged to read the next section, "Converting a Convertible Bond," although it may be skipped without loss of continuity of the book.

Let's assume BCD Corporation is estimated to have earnings per share (EPS) of $4.00 assuming *none* of its convertible bonds are converted, and

$2.80 if *all* the bonds are converted. Assuming the stock is thought to merit a price/earnings ratio of 10×, what is the stock worth?

				Stock value
EPS		P/E		
$4.00	×	10×	=	$40
		or		
$2.80	×	10×	=	$28

Since the bonds have not in fact been converted, the actual EPS is $4, but would you want to pay $40 for the stock knowing that bondholders might convert with the resulting decline in EPS?

One answer is to be conservative and assume the bonds will be converted. Since most investors hate to lose money, why take chances? The most conservative investor would almost always use the lowest EPS figure, and thus, in this case, would judge the value of the stock based on EPS of $2.80. If that investor believes the stock is worth 10 times earnings, he or she would be willing to pay up to $28 for the stock but not higher. If other investors bid the stock up higher, the conservative investor would simply avoid this stock and look for other stocks.

On the other hand, what if the bond is never converted and simply gets redeemed at maturity? In that case, the stock might be attractive up to $40 a share, and therefore is very attractive around $30 a share. So which EPS figure does one use? The Financial Accounting Standards Board[2] has a decision rule that tells companies when to assume conversion and when not to in calculating the EPS figures they publish in their reports to shareholders.

The effect of this rule is to create three definitions of earnings per share, called *basic earnings per share*, *primary earnings per share*, and *fully diluted earnings per share*.

DEFINITIONS

- **Basic earnings per share**—The earnings per share figure that results from dividing the actual net earnings by the number of shares outstanding at the end of the year, without giving any consideration to convertible issues.

---

2 The Financial Accounting Standards Board is the group of accountants and investment people who are authorized by the Securities and Exchange Commission to make the accounting rules that public companies must follow.

- **Primary earnings per share**—The earnings per share figure that results from converting all convertible issues that, according to a detailed decision rule, are likely to be converted to stock at some time.

- **Fully diluted earnings per share**—The earnings per share figure that results from converting all convertible issues, whether or not they are likely to ever be converted.

The latter two definitions are correct as far as they go, but are not complete. Both primary and fully diluted EPS calculations consider a number of other factors that can also give rise to additional shares outstanding. These include convertible preferred stocks (discussed in the next chapter), warrants, rights, and stock options.[3] The latter three items usually have far less impact on EPS than convertible bonds or convertible preferreds, and will not be covered here. Suffice it to say, if the number of additional shares from all these sources is significant, then they would need to be included in the primary and fully diluted earnings per share figures that are reported to the public.

When investors talk about a company's earnings without specifying basic, primary, or fully diluted, it is often because the company has no convertible issues, and therefore has only one earnings figure (which would be the same as basic EPS).

While primary earnings per share was intended to be the single best figure, mechanical decision rules are never perfect, and thus there is no absolute answer to the question of which EPS figure is best. Some investors choose to use primary EPS and some use fully diluted EPS. It comes down to a matter of personal preference. I recommend using fully diluted earnings as the best single choice, unless it is clear that a company's convertible bonds (or convertible preferred stocks) are never going to be converted. This would happen if the company's stock is selling well below the "conversion" price, and the convertible bonds are expected to mature before the stock price rises above the bond's conversion price.

The Financial Accounting Standards Board believes that most investors use fully diluted EPS, and has proposed doing away with the concept of primary EPS. This proposal would require a company to report only *basic* earnings per share and *diluted* earnings per share. The diluted earnings per share figure would be the same as the current *fully diluted* earnings per share.

---

3 Stock options in this case refers to options given by a company to its employees to buy company stock from the company. It has nothing to do with the put and call options you can buy through your stockbroker on the options exchanges. These latter kinds of options have no effect on company earnings, and they are not discussed in this book.

CONVERTING A CONVERTIBLE BOND

Because companies publish both primary and fully diluted earnings figures, most readers will never have occasion to go through the mechanics of converting a bond, and therefore this section may be skipped without losing the continuity of the book. Going through it, however, will improve the reader's familiarity with financial statements, so you are encouraged to read through this section if time allows.

To learn how to convert a convertible bond to stock, let's look at Company EFG. Shown below are EFG's income statement for 1995 and the lower right side of EFG's balance sheet at December 31, 1995, as well as some additional information. The *capitalization* portion of the balance sheet is the only part of the balance sheet that is affected by the conversion process, so that is the only part shown.

EFG (basic EPS—before assuming conversion of bonds)

Income Statement for 1995

Sales		$100,000
Expenses		
CGS	$60,000	
SGA	24,000	
Interest	6,000	
	$90,000	$ 90,000
Profit before tax		$ 10,000
Tax (50%)		5,000
Net profit		$ 5,000

$$\frac{\text{Net profit}}{\text{Shares outstanding}} = \frac{\$5,000}{1,250} = \$4\,/\,\text{share}$$

Part of Balance Sheet at 12/31/95

Capitalization

Long-term debt	
4% Mortgage bonds	$ 50,000
10% Convertible bonds	$ 25,000
Equity	
Common stock at par $1	$ 1,250
(1,250 shs. outstanding)	
Additional paid-in capital	$ 40,000
Retained earnings	$120,000

Other Information to Be Considered:

1. There are $25,000 face amount of convertible bonds outstanding. Since each bond has a face value of $1,000, there are 25 convertible bonds. Note that the amount of *long-term debt* on the balance sheet is always the face value of the bonds outstanding. It is not related to the current price of the bond.

2. Each convertible bond converts into 40 shares of common stock. Since there are 25 convertible bonds outstanding, the total issue of convertible bonds converts into 1,000 shares of stock.

    25 bonds × 40 shares per bond = 1,000 shares

3. The annual interest payable on the convertible bonds is 10% (the coupon rate) times the face value of the bonds outstanding ($25,000). Therefore the total amount of interest on the convertible issue is $2,500 per year.

4. The annual interest on the 4% Mortgage bonds is 4% times its face value of $50,000, which comes to $2,000.

5. The total interest expense for the year, shown on the income statement, was $6,000. This $6,000 includes the $2,500 paid to the convertible bondholders, the $2,000 paid to the mortgage bondholders, and $1,500 paid to holders of some other debt. The $1,500 might represent interest on short-term debt or it may represent interest on some bonds that were outstanding at the beginning of the year but were redeemed sometime during the year, and therefore do not appear on the year-end balance sheet. We do not know, and it does not matter.

The Conversion Process

When EPS are being calculated assuming a bond has been converted, it is always assumed that the bond was converted at the beginning of the year. The following calculations are made:

1. Since the convertible bond is assumed to have been converted to stock at the beginning of the year, the bond would have ceased to exist at that time. Therefore, interest on the bond would not have been paid that year. So the $2,500 interest on the convertible bonds, which was included in the company's total $6,000 interest expense, has to be removed, leaving $3,500 in interest expense for the year. Note that this also changes the pretax profit and hence the taxes and aftertax profit.

2. Since the convertible bond has been converted into 1,000 new shares of stock, the new 1,000 shares must be added to the 1,250 shares already outstanding, giving a new total of 2,250 shares outstanding.

As a result of these changes, the adjusted income statement and balance sheet would look as follows. Numbers that have changed as a result on the conversion process appear in italics.

EFG (after assuming conversion of bonds)

Income Statement for 1995

Sales		$100,000
Expenses		
CGS......................	$60,000	
SGA......................	24,000	
Interest	*3,500*	
	$87,500	*$87,500*
Profit before tax		*$12,500*
Tax (50%)		*6,250*
Net profit		*$ 6,250*

$$\frac{\text{Net profit}}{\text{Shares outstanding}} = \frac{\$6,250}{2,250} = \$2.78 \text{ / share}$$

Part of Balance Sheet at 12/31/95

Capitalization

Long-term debt	
4% Mortgage bonds	$ 50,000
Equity	
Common stock at par $1.................	*$ 2,250*
(*2,250* shs. outstanding)	
Additional paid-in capital	*$ 64,000*
Retained earnings...........................	$120,000

Note that the $25,000 face amount of 10% convertible bonds has been removed from Long-term debt, and the same dollar amount has been added to Equity on the balance sheet. This makes sense because the bonds were converted to equity. The $25,000 was divided between Common at par and Additional paid-in capital according to the rules presented in Chapter 2; i.e., $1,000 was added to Common at par (because par value is $1 and there are 1,000 new common shares) and the remaining $24,000 was additional paid-in capital.

DETERMINING PRIMARY AND FULLY DILUTED EARNINGS PER SHARE

Earnings per share were $4.00 before conversion of the bond and would be diluted to $2.78 after conversion. The Financial Accounting Standards Board has a procedure to help decide which of these EPS figures the company should report to shareholders. As discussed earlier, companies are currently required to calculate and present primary earnings per share and fully diluted earnings per share figures in their reports. To calculate these, the first step is to determine whether the convertible bond is likely, according to a specific rule, to be converted before it matures.[4] Convertible bonds that are deemed likely to be converted under this rule are called *common stock equivalents* (abbreviated C.S.E.s). Convertible bonds that are less likely to be converted are not called by any particular name. They are simply not C.S.E.s. To calculate Primary EPS you must assume conversion (i.e., do the conversion calculation just shown) if the convertible bond is a C.S.E. You do *not* convert it if it is not a C.S.E. To calculate fully diluted EPS, you must assume conversion of the convertible bond *whether or not* it is a C.S.E.

If a company has more than one convertible issue outstanding, primary EPS is calculated by assuming conversion of all the convertible issues that are C.S.E.s, and not converting any issues that are not C.S.E.s. Note that if all of a company's convertible issues are C.S.E.s, then primary EPS would be the same as the fully diluted EPS. In other companies it is possible that none of the convertible issues are C.S.E.s. And, of course, many companies do not have any convertible issues. In this latter case the only EPS figure is the basic EPS and there is no need to use the words *primary* or *fully diluted*.

There is one more consideration when calculating primary or fully diluted EPS. The net result of the conversion process is usually that the EPS of the company are reduced, as was the case for company EFG in the example above. When this happens, we say the convertible issue is *dilutive*. Sometimes, however, going through the conversion calculations

[4] The rule is that if the convertible bond's yield at the time it was issued was less than two-thirds of banks' prime lending rate at that time, then the convertible bond issue will be deemed to be a Common Stock Equivalent as long as it is outstanding.

for a given convertible issue will result in EPS going up, not down. When this happens, we say that particular convertible issue is *antidilutive*. If a convertible issue is antidilutive, it would not be converted when calculating primary or fully diluted EPS, even though it would otherwise need to be converted.

12

Preferred Stock

When JMC raised $20,000 in 1994 to build a new plant, the company chose to sell bonds, a debt financing. The company considered selling common stock, an equity financing, but found debt financing to be the more attractive alternative. Another alternative, not considered by JMC at that time, was to sell preferred stock. When a company sells preferred stock, it is also an equity financing. Preferred stock is in some ways quite different from common stock, having some of the characteristics of common stock, but also having some of the characteristics of bonds.

The treasurer of JMC decided to learn more about preferred stock so the next time JMC wanted to raise money, the company would be better able to consider all the alternatives. The treasurer asked Mr. Gaines for an explanation of preferred stock. Gaines made the following points.

OVERVIEW OF PREFERRED STOCK

Preferred stock is often initially confusing, because at first glance it seems to be more like a bond than like common stock. This is because the dividend on a preferred stock is generally fixed, like the interest on a bond. In addition, some preferred issues are redeemable, may have a sinking fund, and may be callable—again, characteristics more typical of bonds than common stock. Finally, some preferreds are convertible into common stock, yet another characteristic of bonds.

Despite this bondlike appearance, preferred stock is equity, not debt. Perhaps the primary distinction here is that the interest paid on a bond is a contractual obligation of the company and, if it is not paid, bond-holders have the right to demand that the entire bond issue be paid back immediately, and if it is not, they can go to court and have the company declared bankrupt. However, if the preferred dividend is not paid, the preferred shareholders have no right to immediate repayment and no right to have the company declared bankrupt in court. More typically, preferred stocks usually provide that if the preferred dividend has not been paid for a specified number of quarters, typically four or six quarters, then the preferred stockholders will have the right to elect two directors of their choosing to the board.

Another difference between an interest payment and a dividend is that an interest payment is an expense and is deducted from sales in order to calculate profit before tax. A dividend, common or preferred, is *not* an expense; it is something directors may choose to do with the aftertax profit of the company.

Preferreds that are not convertible are called *straight* preferreds. Straight preferreds will be covered first because their characteristics almost always apply to convertible preferreds as well.

Preferred stocks are also sometimes called preference stocks. Usually, if a company has issues of both preferred stocks and preference stocks, the different titles are primarily to help distinguish them. The possible minor difference between them is discussed later.

THE PREFERRED DIVIDEND

The first major difference between a common stock and a preferred stock is the dividend it receives. Whereas the dividend paid on a common stock, called the common dividend, tends to change frequently depending on the success of the company, the dividend on a preferred stock, called the preferred dividend, is usually fixed. Most preferred stocks specify a quarterly dividend, but some pay a semiannual or only an annual dividend. The title of a preferred stock usually states the actual dollar dividend, unlike a bond, where the title specifies the interest as a percent of the face amount. Thus, a typical preferred stock might be called the $3.60 Preferred. This tells you that each outstanding share of this preferred stock issue is entitled to receive an annual dividend of $3.60 per share. So if the dividend is paid quarterly, the holder of a share of this preferred stock would receive $.90 per quarter.

Not all preferreds have a fixed dividend. A few preferreds specify that the dividend automatically goes up or down after a certain year, or if a certain profit level is reached by the company, or if some other specified circumstance is met; but even in these cases the new amount of the dividend is usually specified.

In addition, there are also some preferreds, called *participating preferreds*, that specify that the preferred dividend moves up or down with the company's earnings or with the common stock dividend. Participating preferreds have become rare, and in this chapter we assume that the dividend is always fixed.

In contrast to the fixed dividends of most preferreds, recall that common dividends are frequently increased or decreased at the discretion of the board of directors. Over the long run, increases or decreases in the common dividend are usually related to the profit growth or decline of the company. Thus, if a company's earnings per common share[1] grows, its common stock price will most likely move up in anticipation of increases in the common dividend, or higher dividends in the future if the company is not currently paying a dividend. However, since the preferred dividend is fixed regardless of the earnings of the company, the price of a preferred stock will not move up like a common stock. Rather, the price of a preferred stock tends to behave like the price of a bond, moving up or down to keep its yield in line with the yields of other similar preferred stocks.

Of course, if the preferred dividend is not paid, the preferred stock could go down sharply, just like a bond if its interest payment was not paid.

---

1 We have always used the term *earnings per share* to mean earnings per common share. This is as it should be. As we will see shortly, preferred shares are never added to common shares when calculating earnings per share. Therefore, the term *earnings per share* will always mean *earnings per common share* (EPS).

The preferred dividend, like the common dividend, must be voted on by the board of directors each time it is due. The board is usually neither legally nor contractually required to pay the preferred dividend, but they almost always do, unless the company's earnings in that quarter were not enough to pay the dividend—and even then they often choose to pay it anyway. Thus, when a preferred stock is initially issued, the directors are, in effect, stating that they intend the payment of the preferred dividend to be an extremely high priority use of the company's future profits and cash for as long as the preferred stock is outstanding, which may be forever.

The importance of paying the preferred dividend is that investors who buy preferred stock generally do so with the idea that the dividend has a very high probability of being paid if the company is able to do so. Thus, if the directors failed to vote to pay a preferred dividend payment when the company was able to pay it, investors would be very unlikely to buy preferred stock of that company again, and the company might lose the ability to do a preferred financing the next time the company wanted to raise money. Therefore, the directors want to build a reputation for always paying a preferred dividend even when it is difficult for the company to do so.[2]

Typically, the board of directors first votes to pay the preferred dividend, and then decides how much to pay as a common dividend and how much of the profit, if any, to retain in the company. Preferred stocks always provide that, if the preferred dividend is not paid in a given quarter, then no common dividend can be paid that quarter. If the company earns enough to pay the preferred dividend but not the common dividend, it usually pays the preferred dividend. When a dividend is not paid, we say it is *omitted*.

A preferred stock can be either *cumulative* or *noncumulative*. A non-cumulative preferred stock specifies that as long as the preferred dividend is not paid, the common dividend cannot be paid. But once the preferred dividend has been *resumed* (i.e., the company starts to pay it again), then the company may declare whatever common dividend it wants. A cumulative preferred specifies further that if the preferred dividend has been omitted for one or more quarters, no common dividend can be paid until *all* the omitted preferred dividends from the

---

2 The same thing is true to a lesser extent for the common dividend. The dividend on a common stock, while less important to investors than that on a preferred stock, is nevertheless an important consideration in buying a stock. A company that has a reputation of paying its common dividend through good times and bad is likely to attract a wider group of investors and, therefore, possibly sustain a higher common stock price than it might have if the common dividend were periodically reduced or omitted.

past are paid up. When a preferred dividend has been omitted for one or more quarters, we say the preferred is *in arrears*. When all the arrearages have been paid, the company is once again free to declare any common dividend it wants. Thus, the first reason for the word *preferred* is that preferred stock has a prior right to dividends ahead of common stock.

ISSUING PREFERRED STOCK

Issuing preferred stock is just like issuing common stock in that, first, it has to be approved by the shareholders, and then, if it is going to be sold to the public, it must be registered with the Securities and Exchange Commission. Like common stock or bonds, public issues of preferred stock are also usually sold through investment bankers.

There is no limit to the number of issues of preferred stock that a company can have outstanding. Nor is there a limit to the number of shares each issue can have. Each issue and its number of shares, however, must first be authorized by the stockholders. Each issue of preferred stock may have different characteristics or the same characteristics. They may have different dividends. One or more may be convertible, while others are not.

One reason a company issues preferred stock is that it wants to raise money, but it already has a lot of debt outstanding and does not want any more, or it may be prohibited from issuing more debt by the covenants in its existing debt. In addition, the company may not want to issue common stock because this would cause too much dilution of earnings per share, or would give up more voting control than the current common shareholders care to give up. Preferred stock represents a compromise. It is not debt because if the preferred dividend is not paid due to lack of profits, the preferred stockholders cannot ask a court to declare the company bankrupt. Yet preferred stock is not exactly common stock because the dividend it receives will not increase with the success of the company, and preferred stockholders do not have the same voting rights as common stockholders at stockholder meetings.

Another common reason for preferred stock to be issued is in exchange for acquiring another company. For example, suppose JMC wanted to buy the Swift Rat Trap Company (SRC). SRC is a small, private company owned by Mr. and Mrs. Swift and their eight investors. They are

willing to sell the company (all their stock) to JMC, and a price for the
SRC stock has been agreed on. If JMC did not have enough cash to pay
for SRC, it could offer to pay SRC shareholders with common stock of
JMC worth the agreed upon value. But if SRC stockholders did not want
JMC common stock, or if JMC did not want to issue more common
stock because of dilution or voting control considerations, then JMC
might create a new issue of preferred stock to give to the SRC stockholders in exchange for their SRC stock.

If Mr. and Mrs. Swift and their investors were willing to take a preferred, JMC and SRC would then negotiate what dividend and how many
shares would be agreeable to both parties. Note that since only ten people,
(the ten SRC stockholders) will be getting this issue of JMC preferred, it
could be a private issue of stock, and therefore would not have to be
registered with the SEC. Later on, of course, if any of the ten stockholders wanted to sell their preferred to the public, it would first have to be
registered.

A preferred stock can be sold for whatever price the buyer and seller
agree on. Many preferred issues are initially sold at $100 per share, but it
is getting more common to see a preferred that is issued at $40 or $25 or
some other figure. When a preferred is initially issued by a company
(sold for cash or exchanged for another company or other asset), it is a
primary offering. When any individual who owns the preferred stock
sells it to another individual, it is a secondary offering, just as with bonds
or common stock. The amount of money (or value) a preferred stock is
initially sold for (or exchanged for) is often declared to be its *par value* or
stated value. However, many companies treat preferred stock the same
as common stock and declare only a small par value and put the rest of
the amount it was sold or exchanged for into Additional paid-in capital.
The par or stated value of a preferred stock, like a common stock, has
little or no investment significance.

PREFERRED STOCK TITLES

Companies that issue preferred stock often have more than one issue of
preferred outstanding. This is because each time that the company wanted
to issue preferred stock it was necessary to have different dividends and
other characteristics in order to sell the stock. Thus the capitalization
section of a company's balance sheet might look something like this:

Long-term debt:	
8% Mortgage bonds	$16,000,000
10% Sinking fund debentures	25,000,000
Equity:	
$2.40 Noncumulative preferred (authorized 60,000 shares, issued and outstanding 55,200 shares)	$?
$3.20 Cumulative preferred Series A (authorized 40,000 shares, outstanding 16,020 shares)	?
$4.20 Cumulative preferred Series B (authorized 40,000 shares, outstanding 34,000 shares)	?
$9.50 Cumulative preferred Series C (authorized 100,000 shares, none issued)	—
$7.75 Cumulative convertible preferred (authorized 30,000 shares, outstanding 6,312 shares)	?
Common at par $2 (authorized 2,000,000 shares, issued 1,000,000, outstanding 1,000,000 shares)	2,000,000
Additional paid-in capital	17,650,000
Retained earnings	33,473,000

The words *Series A* and *Series B* and the like have no meaning by themselves, but are just titles to distinguish the different issues. Notice that the Series C has been authorized by the shareholders, but as yet none has been issued. The Series A and Series B information does not tell you how many shares were originally issued, but in both series there are fewer shares outstanding than were authorized. There is no way to tell from the information given if more of the Series A and B were issued and outstanding at one time. The company also has a convertible preferred; this also has fewer shares outstanding than authorized, and there is no way to tell from this information if the currently outstanding 6,312 shares were all that were ever issued, or if more were issued but some were converted or bought back by the company and retired.

Notice also the question marks where the dollar figures should be, next to the preferred issues. Different companies use different dollar figures. Some companies will use the amount of money the preferred was sold for, or the value of the preferred if it was exchanged when acquiring a company. Other companies will use the liquidating value (discussed shortly). Other companies will only use part of the amount of money the preferred was sold for and put the rest in Additional paid-in-capital. Since the dollar figure beside the preferred stock can represent any of these things, we have used question marks to indicate the confusion that may exist. Regardless of the figure put there, preferred stock is classified as equity, although, as will be seen, in some cases it is questionable whether this is appropriate.

CALCULATING EARNINGS PER SHARE WHEN THERE IS A PREFERRED STOCK OUTSTANDING

The term *earnings per share* (EPS) means earnings per *common* share. The number of preferred shares outstanding is *not* added to the number of common shares when calculating earnings per share. The reason is as follows. Earnings per share is calculated to give the common stock investor an indication of the possible dividend per common share, and it is ultimately the current and potential future dividends per common share that determine what a common stock is worth. Thus, when we calculate or project future earnings per share, we are really asking how much earnings will be available to pay to common shareholders. The earnings available to pay to common shareholders is equal to the net earnings after tax *less the preferred dividend*. This is because the preferred dividend must always be paid before any common dividend can be paid. Thus, the portion of earnings that must be paid as preferred dividends can never be available to be paid as common dividends. Therefore, a correct calculation of earnings per common share (shown on page 155) always uses only the earnings available for common dividends, which, again, is net earnings minus all preferred dividends.

Similarly, the correct calculations of earnings per share uses only the number of *common* shares outstanding, *not* common shares plus preferred shares. This is because after the preferred shares have received their fixed dividend, they do not get to take advantage of any growth in profit available for common dividends. For example, let's look at ABC Company, which has two issues of stock outstanding.

Issue	Shares outstanding	Required dividend per share	Total required dividend
Preferred	40	$2	$80
Common	100		

Company ABC's income statement is shown in Column A and the calculation of earnings per share is shown in Column B.

	Income statement (A)	Calculation of earnings per share (B)
Sales	$1,000	$1,000
Cost of goods sold	− 400	400
Selling and admin. expense	− 150	150
Interest expense	− 50	50
Pretax profit	400	400
Taxes (assuming 50% rate)	− 200	200
Net profit	$ 200	$ 200
Less: Preferred dividend		80
Equals: Profit available for common		$ 120

$$\frac{\text{Profit available for common}}{\text{Common shares outstanding}} = \frac{\$120}{100} = \$1.20\,/\,\text{share}$$

For another example let's look at XYZ Company, which has the following stock issues outstanding.

Issue	Shares outstanding	Required dividend per share	Total required dividend
Series A preferred	200	$5	$1,000
Series B preferred	100	6	600
Common stock	1,000		

Income Statement and Calculation of Earnings per Share

Sales	$100,000
Less: CGS	60,000
SGA expense	18,000
Interest expense	2,000
Earnings before income tax	20,000
Income tax	10,000
Net earnings	10,000
Less: Total preferred dividend	1,600
Equals: Earnings available for common	$ 8,400

$$\frac{\text{Earnings for common}}{\text{Common shares outstanding}} = \frac{\$8,400}{1,000} = \$8.40\,/\,\text{share}$$

In this calculation, the entire preferred dividend of both preferred is-sues was subtracted to get earnings available for common. The *earnings for common* is then divided by only the common shares outstanding. If one had incorrectly used net earnings of $10,000, and also incorrectly used the combined common and preferred shares outstanding, the calcu-lated EPS would be: $10,000 divided by 1,300 shares = $7.69/share. This is a meaningless number.

To repeat, the term *EPS* or *earnings per share* always means per *com-mon* share.

Question: What is the net earnings of XYZ Company? Answer: $10,000. Do not confuse the net earnings of a company with the earn-ings available for common. The difference, the preferred dividend, is one of the things the directors choose to do with company profit. In XYZ Company, the board chose a long time ago, when the Series A and Series B preferreds were issued, to use some of future profits to pay preferred dividends.

LIFE OF A PREFERRED STOCK

Some preferred stock issues, like common stock, may be outstanding for-ever unless the company buys them back on the secondary market and retires them. These preferreds are called *perpetual preferreds*. Other preferreds are more like bonds, in that they have a fixed life and maturity date. Such preferreds, like bonds, may have a sinking fund or may be left outstanding until their guaranteed redemption date (which is the same thing as final maturity on a bond, i.e., the day the company must buy back all the outstanding preferred stock or bonds). Some preferreds are also similar to bonds in that they may have call features and nonrefunding provisions (review call and refunding features in Chapter 10).

When a preferred stock has a guaranteed redemption date, it would seem more appropriate to treat it as long-term debt rather than as an equity item. Debt is generally thought of as money put into the company that will be paid back eventually. Equity is generally thought of as money put into the company permanently. Perhaps the reason that a preferred with a guaranteed redemption date is thought of as equity is that, if the company is unable to pay the preferred dividend, the preferred stock-holders cannot have the company declared bankrupt; whereas, if the com-pany is unable to pay a bond's interest, the bondholders may be able to have the company declared bankrupt.

A company issuing a preferred would like the flexibility to call it, either to *refund* it by selling a new preferred with a lower dividend, or simply because the company has excess cash available and, by calling and retiring the preferred stock, the company will no longer have to pay the preferred dividend. The benefit to the company of refunding is this: Suppose the company had outstanding 1,000,000 shares of a preferred stock with a dividend of $8 per share. Assuming the preferred was sold at $100/share, it would have had an initial yield of 8 percent. Now, suppose interest rates for similar preferreds fell to 7 percent. If the company had the right to call the preferred for refunding, it would be able to sell a new 1,000,000 share issue of preferred at $100 per share, but with a $7 dividend, and use the proceeds to call and pay back (redeem) the $8 preferred shares. Thus, the company could lower its preferred dividend payments from $8,000,000 per year to $7,000,000 per year. While the company would obviously like this flexibility, the buyers of the $8 preferred stock would just as obviously not want to have their $8 preferred (which is yielding them 8 percent on their initial purchase price) called away when they could only reinvest their money at the current market rate of 7 percent. As we saw with bonds in Chapter 10, the more flexibility the company wants, the higher dividend it will have to pay in order to sell the preferred.

LIQUIDATING PREFERENCE

The second way in which a preferred stock has priority over a common stock is in its right to receive money in the event the company liquidates. Recall that when a company liquidates, either voluntarily or in the event of bankruptcy, first it sells off all its assets and then pays off all its liabilities. Any money left over goes to the common stockholders. However, if there is any preferred stock outstanding, the preferred shareholders get a certain amount of money before the common shareholders get anything. The amount of money each preferred share gets is called its *liquidating preference* or *liquidating value*. Each share of preferred stock outstanding in a given issue has the same liquidating preference (i.e., gets the same amount of money in the event of liquidation). But different issues of preferred stock may have different liquidating preferences. The liquidating preference is set when the preferred is initially issued and, like the preferred dividend, rarely ever changes except in the case of a few unusual preferreds. A preferred issue's liquidating preference may be unrelated to how much the preferred was initially sold for.

A typical preferred stock portion of a balance sheet of a company with more than one issue of preferred stock outstanding may look as follows:

Equity

$3.75 Noncumulative preferred Series A (authorized 60,000 shares, outstanding 10,000 shares) (liquidating preference $50 per share) ....

$6.00 Cumulative preferred Series B (authorized 10,000 shares, outstanding 8,000 shares) (liquidating value $20 per share) ....

$5.00 Cumulative convertible preferred Series C (authorized 40,000 shares, issued and outstanding 1,500 shares) (liquidating value $10 per share) ....

If this company were liquidated, the following amount of money would be paid to the preferred shareholders, assuming there was enough available after all the other liabilities had been paid off.

	Shares outstanding		Liquidating preference		Total
Series A:	10,000	×	$50	=	$500,000
Series B:	8,000	×	$20	=	$160,000
Series C:	1,500	×	$10	=	$ 15,000
Total liquidating value				=	$675,000

After the $675,000 was paid to the preferred shareholders, any remaining money would be split up among the common shareholders.

If there had been less than $675,000 available for the preferred stockholders, then there might be a predetermined priority among each series of preferred as to which gets paid first, or they might all have equal priority, in which case each series would get an equal portion of its liquidating value. When there is a priority of one preferred over another in the event of liquidation, the one with the lower priority is sometimes called a preference stock instead of a preferred.

BOOK VALUE PER COMMON SHARE

In Chapter 4, book value per common share was defined as total assets less total liabilities divided by the number of common shares outstanding. Now that definition must be modified to consider the liquidating value of the preferred. Thus, *book value per common share* is now defined as total assets, less total liabilities, less liquidating value of preferred (if any), divided by common shares outstanding.

DEFINITION

• **Book value per common share**—Total assets, less total liabilities, less liquidating value of preferreds (if any), divided by common shares outstanding.

Book value per common share is usually available from financial services your stockbroker has, but published book value figures sometimes do not correctly consider the liquidating value of the preferred, so you might want to learn to do it yourself.

To calculate book value per common share, first calculate the book value (step 1) and then divide the book value by the number of *common* shares outstanding (step 2). Do *not* add the preferred shares to the common shares.

Example: You can calculate the book value per common share of company MNO, given the following information.

Assets			Liabilities		
Current Assets			**Current Liabilities**		
Cash	$	100	Bank debt payable	$	150
Accounts receivable		200	Taxes payable		50
Inventory		300	Other liabilities		100
Total current assets	$	600	Total current liabilities	$	300
Fixed Assets			**Long-Term Debt**		
Property	$	100	8% Mortgage bonds	$	200
Plant		250	9% Debentures		140
Equipment		850	11% Subordinated		
	$	1,200	debentures		60
			Total Long-term debt	$	400
TOTAL ASSETS		$1,800	**Ownership Equity**		
			$2.50 Preferred	$	100
			Outstanding 50 shares		
			Liquidating value $5/share		
			Common @ par $.50	$	100
			Outstanding 200 shares		
			Additional paid-in capital		250
			Retained earnings		650
			Total equity		$1,100
			TOTAL LIABILITIES AND OWNERSHIP EQUITY		$1,800

Book value per common share of Company MNO would be calculated as follows:

Step 1. Total Assets.........................	$1,800		
less: total liabilities.........	$ 700		
less: liquidating value of preferred	$ 250	(50 preferred shares × $5 liq. value/share = $250)	
Equals: book value	$ 850		

$$\text{Step 2.} \quad \frac{\text{Book value}}{\text{Common shares outstanding}} = \frac{\$850}{200} = \$4.25\,/\,\text{share}$$

Thus, if company MNO were to liquidate, and assuming it could sell all its assets for exactly their carrying value on the books, each share of common stock would receive $4.25 after all the liabilities had been paid off and after the preferred shares had received their liquidating value.

CONVERTIBLE PREFERRED

Some preferred stocks, like some bonds, are convertible into common stock. Convertible preferreds have all the features of straight preferreds described thus far, but have the added feature that they may be converted into common stock. Convertible preferreds are usually convertible at any time by the preferred stockholder, although in some cases they may only be convertible before or after a specified date. Most convertible preferreds convert into a fixed number of common shares, but like convertible bonds, one occasionally sees an issue where the conversion ratio changes over time or depends on the company's profit level or some other factor. For example, an unusual convertible preferred might say the following:

> "This convertible preferred may not be converted before January 1, 1999. After that date, the holder may convert them, at his option, at the rate of 2 common shares for each share of convertible preferred up until December 31, 2001. Beginning January 1, 2002, these convertible preferred shares may be converted into common stock at the ratio of 2.4 shares for every share of convertible preferred."

For the remainder of the chapter it is assumed that the conversion rate is fixed.

Calculating earnings per share for a company with one or more convertible preferreds outstanding presents the same problem as a company with convertible bonds outstanding: That is, do you assume the preferreds are converted or not converted? The answer is that the same procedures that apply to convertible bonds also apply to convertible preferreds. Therefore, the presence of one or more convertible preferreds, like convertible bonds, may give rise to both a primary EPS figure and a fully diluted EPS figure, as well as basic EPS, and the investor must choose which figure to focus on for evaluating stock prices. Basic, primary, and fully diluted EPS can be reviewed in Chapter 11. Some companies have both convertible bonds and convertible preferred stocks outstanding. In these companies, each convertible issue is looked at separately to determine if it should be converted when calculating earnings per share.

CONVERTING A CONVERTIBLE PREFERRED

As in the previous chapter on convertible bonds, readers not interested in the mechanics of converting convertible preferreds can skip the remainder of this chapter without losing continuity of the book. Going through the process, however, will further familiarize you with the concepts, and thus it is presented here for readers who wish to go through it.

When calculating EPS for a company with a convertible preferred, one must, again, apply the decision rules given in the last section in Chapter 11. To calculate basic EPS, the convertible preferred or preferreds are not assumed converted. To calculate primary and fully diluted EPS, one must first determine if a convertible preferred is a common stock equivalent. If a convertible preferred is a C.S.E., then it must be converted, as shown in Example 1 below, when determining primary EPS. If it is not a common stock equivalent, then it is not converted when determining primary EPS, as in Example 3. When calculating fully diluted EPS, all convertible preferreds are converted whether or not they are common stock equivalents, as in Examples 2 and 4. In these examples, assume first that company PQR's Series B convertible preferred is a common stock equivalent, and then assume that it is not. Note that the Series A preferred is not convertible.

Company PQR		Company PQR	
Income Statement		Stock Outstanding	
Sales	$10,000	**$4 Series A Preferred**	
CGS	5,000	Outstanding: 50 Shares	
SGA	2,000		
Interest expense	1,000	**$1 Series B Convertible Preferred**	
Pretax profit	$2,000	Outstanding: 100 shares	
		Conversion ratio: each share	
Income tax	1,000		converts into
Net profit	$1,000		2 shares of
			common.

Common Stock
Authorized: 800 shares
Outstanding: 500 shares

Example 1:   Calculate Primary EPS, Assuming Series B Preferred Is a Common Stock Equivalent

Step 1. Calculate profit available for common

Net profit	$1,000
Less: Pfd.Div. (Series A only)	200
Profit available for common	$ 800

Note: There is no Series B Pfd. dividend because the Series B is assumed to have been converted.

Step 2. Calculate number of primary shares outstanding

Common shares: 500 originally outstanding
+ 200 from conversion of Series B Preferred
(100 preferred shares × 2 common
shares per preferred share)
700 total common shares for primary EPS

Step 3. Calculate primary EPS.

$$\frac{\text{Profit available for common}}{\text{Primary shares}} = \frac{\$800}{700} = \$1.14 \text{ per common share}$$

Example 2: Calculate Fully Diluted EPS, Assuming Series B Preferred Is a Common Stock Equivalent

Answer: Same as primary EPS. Because the Series B Preferred is a common stock equivalent, it would be assumed to be converted in either case.

Example 3: Calculate Primary EPS, Assuming Series B Preferred Is *Not* a Common Stock Equivalent

Step 1.   Calculate profit available for common

Net profit	$1,000
Less: Pfd. dividend on Series A	200
Less: Pfd. dividend on Series B	100
Profit available for common	700

Note: The Series B in this example is not a common stock equivalent and therefore it is not assumed converted. Since it is therefore still outstanding, its dividend would have to be paid before any dividend could be paid to the common stockholders.

Step 2.   Calculate number of primary shares outstanding

Common shares: 500 originally outstanding. There is no change. The Series B is not assumed converted because it is not a common stock equivalent.

Step 3.   Calculate primary EPS

$$\frac{\text{Profit for common}}{\text{Primary shares}} = \frac{\$700}{500} = \$1.40/\text{share}$$

In this case, primary EPS is the same as basic EPS.

Example 4: Calculate Fully Diluted EPS, Assuming Series B Preferred Is *Not* a Common Stock Equivalent

Answer: For fully diluted EPS, all convertible issues are converted whether or not they are common stock equivalents. Therefore, the Series B Preferred must be converted and fully diluted earnings are $1.14 per share, the same as in Examples 1 and 2.

PART 3

Company Assets and Cash Flow

13

Fixed Assets, Depreciation, and Cash Flow

The topics covered in this section are not the kinds of things that are generally heard in investment discussions at cocktail parties. In fact, these topics may seem more like accounting issues than investment-related concerns. But it is necessary to learn how accountants present these items in the financial statements in order to understand and interpret them. Many of these topics are covered in a generalized manner, so the reader will be better able to understand the wide variety of specific issues that are certain to be encountered in most companies' financial statements. An informed investor must know when something is, in fact, simply an accounting detail, and when it may have an impact on company earnings and hence, investment results. In this chapter, we will see how to account for wear and deterioration and disposal of a company's plant and equipment, and how it affects a company's earnings and, therefore, its stock price. We will also see that cash flow is not the same as earnings.

DEPRECIATION

When we looked at the balance sheet of JMC in Chapter 3, Fixed assets appeared as follows:

Fixed assets:	
Property	$ 3,000
Buildings	13,000
Equipment	44,000
Total fixed assets	$60,000

The figures for property, buildings, and equipment reflect JMC's initial cost of these assets. With the passage of time, however, these assets change in value from what they originally cost. Buildings and equipment deteriorate. A plant becomes old and inefficient in terms of the current needs of the corporation. It must be rebuilt or replaced. A machine tool wears out in time, or better manufacturing techniques are developed and the old machine tool becomes obsolete and worthless. Land (property), on the other hand, frequently increases in value.

When buildings or equipment wear out and become worth less than their original cost, the company has obviously lost something of value. This loss to the company must be reflected on the financial statements. Suppose, for example, Company ABC bought a machine tool for $10,000. At the time of purchase, $10,000 is added to the Equipment account. From experience, the company knows the tool will last about 10 years before it is worn out and must be replaced. The company could carry the tool on the books (in the Equipment account) at $10,000 for 10 years, and then, when the tool is disposed of, reflect the loss as an expense of $10,000 in the income statement. But in reality the tool wears out gradually over the 10 years, and thus it would be more reasonable to gradually reflect the loss in value of the tool over the 10 years. Let us assume the machine wears out evenly over the 10 years. Using that assumption, since it cost $10,000 and is expected to last 10 years, we can say it is losing its original value at the rate of $1,000 a year, or, in the language of Wall Street, it is *depreciating* by $1,000 a year. How do we show this depreciation on the financial statements?

For simplicity, let us assume this is Company ABC's only asset, and that it was acquired January 1, 1992. At the time the asset was acquired, the Fixed assets account would appear as follows:

Company ABC
Part of January 1, 1992, Balance Sheet

Fixed assets:
  Plant and equipment $10,000

During the year the tool would be depreciated by $1,000, so the Fixed asset account at the end of the year would look like this:

Company ABC
Part of December 31, 1992, Balance Sheet

Fixed assets:
  Gross plant and equipment $10,000
  Less: Accumulated depreciation   1,000
  Net plant and equipment .... $ 9,000

DEFINITIONS

- **Gross plant and equipment**—*Gross* refers to initial cost. As long as a company owns an asset, that asset's *original* cost is included in Gross plant and equipment, regardless of how much it has been depreciated.

- **Accumulated depreciation**—The total amount by which all the assets in the Gross plant and equipment account have been depreciated down through the years. One can also talk about the accumulated depreciation of *one* piece of equipment, which is the total amount by which *that* asset has been depreciated down through the years. Here, the company has only one asset, so the accumulated depreciation of that asset is equal to accumulated depreciation of the company—in this case, $1,000.

- **Net plant and equipment**—This is simply Gross plant and equipment less Accumulated depreciation. When computing the book value of the company, it is the Net plant and equipment that is used, not the gross. Similarly, the book value of a *single piece of equipment* is equal to the original cost of *that piece of equipment* less the accumulated depreciation of that piece of equipment. Thus, the book value of Company ABC's machine tool was $9,000 at December 31, 1992.

The $1,000 of depreciation taken on the machine tool also appears as an expense on the income statement for 1992.

Company ABC Income Statement from January 1 to December 31, 1992		
Sales		$10,000
Expenses:		
Cost of goods sold	$4,000	
SG&A	1,500	
Interest expense	500	
Depreciation expense...........	1,000	
Total expenses	7,000	7,000
Profit before taxes		3,000
Tax expense		1,500
Profit after taxes		$ 1,500

Depreciation is almost always listed as a separate expense item, as in this example, but some companies include it in Cost of goods sold (CGS) or in Selling, general, and administrative expense (SG&A), or both, such as shown here.

Company ABC Income Statement from January 1 to December 31, 1992		
Sales		$10,000
Expenses:		
Cost of goods sold	$4,600	
SG&A.................................	1,900	
Interest expense	500	
Total expenses	7,000	7,000
Profit before taxes		3,000
Tax expense		1,500
Profit after taxes		$ 1,500

In this income statement, $600 of depreciation expense has been included in Cost of goods sold, and $400 of depreciation expense has been included in the SG&A account. In a real company, there would be no way to know how much of the depreciation expense was in each category.

In its second year, 1993, the machine tool would be depreciated by another $1,000. Assuming there was still only the one asset in the company, the fixed assets portion of the balance sheet at the end of the second year would look like this:

Company ABC
Part of the December 31, 1993, Balance Sheet

Fixed assets:	
Gross plant and equipment	$10,000
Less: Accumulated depreciation	2,000
Net plant and equipment	$ 8,000

Note that accumulated depreciation *on the balance sheet* is the total of all the depreciation for this year and past years. On the other hand, the depreciation expense on the 1993 *income statement* would still be only $1,000. The depreciation expense on a given year's income statement is only *that year's* depreciation.

At the end of 10 years, Fixed assets would appear as follows:

Company ABC
Part of the December 31, 2001, Balance Sheet

Fixed assets:	
Gross plant and equipment	$10,000
Less: Accumulated depreciation	10,000
Net plant and equipment	0

What happens if the machine tool is still working? The answer is, nothing changes. Since the asset has been depreciated down to $0, it is not depreciated further. Thus, in each succeeding year the fixed assets portion of the balance sheet would remain the same as at December 31, 2001, until the machine tool was sold or thrown away and no longer belonged to the company. Then all its numbers are taken off the balance sheet.

In a real company, of course, there would be many assets. In some companies they are all lumped together into one category—*Property, plant, and equipment.* More frequently, companies categorize their assets into separate property, plant, and equipment accounts, or other titles depending on the nature of their assets. The fixed assets portion of a typical balance sheet may look like this:

XYZ Corporation Part of the December 31, 1993, Balance Sheet		
Fixed assets:		
Gross property		$ 5,000
Gross plant and equipment		
Plant	$ 50,000	
Equipment	100,000	
	150,000	
Less: Accumulated depreciation	60,000	
Net plant and equipment	90,000	90,000
Net property, plant, and equipment ...		$95,000

There is no way to tell how much of the $60,000 of accumulated depreciation on the balance sheet reflects depreciation of the plant and how much reflects depreciation of the equipment. There is also no way to tell how many years' worth of depreciation are included in the $60,000. All we know for sure is that the total of the depreciation for all the assets still owned by the company is $60,000.

Notice that property (land) is recorded separately and not depreciated. This is because property does not wear out, in the usual sense. In fact, we said earlier that its value frequently increases over time. No account is kept on the balance sheet to reflect this increase. Land is almost always carried on the books at initial cost until it is sold.

DEPRECIATION'S IMPACT ON COMPANY EARNINGS

Understanding depreciation and watching the annual changes in a company's depreciation expense are important to investors because depreciation changes can give hints about upcoming changes in company earnings. This, in turn, can directly impact the price of the company's stock. Look, for example, at High Flying Airlines Corporation (HFA). HFA's income statement for the past four years looks as follows. HFA has 100 shares of common stock outstanding.

HFA
Income Statements for 1992–1995

	1992	1993	1994	1995
Sales	$10,000	$11,000	$12,000	$10,000
Cost of goods sold	5,000	5,500	6,000	5,000
SG&A	1,000	1,100	1,200	1,000
Depreciation	3,000	3,000	2,800	2,400
Total expense	9,000	9,600	10,000	8,400
Pretax profit	1,000	1,400	2,000	1,600
Tax (at 50%)	500	700	1,000	800
Net income	$ 500	$ 700	$ 1,000	$ 800
EPS	$ 5	$ 7	$ 10	$ 8

From 1992 to 1994 the company's sales and earnings grew. In 1995, however, HFA lost business to other airlines (lost market share) and sales and earnings fell. Looking at the individual expense numbers, however, we see some interesting differences, which can help investors project future results.

Notice that cost of goods sold in each year increased by the same percent as the sales increased. Thus the cost of goods sold remained at a constant 50 percent of sales. Similarly, the selling, general, and administrative expense also went up by the same amount as sales each year, and therefore remained at a constant 10 percent of sales each year. But depreciation expense from 1992 to 1993 did not go up. And in 1994 and 1995 depreciation expense began declining by increasing amounts. What this almost certainly indicates is that an increasing number of the company's airplanes are becoming fully depreciated, and therefore no further depreciation is being taken on them. As investors, if we read the annual report and other company releases carefully and see that HFA is not currently planning any major new purchases of airplanes, we can reasonably conclude that depreciation expense should continue to fall. Thus, if we assume that air travel is up in 1996 and that HFA's market share recovers, then HFA's sales are likely, at least, to return to the 1994 level. If we further assume that Cost of goods sold and SG&A will continue to be about the same percentage of sales as in past years, we can come up with the following earnings estimate for 1996.

	1995 Actual	1996 Estimated earnings
Sales	$10,000	$12,000
Cost of goods sold	5,000	6,000
SG&A	1,000	1,200
Depreciation	2,400	2,200
Total expense	8,400	9,400
Pretax profit	1,600	2,600
Tax (at 50%)	800	1,300
Net income	$ 800	$ 1,300
EPS	$ 8	$ 13

Of course, we don't know for certain by how much depreciation will decline, nor for that matter do we know for certain that sales will recover in 1996. But each of the assumptions in the 1996 estimated earnings appears reasonable, based on past trends. Thus, as investment analysts, we can foresee that HFA's earnings per share could jump substantially in 1996 to a new high level, considerably above the previous peak in 1994. This could be a great opportunity to buy the stock.

On the other hand, we can also foresee that HFA will soon have to sell its old aircraft and purchase a new generation of more modern airplanes if it wants to remain competitive. In that case, depreciation expense would increase *sharply* in the year HFA begins depreciating its new aircraft. The increased depreciation expense would lower earnings. In addition, interest expense would go up if HFA needed to borrow money to buy the new airplanes. Thus, earnings could fall sharply in 1997 or 1998 even if air travel continues to rise and HFA maintains its market share. Realizing this, investors would be suspicious of the high 1996 earnings, and the stock might not do well despite those record earnings.

In sum, an investor should always watch changes in a company's depreciation to see what impact it might have on future reported earnings. Investors should also look at all the company's reports and press releases, and read business newspapers and industry journals that might give hints of company plans, such as HFA's need to buy new airplanes. With all this available information, the investor is then in a better position to make an informed judgment about the prospects for the company's earnings, and how that might influence the price of the stock.

SELLING OFF AN ASSET

When a company sells an old building or piece of equipment, or otherwise disposes of it, its gross cost, accumulated depreciation, and net book value are all removed from the balance sheet. To see how this is done, let's start with the fixed assets portion of XYZ Corporation's 1993 balance sheet on page 172, and see how the following changes are reflected.

1. During 1994, a piece of equipment that had cost $20,000 and had been depreciated down to a book value of $6,000, was sold for $7,000 cash.

2. XYZ Corporation made no new purchases of property, plant, or equipment in 1994.

3. Depreciation for 1994 was $5,000.

   To reflect these events, the following accounting changes would occur:

Gross plant and equipment at 12/31/93	$150,000
Less: Original cost of equipment sold	20,000
Gross plant and equipment at 12/31/94	130,000

Accumulated depreciation at 12/31/93	60,000
Less: Accumulated depreciation of equip. sold off	14,000
	46,000
Plus: Depreciation for 1994	5,000
Accumulated depreciation at 12/31/94	51,000

Net plant and equipment at 12/31/93	90,000
Less: Book value of equipment sold off	6,000
	84,000
Less: Accumulated depreciation expense for 1994	5,000
Net plant and equipment at 12/31/94	79,000

Thus, at the end of 1994, the fixed assets portion of the balance sheet would appear as follows.

XYZ Corporation		
Part of the December 31, 1994, Balance Sheet		
Fixed assets:		
Gross property		$ 5,000
Gross plant and equipment		
Plant	$ 50,000	
Equipment	80,000	
	130,000	
Less: Accumulated depreciation	51,000	
Net plant and equipment	$ 79,000	79,000
Net property, plant, and equipment....................		$84,000

In addition to these changes in fixed assets, there will also be some other changes in the financial statements. First, the price for which the equipment was sold is added to the cash account under Current assets. Note that the price for which the equipment was sold has no effect on the fixed assets portion of the balance sheet. Also, since the piece of equipment was sold for $7,000 and had a *book value* of $6,000, a profit of $1,000 must be recorded on the income statement. Had the equipment been sold for $2,000, a loss of $4,000 would have been recorded. The amount of profit or loss recorded in selling off used equipment is usually very small compared to the overall profit or loss of the corporation. Unfortunately, there is often no way to tell from the financial statements how much this profit or loss was. If it were large it could give a false impression of the company's earnings growth, but the company would probably be required to note it in a footnote.

Frequently, when an asset wears out or becomes obsolete before it is fully depreciated (down to $0 or near $0), it cannot be sold and must be thrown out or *retired*. In this case the accounting would be the same as if the asset were sold for $0. This is sometimes called *writing-off* an asset. For example, if XYZ Corporation had a piece of equipment costing $5,000, which had been depreciated to $2,000, and had become worthless, the company would *write-off* the remaining $2,000, (i.e., bring $2,000 to the income statement as an expense and add $2,000 to *Accumulated depreciation* to bring the asset's net book value to $0).

When the piece of equipment is actually thrown out, or otherwise disposed of, the $5,000 would be removed from both the *Gross plant and equipment* and the *Accumulated depreciation* accounts. It is possible that a piece of equipment can be written off or written down to $0, even though it is not actually being disposed of. This might occur when an old machine tool is not being used but the company wants to keep it around, just in case it should be needed in a time of unexpectedly strong demand for the company's products. We will return to the subject of write-offs in Chapter 14.

METHODS OF DEPRECIATION

Depreciation, we said, reflects the declining value of an asset to the company. Earlier, we assumed that company ABC's machine tool depreciated evenly over a period of 10 years. This is not necessarily a valid assumption. Often it is not possible to say how rapidly the value of an asset deteriorates. In the case of a company car, for example, as long as the car can get a salesperson from one place to another it might be said that the value of the car to the company has not depreciated at all. On the other hand, as the car gets older it is worth less in the used car market if the company decides to sell it. Further, since the car is older, it is more likely to break down and become worthless all at once.

How does a company decide how quickly to depreciate an asset? Should depreciation be taken evenly over the estimated life of an asset, as in Company ABC's machine tool? Or should more depreciation be taken in the early years and less in the later years? Or less in the early years and more in the later years? The first two methods are both commonly used and the third almost never.

When an asset is depreciated evenly over its estimated useful life, it is called *straight-line depreciation*. When the asset is depreciated more in the early years and less in the later years, it is called *accelerated depreciation*. The rationale for using accelerated depreciation is that: (1) equipment frequently wears out sooner than expected; (2) resale value generally declines at a more rapid rate in the early years; and (3) equipment often becomes obsolete sooner than expected, possibly because a better piece of equipment comes along to replace it, or possibly because the company stops making the product the equipment was used for. Another, perhaps more important reason for using accelerated depreciation is the tax advantage it gives, which will be explained shortly.

Three of the more common methods of computing depreciation are: (1) straight-line, (2) double-declining-balance, and (3) sum-of-the-years'-

digits. The latter two are different methods of accelerated depreciation. To compare these methods, let's look at BCD Corporation, which bought a machine tool costing $10,000 at the beginning of 1995. The expected life of the tool is five years. Therefore, if straight-line depreciation is used, the tool would be depreciated by $2,000 each year, or 20 percent per year.

The computation of double-declining-balance and sum-of-the-years'-digits depreciation can be found in any good accounting text and will not be shown here. Rather, we will just show their results in Table 13.1.

Table 13.1 Depreciation Comparison Table

	Straight-line depreciation	Accelerated depreciation	
		Double-declining-balance	Sum-of-the-years'-digits
Original cost............ $10,000		$10,000	$10,000
Depreciation yr. 1..	$2,000	$4,000	$3,333
Book value (end yr. 1)	8,000	6,000	6,667
Depreciation yr. 2..	2,000	2,400	2,667
Book value (end yr. 2)	6,000	3,600	4,000
Depreciation yr. 3..	2,000	1,440	2,000
Book value (end yr. 3)	4,000	2,160	2,000
Depreciation yr. 4..	2,000	864	1,333
Book value (end yr. 4)	2,000	1,296	667
Depreciation yr. 5..	2,000	518	667
Book value (end yr. 5)	0	778	0

Note the difference between straight-line and accelerated depreciation. Using either method of accelerated depreciation, the depreciation charge (expense) in the early years is greater than what it would be using straight-line depreciation. Conversely, in the later years, accelerated depreciation is less than straight-line. For the remainder of the discussion we will use only double-declining-balance for comparison of the effects of accelerated and straight-line depreciation.

There are unlimited other ways of calculating depreciation. In fact, any method that appears "reasonable" to the Internal Revenue Service and the company's accountants is acceptable. For a company that wants to depreciate assets as rapidly as possible, the IRS publishes a set of guidelines that gives the maximum allowed depreciation rate (i.e., the minimum expected life for every type of asset: cars, tools, buildings, electric generators, office furniture, and so on). Use of the guidelines for maximum depreciation is quite common among corporations, thereby eliminating the need of long theoretical discussions with the IRS and the company's accountants.

Note that at the end of the fifth year, the double-declining-balance method of depreciation has not fully depreciated the asset to $0, but has left a small book value of $778. This is called a *residual value*. These residual values are sufficiently small that they do not affect the company's decision to use straight-line or accelerated depreciation.

Why should a company choose straight-line rather than accelerated depreciation, or vice versa? Consider the following case. In 1995, BCD Corporation had sales of $40,000. Its combined cost of goods, SG&A, and interest expense were $20,000. Since none of these will be affected by the choice of depreciation method, we will lump them together in the income statement following. The company has 1,000 shares of stock outstanding. BCD's income statement, depending on whether the company chose straight-line or accelerated-depreciation, would be as follows:

BCD Corporation
Income Statement for 1995

	Straight-line	Accelerated
Sales	$40,000	$40,000
CGS + SG&A + Interest expense	20,000	20,000
Profit before depreciation and taxes	20,000	20,000
Depreciation	2,000	4,000
Profit before taxes	18,000	16,000
Taxes (at 50%)	9,000	8,000
Profit after taxes	$ 9,000	$ 8,000
Earnings per share	$ 9	$ 8

If BCD wants to show the highest possible earnings per share, it would use straight-line depreciation, but it would have to pay higher taxes. If it wanted to pay the lowest possible taxes, it would use accelerated depreciation. Since both these alternatives are desirable, what does the company do? The answer is, both. When filing its income tax return, the company uses accelerated depreciation. When reporting earnings to the public, it use straight-line depreciation.

DEFERRED TAXES

Using both methods, straight-line depreciation for reporting to shareholders and accelerated depreciation for tax purposes, creates an interesting problem. The income statement in the company's annual report to
shareholders would show taxes of $9,000, as in the left column on page
179. But the actual taxes payable would only be $8,000 (assuming that
the taxes had not been paid yet). This difference is reconciled by setting
up a new account on the liability side of the balance sheet called *Deferred taxes* (which in this case would equal $1,000). The reason for this
is as follows. By using accelerated depreciation for tax purposes, but not
for reporting to the shareholders, BCD ends up paying lower taxes in the
early years of the asset's life (compared to what it would have paid if it
used straight-line depreciation for tax purposes) but will then make up
for this by paying higher taxes in the later years of the asset's life. In
effect, then, by choosing to pay taxes using accelerated depreciation,
BCD is simply deferring the time when it actually has to pay a portion of
its tax, relative to when the income statement says the taxes were paid
under straight-line depreciation.

The deferred taxes, then, will be "paid off" in the third, fourth, and
fifth years of the asset's life, which are the years when accelerated depreciation becomes less than straight-line depreciation for the assets (see
Table 13.1). In these later years, the income statement using straight-line
depreciation will show lower taxes than are actually being paid.

The Deferred tax account is usually placed between Long-term debt
and Equity on the balance sheet, as shown here. Thus, the capitalization
portion of BCD's balance sheet might look like this:

Capitalization	
Long-term debt	
6% Mortgage bonds..........................	$20,000
9% Debentures...................................	4,000
Deferred tax..	1,000
Stockholders' equity	
Common stock ($2 par)	
(authorized 2,500 shares;	
outstanding 1,000 shares)	2,000
Additional paid-in capital	14,000
Retained earnings	40,000
Total stockholders' equity	$56,000

To review, the Deferred tax account in the capitalization portion of the balance sheet arises on the reports to shareholders only because the company has chosen to use a different method of depreciation accounting when preparing its tax returns for the IRS than it uses when reporting to shareholders.

To state it yet another way, the presence of a Deferred tax account in the capitalization section of the balance sheet is telling investors that some portion of the income tax expense shown on the income statement in the reports to shareholders has not yet been paid, but will be paid in some future years. This is important because if the company is actually paying less money for taxes than the income statement shows it is paying, it implies that the company is currently earning more cash than the income statement indicates. This will be discussed more fully in the "Cash Flow" section and again in Chapter 15.

CHANGING THE METHOD OF DEPRECIATION ACCOUNTING

From an investment point of view, it is important to realize that a company can have a large degree of control over its earnings when choosing or changing its method of depreciation. A company that has always used accelerated depreciation for both tax and shareholders' report purposes might be able to mask a decline in earnings per share in a bad year by changing its depreciation method for shareholders to straight-line, and thus show an earnings increase.

Identifying this type of accounting change, which can distort the reported earnings per share and give a misleading impression of a company's growth, is an important task for any investor. Fortunately, accounting rules require that a change in the method of depreciation (or any other accounting change) that produces a "significant distortion" in earnings, must be explained in the footnotes to the financial statements. While a "significant distortion" has not been precisely defined, it is usually taken to mean a change that affects earnings by more than 5 percent or 10 percent of the reported figure.

Of course, a company cannot keep changing accounting techniques back and forth to suit its needs. One of the basic principles of accounting is that a company, having once selected a method of accounting, must apply it consistently over the years. Occasional changes are acceptable, however, and it is this occasional change that must be watched closely because a company may do it to "hide" a decline in earnings in a bad year.

Of the two methods of calculating depreciation, *accelerated* is considered the more conservative. In general, when choosing among accounting options, the more conservative method is the one that shows lower earnings in the current year, even though allowing higher potential earnings in future years. The opposite of conservative accounting is called liberal accounting. Companies that use liberal accounting techniques will show maximum possible earnings in the current year, which to some extent will result in lower earnings in future years. Other things being equal, companies with conservative accounting generally tend to get higher price/earnings ratios than companies with liberal accounting.

CASH FLOW

Cash flow means money flowing into and out of a company. When Company BCD purchases raw material for inventory and pays cash, that is a cash flow out of the company. If BCD purchases raw material on May 15 but does not plan to pay for it until June 15, the cash flow-out will not take place until June 15.

Similarly, when BCD sells finished good to a customer, if the customer pays cash or writes a check, that is immediate cash flow-in for BCD. If the customer does not pay for the goods at the time of purchase, there is no cash flow-in at that time. The cash flow-in will take place perhaps 30 or 60 days later, or whenever the customer actually pays cash or delivers a check to BCD.[1]

Although it is natural to think of cash flow as being the same as the "earnings" of a company, cash flow is in fact different from earnings. Depreciation expense in particular can cause cash flow to be quite different from the earnings that companies report to shareholders. To see how cash flow can differ from earnings, lets look again at Company BCD's income statement for 1995. For now, assume BCD uses accelerated depreciation for both tax purposes and reporting to shareholders.

---

1 It could be argued that the cash flow-in does not really take place until the check is cashed, but that is just a matter of a day or two and is a minor distinction that investors can ignore.

Company BCD Income Statement from Jan. 1, 1995 to Dec. 31, 1995 (Using Accelerated Depreciation)		
Sales		$40,000
Expenses		
CGS	$14,000	
SG&A	4,000	
Interest	2,000	
Depreciation	4,000	
	$24,000	$24,000
Profit before tax		$16,000
Tax (at 50%)		$ 8,000
Net profit		$ 8,000

This income statement shows a profit of $8,000, but the cash flow will turn out to be greater. To calculate the cash flow for 1995, let's look at each item on the income statement and see how it impacts cash flow.

— Sales

The sales figure fairly accurately reflects the cash that "flowed" into the company. It is not perfectly accurate because some of BCD's customers in December 1995 had probably not paid for their purchases by year end. In that case, the money owed to BCD would be reflected in BCD's accounts receivable on the December 31, 1995, balance sheet. On the other hand, the accounts receivable that had been on the balance sheet at the *beginning* of 1995 (reflecting sales made in late 1994) were probably received in 1995. Therefore, BCD's cash flow-in in 1995 was probably reasonably close to the sales figure, with cash not yet received from late 1995 sales being made up by cash received in early 1995 from late 1994 sales. The cash flow-in is usually close enough to the sales figure that investors can simply treat sales as cash flow-in.

— Cost of Goods Sold

Cost of goods sold reflects cash paid out of the company to purchase raw material and pay wages, but does not equal cash flow-out exactly, because BCD may not have paid for all its purchases yet. In addition, the company might have sold some goods in 1995 for which the raw material and labor costs had been paid in 1994. Similarly, BCD might have paid in 1995 for goods that are still in inventory at year end, December 31, 1995, and will not be sold (and therefore become cost of goods sold) until 1996. Despite these timing differences, the Cost of goods sold (shown as CGS on the income statement) figure is usually close enough to the actual cash that flowed out of the company during the year that investors can treat it as if it were a cash flow-out item.

— Selling, General & Administrative Expense

This reflects cash paid out for some labor, such as company bookkeepers and security guards; some goods, such as office supplies; and probably some services, such as advertising, printing the company's annual report, and the like. SG&A expense, like CGS expense, is not a perfect indication of cash flow-out, but it is likely to be close enough that investors can treat it as a cash flow-out item.

— Interest Expense

Interest expense can also be treated as a cash flow-out item. Again, it may not be perfectly accurate, but it is close enough.

— Depreciation Expense

This expense item is different. Depreciation expense does not reflect cash flow-out in 1995. Depreciation is an accounting entry reflecting the wearing out of fixed assets that were purchased over a number of past years. There is no cash flow-out as a result of depreciation expense. The cash flow-out took place in past years when the company purchased the plant and equipment.

In the language of Wall Street, depreciation is a *noncash expense*, meaning that no cash flows out of the company as a result of depreciation expense. By contrast, cost of goods sold expense, selling, general, and administrative expense, and interest expense are considered *cash expenses* because they reflect cash paid for such goods and services.

— Taxes

For the most part, corporations pay taxes in the year the profit is earned. Thus, for now, *tax expense* should be treated as a cash flow-out item. We will see shortly that an adjustment may need to be made.

Now that we have examined how to handle each item separately, let's go back and compare Company BCD's income statement to its cash flow statement.

Company BCD Income Statement for 1995 (Using Accelerated Depreciation)			Company BCD Cash Flow Statement for 1995 + = cash flow in − = cash flow out		
Sales		$40,000	Sales................ + $40,000		
Expenses					
CGS	$14,000		CGS .... − 14,000		
SG&A.............	4,000		SG&A .... − 4,000		
Interest	2,000		Interest .... − 2,000		
Depreciation	4,000				
	$24,000	$24,000			
Profit before tax ..		$16,000			
Tax (at 50%)		$ 8,000	Taxes .... − 8,000		
Net profit		$ 8,000	Cash flow .... + $12,000		

The cash flow statement shows a net cash flow-in of $12,000, which is $4,000 greater than the net profit of $8,000. This is because in the calculation of net profit (in the left-hand column), depreciation expense of $4,000 was deducted from sales even though depreciation does not represent cash flow-out. Thus, to calculate cash flow, one can either subtract all the cash expenses from sales, as we did in the right-hand column here, or one can use a short-cut method—that is simply to take the net profit ($8,000) and *add back* the depreciation ($4,000), which gives the same $12,000 net cash flow-in. The reason this short-cut method works is that it is just adding back the $4,000 of depreciation expense that had been subtracted out on the income statement.

The calculation of cash flow becomes a little more complicated when investors are given financial statements that use straight-line depreciation accounting, even though the company pays taxes based on accelerated depreciation. In this case, the only difference in the cash flow calculation from that presented in the cash flow statement above is how taxes are handled. Recall from earlier in this chapter that when a company uses accelerated depreciation for tax calculations, but straight-line depreciation for shareholder reporting, the tax expense reported to shareholders is usually greater than the actual tax paid, and when this happens the company must create a new account called *Deferred tax* on the balance sheet to reflect the difference. When calculating cash flow for a company that uses both methods of depreciation, *it is necessary to add the increase in deferred taxes for the year to get the correct cash flow for the year.* Why this is so is not always easy to grasp at first, but the procedure is easy to follow, as shown here.

Example: Calculate the cash flow for Company BCD assuming BCD uses straight-line depreciation for reporting to shareholders and accelerated depreciation for tax purposes.

	Company BCD Income Statement for 1995 (Using Straight-Line Depreciation)	
Sales		$40,000
Expenses		
CGS	$14,000	
SG&A	4,000	
Interest	2,000	
Depreciation	2,000	
	$22,000	$22,000
Profit before tax		$18,000
Tax (at 50%)		$ 9,000
Net profit		$ 9,000

Answer: Using the short-cut method

Net profit	$ 9,000
Add back:	
Depreciation	2,000
Deferred tax	1,000[2]
Net cash flow	$12,000

Note that the cash flow works out to the same $12,000 figure whether the company uses straight-line depreciation or accelerated depreciation for reporting to shareholders.[3] The cash flow that we have just calculated is usually called *cash flow from operations.*

---

2 Recall from page 180 that BCD's Deferred tax for 1995 was $1,000.

3 The reason they work out to the same figure is this: When using straight-line depreciation, as compared to accelerated depreciation, Net profit from the income statement is higher by $1,000, and Deferred tax "adds" another $1,000 to the Cash flow calculation. This combined $2,000 is exactly offset by Depreciation being $2,000 lower; and the Cash flow correctly works out to $12,000 either way. Also, technically speaking, Deferred tax does not "add" $1,000. It is actually an adjustment that corrects the $9,000 of Taxes stated on the income statement to the $8,000 actually paid.

DEFINITION

- **Cash flow from operations**—the amount of cash generated by the company from making and selling its products or services. It does *not* include cash raised by selling new stock or bonds. Those would be called *cash flow from financing*.

It is important to be able to calculate cash flow, because, as we will see in Chapter 15, what a company *needs* to do with some (and possibly all) of its cash flow, and what it *chooses* to do with the rest of its cash flow (if there is any extra), can have a significant impact on its stock price.

REVIEW OF KEY POINTS

Depreciation is an expense reflecting the wearing out of fixed assets. Because depreciation expense is deducted from sales to calculate earnings, *but does not represent an expenditure of cash*, the amount of cash that the company earns from operations will usually be greater than the earnings shown on the company's income statement. The amount of cash a company earns making and selling its products or services is called *cash flow from operations*. Cash flow from operations is most easily calculated by starting with the company's reported earnings and adding back Depreciation and any increase in deferred taxes during the year. By adding back the increase in deferred tax, the investor does not have to worry about whether the company is using straight-line depreciation or accelerated depreciation.

14

Cost versus Expense, Capitalizing Assets, and Write-offs

THE DIFFERENCE BETWEEN A COST AND AN "EXPENSE"

In general conversation, the words *cost* and *expense* mean about the same thing. In an accounting sense, they have very precise and different meanings. Nevertheless, even Wall Streeters use the words loosely and often use one when they mean the other. When you understand clearly the difference between a cost and an expense, two things will happen. First, a great deal of accounting will begin to make more sense, and second, you can use the words interchangeably because you will usually know from context which is meant.

The following definitions of cost and expense often initially create confusion in the mind. Following the definitions, examples are given to further clarify this distinction. Finally a specific company example, SFC Corporation, is presented to show the investment importance.

DEFINITIONS

- **Cost**—A cost is incurred when a company pays for something, or becomes obligated to pay for something. When a cost is incurred, it may or may not also be an expense.

189

- **Expense**—An expense is any and all dollar figures that are deducted from sales to reach net profit. An expense always reflects a cost, but he cost may not have occurred in the same year. It may have occurred in a prior year, or it may be expected to occur in a future year.

When a company makes a purchase, it may pay in cash, or incur an account payable (which of course must be paid off later). In either case, a cost has been incurred. Another example of a cost is when a company declares a cash dividend. The cash might not actually be paid for three weeks, but the company has placed this obligation upon itself and therefore has incurred a cost. Note that we say the cost is incurred when the dividend is declared, not when it is actually paid out three weeks later.

When Jones Mousetrap buys some wood to use to make mousetraps, the price of the wood is put in Inventory. Since JMC is obligated to pay for that wood, whether paid in cash now or later, the purchase of inventory is definitely a cost. It is not an expense because nothing has to be brought to the income statement to be deducted from sales. That does not happen until the finished goods in inventory are sold. When finished goods are sold, their dollar value comes out of inventory, and goes into cost of goods sold expense, but not until then. Since inventory is usually converted to finished goods and sold within one year, some people think of an inventory purchase as an expense as well as a cost, but this is not accurate.

An easier example is the payment of interest. When interest is paid, it is both a cost and an expense. It is a cost because the company becomes obligated to pay it when it is due. It is an expense because it is deducted immediately from sales in order to calculate profit.

What about the wages earned by an employee? If wages are paid for building mousetraps that have already been sold, then the wage is both a cost and an expense. If it is paid for building mousetraps that have not yet been sold, it is a cost but not yet an expense. That cost will be carried in Finished goods on the balance sheet until those mousetraps are actually sold. When those mousetraps are sold, both the wage cost and the raw material cost will be taken out of Finished goods and become *cost of goods sold expense*. In sum, the costs of making the mousetraps do not become an expense until the traps are sold.

When wages are paid for general and administrative work, such as a portion of the wage paid to Arbetter in the example in Chapter 1, it is both a cost and an expense. It is an expense because it is brought directly to the income statement and deducted from sales at the time (or in the period) it was paid. Thus SG&A expense is called a *period expense* because it is deducted from sales in the period in which the cost is incurred. This is not true of wages paid for building mousetraps, which *might* become Cost of goods sold expense in the period the cost was incurred, or might become Cost of goods sold expense in a later period, depending on when the traps were sold.

CAPITALIZING AN ASSET

When a company buys a machine tool, a cost is incurred. Because the machine tool will be used for many years, the cost of the machine tool is put under Fixed assets on the balance sheet. This cost will *not* be deducted from sales that year in deriving net profit. Therefore, when a fixed asset is purchased, a cost is incurred but *not* an expense. In the language of Wall Street, the cost of the machine tool is *capitalized*, not *expensed*. In other words, the cost of the asset will go on the balance sheet as a fixed asset and will be depreciated over the appropriate number of years.

DEFINITION

* Capitalizing an asset—means putting the asset's cost on the balance sheet under Fixed Asset (or Long-Term Assets, or Property, Plant, and Equipment, or some similar title). When an asset is capitalized, it will usually then be depreciated over an appropriate number of years. Land is an exception. Its cost is capitalized, but it is not subsequently depreciated.

When a capitalized asset is depreciated, the depreciation taken in any given year *is* an expense, but *not* a cost. The depreciation is an expense because it is deducted from sales in deriving net profit. Depreciation is not a cost because there is no obligation to pay for something. The obligation to pay for the machine tool was incurred in a prior year. Thus, when the cost of an asset is capitalized and then depreciated in later years, what has really happened from an accounting point of view is that *the expensing of the cost has been deferred to later years*. Practically all costs eventually have to be expensed. Exceptions are: (1) the purchase of land, (2) the declaration of a dividend, and (3) repayment of the principal portion of a debt obligation.

The rationale for capitalizing the cost of the machine tool and expensing it gradually over a period of years is that since the machine tool is going to be used to help generate sales over a period of years, it would seem fair to account for its "cost" over the same period of years. The way this is done is by reflecting its cost, through depreciation expense, over the period of years that the machine tool is expected to be used.

DEFERRED EXPENSE

In the previous chapter we said an asset is depreciated because it wears out. While that is true, it is also accurate, from an accounting viewpoint, to say that an asset is depreciated because its cost is being expensed over a period of years, which perhaps equals the estimated time it takes to wear out.

Thus, any capitalized asset may be thought of as creating a deferred expense. In fact, many balance sheets contain an asset category called *Deferred expense*. This title does not tell you much. It only tells you that a cost was incurred for something and has not yet been expensed.

Sometimes a balance sheet will use the title "Deferred costs" or "Deferred charges" instead of "Deferred expenses." They mean the same thing but are not as precise. *Charge* is a loose word that can mean a lot of things depending on context, but usually means "expense." If the conceptual difference between cost and expense is understood, one can usually tell from context what is meant by *charge, cost,* or *expense.*

Deciding whether to capitalize an asset or to expense it is not always as clear-cut as one might assume. A machine tool will last for years, but certain parts, such as the cutting edges, have to be replaced monthly, or even daily. If the company buys a large supply of cutting edges at one time, should their cost be capitalized or expensed? What about the tires on a company truck that might last 6 months or 18 months, depending on usage and whether they are retreaded? Without trying to answer these questions, it should be apparent that there is some discretion involved in making the decision. This creates an opportunity for management to control its earnings. A conservative company would *expense* all these discretionary items (i.e., deduct them from sales in the year they were purchased, either as CGS or SG&A) and show a lower profit. A company with liberal accounting would *capitalize* such items and depreciate (expense) them over a period of years. Hence, the company with liberal accounting would show higher earnings in the initial year because it only expensed a small portion of the discretionary items (through depreciation), but would show lower earnings in the later years because it would have to continue deducting the depreciation expense (which the conservative company had fully expensed or written off in the first year).

The term *written off*, therefore, simply means "expensed." A write-off usually refers to expensing the full amount of an asset, as in the discretionary items previously mentioned. But it would be equally correct to say "20 percent of a machine tool was written-off in one year," meaning the machine tool was depreciated by 20 percent in that year. For example, assume the machine tool cost $10,000 and was depreciated on a straight-line basis over five years. All the following sentences say the same thing:

1. The tool is being depreciated by $2,000 per year.

2. The tool is being written off by 20 percent, or $2,000 per year.

3. The capitalized value of the tool is being charged to earnings at the rate of $2,000 per year.

4. The cost of the tool is being deferred and expensed evenly over a five-year period.

Capitalizing the cost of a plant or a piece of equipment is not the only thing that can create a deferred expense or deferred charge. Two other common examples of deferred expenses are as follows.

A Specific Example: Deferred Research and Development Expense

To understand the investment significance of capitalizing a cost (putting its cost on the balance sheet), as opposed to expensing it, let us look at the example of research and development costs at Super Fast Computer Corporation (SFC). When SFC spends money on research and development (R & D) of new products, should the cost be capitalized or expensed? The cost, of course, is incurred now, but the benefits of the R & D may not be realized until many years later, when the products that were being developed are actually sold. Therefore, it would seem reasonable to "recognize the cost" (i.e., do the expensing) at the same time that the profits are realized. But what if the products being developed are never successfully sold? How does one decide how much of the R & D cost was actually spent developing successful products and how much was spent developing unsuccessful products? Further, how do you know in advance which products will be successful and which will not, and for how long a period of time will the successful products be successful? If you capitalize R & D, over what period of time do you expense it? Since these questions are usually unanswerable, it is common practice to write off R & D when it is incurred (i.e., expense the cost in the year it was incurred).

When a company does capitalize R & D (liberal accounting), the expense it takes in later years is called *amortization*, rather than depreciation. Depreciation usually refers to writing off, or expensing, the cost of hard assets, such as plant and equipment that are deteriorating in value. R & D is not a hard asset and, in fact, may increase in value as new improvements are built into old products. *Amortization* does not imply a deterioration, but just refers to the deferred expensing of a cost incurred in an earlier year. Thus, depreciation may be thought of as one kind of amortization. The distinction is minor.

An example of where a company might capitalize R & D is in the case of a small, high-technology company that was formed to develop a particular product and has little or no other sales yet. Super Fast Computer Corporation, for example, was formed in 1994 by three engineers who all quit a large computer company because they thought they could manufacture a better computer, and by having their own company they would make more money. During 1994 SFC spent $100,000 on R & D on the new computer. Also that year, the company manufactured some small components at a cost of $30,000, which were sold for $40,000 to raise some cash. If the $100,000 R & D cost had been capitalized, the company would have shown a profit and the simplified financial statements of SFC would appear as follows:

SFC Corp. Income Statement 1994
R&D Capitalized

Sales	$ 40,000
Expense	30,000
Profit before tax	10,000
Tax	5,000
Net profit	5,000

Long-term Assets Portion of Balance Sheet
12/31/94

Plant and equipment	$ 50,000
Deferred R & D	100,000
Total long-term assets	$150,000

Had R & D been expensed, the same simplified statements would appear as follows:

SFC Corp. Income Statement 1994 R&D Expensed	
Sales	$ 40,000
Expense	130,000
Net *loss*	(90,000)

Long-term Assets Portion of Balance Sheet 12/31/94	
Plant and equipment	$ 50,000
Total long-term assets	$ 50,000

Note the convention of putting the loss in parentheses.

There are no real benefits of capitalizing R & D to show a profit. Potential investors should know that SFC is actually spending far more than it is taking in. If it does not begin making a "real" profit soon—rather than the "accounting" profit of 1994—the company will soon run out of money and either have to raise more or go out of business. Such a stock is an extremely risky venture.

In the Long-term assets portion of the balance sheet, Deferred R & D might have been called "Deferred charges" or "Deferred costs," or even "Deferred assets." Obviously, Deferred R & D is the most descriptive title because it tells what kind of "asset" is having its expensing deferred. Deferred R & D might also be called an *Intangible asset*. Although the information or know-how learned as a result of the R & D cost is definitely as asset, it is not clear when and how much of it will eventually be converted to products.

The process of capitalizing SFC's $100,000 of R & D cost and amortizing it on a straight-line basis (evenly) over 10 years could be stated in any of the following ways. Each statement says the same thing.

1. SFC capitalized $100,000 of R & D costs and is expensing it by 10%, or $10,000, per year.

2. SFC is carrying its R & D costs as a deferred charge (or deferred expense) on the balance sheet and will write it off evenly over 10 years.

3. The capitalized value of R & D is being amortized evenly over 10 years.

4. Intangible assets reflect R & D costs and will be amortized straight line over 10 years.

5. SFC has deferred the cost of its R & D and is writing it off evenly over 10 years.

This latter way is technically incorrect. SFC has not deferred the *cost* of its R & D. It has deferred the *expensing*, or *amortizing*, of the cost. Wall Street language is sloppy, however, so you might hear it this way.

Although each of the five sentences provides the same information, footnotes in company annual reports, unfortunately are not always as clear. For example, the same information might be presented as a footnote that says something like, "Deferred Expenses reflect the cost of certain assets which will be amortized to in a manner reflecting their expected benefit to the company." This is vague and gives no clue as to the reason for the deferred expense, or the possible impact on earnings.

The point here for investors is that the sudden appearance on the balance sheet of a deferred asset account, or a sharp increase in such an account, whether called deferred costs, deferred expenses, deferred charges, deferred R & D, intangible assets, or something similar, is a warning flag that even though the company's reported earnings may be increasing, there might be some large outflow of cash (a cost) that is not yet being expensed on the income statement. Therefore, the company's financial condition or future earnings, or both, might not be as strong as expected. In such a case, investors should ask the company how big an impact the deferred expense will have on future years' earnings.

For most companies, amortization expense is small relative to depreciation expense. Also, since both are similar in that they reflect the expensing of costs incurred in prior years, most companies lump them together on the income statement. Thus, you are likely to see something like "Depreciation & amortization expense" as a single item rather than have each listed separately. Where amortization is large, it may be broken out separately.

Intangible Assets

Deferred R & D is just one kind of intangible asset. An intangible asset might also be a patent, a copyright, or a brand name. The presence of an intangible asset account on the balance sheet, however, usually indicates that the intangible asset was purchased, rather than developed by the company. When Regal Drinks, Incorporated (RDI) develops a successful brand, they enjoy all the benefits of owning that brand, but they do not show it as an intangible asset on the balance sheet. On the other hand, if RDI were to acquire a brand name by purchasing another company, then RDI might have to show an Intangible asset account on the balance sheet. This would arise as follows. Suppose RDI bought a company that sold instant coffee under a well-established brand name. The book value of the coffee company was $1,000,000, but RDI paid the original owners of the coffee company $1,400,000. What has happened? RDI has purchased $1,000,000 worth of net property, plant, and equipment, but it has also purchased the coffee company's brand name. The $400,000 of cost above the $1,000,000 worth of net assets (i.e., the cost in excess of the book value of the acquired assets) would be attributed to the value of the brand name, and would be called an *intangible asset* or *goodwill*, and in this case be equal to $400,000.

The $400,000 cost of this intangible asset must eventually be deducted from sales as an expense, just as the property, plant, and equipment, which were acquired for $1,000,000, will have to be deducted as a depreciation expense. In the case of the $1,000,000 of PP&E, the depreciation expense can be taken over the estimated lives of the assets. But what is the estimated life of the brand name? In the case of an instant coffee, the brand name might be good for 10 or even 20 or more years, or it might lose its appeal in six months. Thus, a conservative company might write off, or "expense," the $400,000 right away and not carry it on the balance sheet at all. A company with liberal accounting policies that wants to show the highest possible earnings immediately would want to amortize the cost of the brand name over as many years as possible, in order to have the lowest possible amortization expense each year.

It is up to the company and its accountants to decide over what period of time the brand name, or goodwill, should be amortized. What if the brand name were Coca-Cola? The life expectancy of this brand name is indefinite. It is, however, a generally accepted accounting principle that goodwill should be amortized over a period of no more than 40 years.

DEFINITION

- **Goodwill**—When Company A acquires Company B, and pays more for it than Company B's book value, the difference between what

Company A pays and Company B's book value is called *goodwill* and goes on Company A's balance sheet. Goodwill is an intangible asset. It is worth something, but you cannot touch it.

Goodwill may be thought of as a deferred charge because its cost—$400,000 in this case—will not be expensed (charged to profit) immediately but will be amortized over a period of years. Goodwill, however, is almost always called *goodwill* rather than *deferred charge*. Only in the case where the dollar value of goodwill is very insignificant might it be lumped together with other things under a heading such as "Deferred assets" or "Deferred charges."

The investment significance of goodwill can be minimal or substantial. Although goodwill is carried as an asset on the balance sheet, it may or may not truly reflect something that is actually worth the dollar amount shown for it on the balance sheet. For example, if the well-established brand name of the instant coffee company acquired by RDI enabled RDI to generate substantial sales and earnings, the intangible asset goodwill would then be well worth the $400,000 that RDI paid for it. But what if the brand name suddenly lost favor and no more coffee could be sold under that name? The balance sheet would continue to reflect an "asset" of $400,000, but now it would be worthless and the company might decide to write it off immediately (expense the entire $400,000 that year) rather than continue to amortize it over a number of years. The immediate write-off of $400,000 would lower earnings a lot more than the small yearly amortization, and could hurt the stock price

The appearance of *goodwill* on a balance sheet, then, is a flag to the investor that the company's book value might be overstated if, in fact, the value of the item reflected in goodwill has declined. This is important because some investors look at book value per share as a price against which to value the price of the stock. This gives rise to an improved definition of book value called *tangible book value*, which is discussed shortly.

While the balance sheet term *deferred charges* may include goodwill, it can also refer to something like an insurance premium that was paid in advance. Suppose, for example, RDI pays an insurance premium of $12,000 for three years of insurance in advance. Since RDI is now insured for three years, it would seem reasonable that the cost of the insurance should be amortized or charged to earnings (expensed) evenly over the three years. Thus, RDI would set up a new asset account on the balance sheet called "Deferred charges" or "Prepaid insurance," which it would amortize evenly over three years, or $4,000 a year. RDI's balance sheet might look like this:

RDI			
Balance Sheet at 12/31/94			
Assets		**Liabilities**	
Current assets:		Current liabilities:	
Cash	$ 1,000,000	Short-term debt	$ 500,000
Accounts receivable	3,000,000	Accounts payable	4,000,000
Inventory	4,500,000	Total current liabilities	4,500,000
Total current assets	8,500,000	Long-term debt:	
Fixed assets:		7% bonds due 2008	7,000,000
Gross PP&E	21,000,000	**Stockholders' Equity**	
Less: Accum. depr.	7,000,000	Equity:	
Net PP&E	14,000,000	Common stock	500,000
Intangible assets:		Additional paid-in capital	4,604,000
Goodwill	400,000	Retained earnings	6,308,000
Deferred charges	12,000	Total equity	11,412,000
	412,000	Total liabilities	
Total assets	$22,912,000	and equity	$22,912,000

BOOK VALUE AND TANGIBLE BOOK VALUE

In Chapter 12, book value was defined as total assets, less total liabilities, less liquidating value of preferred stock. When calculating book value, it is more prudent to also subtract intangible assets and call the result *tangible book value* instead of just *book value*.

DEFINITIONS

- **Book value**—Total assets less total liabilities less liquidating value of preferred stock.

- **Tangible book value**—Total assets less intangible assets less total liabilities less liquidating value of preferred stock.

Since RDI does not have any preferred stock, its book value and tangible book value can be calculated as follows:

	Book value	Tangible book value
Total assets	$22,912,000	$22,912,000
Less: Intangible assets		412,000
		22,500,000
Less: Total liabilities	11,500,000	11,500,000
	$11,412,000	$11,000,000

Note that people frequently say "book value" when they mean "tangible book value." Tangible book value is the more conservative calculation. It is preferred by most investors, first, because it is hard to know whether the intangible assets really have any current worth, and second, because intangible assets, such as deferred R & D and goodwill, more often than not, cannot be sold for anything if the company goes bankrupt.

Tangible book value is sometimes called *tangible net worth*. Net worth just means equity. Therefore, *tangible net worth* means equity less intangible assets. The terms *book value*, *net worth*, and *tangible net worth* are often used interchangeably. The tangible book value of RDI of $11,000,000 is very close to its total book value or net worth of $11,412,000. This is frequently the case when there are few or no intangible assets. Nevertheless, it is not a good idea to assume that the book value equals equity or net worth. It is always safer to calculate it yourself, particularly when there is preferred stock outstanding or a large amount of intangible assets.

AMORTIZATION AND CASH FLOW

In Chapter 13 we saw that the *cash flow from operations* that a company generates is usually greater than the reported profit. This is because depreciation expense is deducted from sales, which reduces profit, even though it does not represent a cash flow-out. Amortization of capitalized costs (deferred expenses) produces a similar result. Amortization is an accounting entry reflecting the expensing of some cost or costs incurred in prior years. Amortization is deducted from sales, which reduces profit, but it does not reflect a cash outlay. The cash outlay that gave rise to the capitalized cost or deferred expense may have occurred many years ago. As a result, when calculating a company's cash flow from operations, amortization is treated the same way as depreciation. Using the short-cut method of calculating cash flow-in shown in the cash flow from operations section in Chapter 13, amortization would be "added back" to earnings the same as depreciation. Thus, a company's cash flow-in statement might look as follows:

Cash flow from operations using the short-cut method:	
Net profit	$ 9,000
Add back:	
Depreciation and amortization	$ 2,000
Deferred tax	$ 1,000
Net cash flow-in	$12,000

EXTRAORDINARY WRITE-OFFS

The terms *write-off* and *write-down*, like many other words used in the investment community, have a variety of meanings or connotations depending on how they are used. The normal depreciation of assets, we said, can be thought of as a write-down. This type of write-down is quite regular, in that assets are continuously being depreciated or written down.

Write-off or write-down is used more frequently, however, in a case where an asset has become useless and is being written down to either $0 or scrap value all at once. For example, assume a machine with an expected life of eight years breaks down after five years and the company does not want to repair it because other machines can pick up the load. Since this machine was not yet fully depreciated to $0 or scrap value, the company must now write it down to $0 or scrap value because that is all it is now worth. Another example might be a company car that is only one year old and is in an accident that is not covered by insurance. The company could get the car repaired, but decides to replace it with a new car. The old car would have to be written off. As a final example, consider a furniture company that has a large inventory of a certain style of bedroom set that is not selling well. After trying different advertising approaches without success, management finally decides this style is unlikely to ever sell well and the product is taken off the market to be used for scrap wood. Therefore, its dollar value in *finished goods inventory* must be written down to scrap value.

These three kinds of write-offs are not as regular as depreciation, and most often amount to a small dollar figure relative to the company's overall financial results. When the amount is small, the company would simply include them in the income statement as part of the cost of goods sold, or selling, general, and administrative expense, or depreciation, depending on the company's normal accounting procedures. In practice there are probably a few such small write-offs in every quarter for every company, so their effects would not be noticeable in the company's pattern of reported EPS, and therefore would not be misleading to investors.

Typically, however, most companies make more of these adjustments in the fourth quarter. Perhaps it is just human nature for management to put off admitting it made a mistake on that style of bedroom set, for example. Or perhaps it is simply human nature to put off making any noncritical decisions until year-end when the accountants require it. Also, of course, it is possible that management is intentionally delaying such write-offs because they want to get the stock as high as possible early in the year and therefore want to show the maximum possible earnings. This could be done either because the company plans to have a stock offering or because members of the company's management want to sell some of their own personal stock. Of course, it is unethical and illegal to show artificially high earnings for either of these last two reasons. In any case, these fourth quarter write-offs can make a company's fourth quarter earnings harder to predict than any of the first three quarters.

In the event that such write-offs come to a significant proportion of income, perhaps 5 percent or more, the company should mention it in a footnote. In a case where such write-offs were extremely large, the company would be required by accounting rules to note them separately as extraordinary items. This would typically occur in unusual cases, such as if a fire or explosion destroyed a plant totally and it had to be written off. It can also occur when a company sells off or closes a division that is no longer making a profit. This kind of write-off is sometimes called a *restructuring cost*.

These extraordinary write-offs and restructuring costs are sometimes called *nonrecurring costs*, meaning that they do not occur regularly in the normal operations of the company. Nonrecurring write-offs can badly distort the progression of a company's earnings, and therefore impact the stock price. So it is important for investors to understand the effects on reported earnings of an extraordinary or nonrecurring write-off.

For an example, let's look at Boom Boom Dynamite Company, which had an explosion in one of its four plants in December of 1995. The plant was not insured.

Had there not been an explosion, the year-end financial statements would have looked like this:

Part of Balance Sheet
BBD COMPANY 12/31/95

Fixed assets:
    Gross property, plant, and equipment $12,000,000
        Accumulated depreciation 7,000,000
    Net property, plant, and equipment 5,000,000

BBD COMPANY
Income Statement for 1995

Sales	$6,000,000	
Expense:		
CGS	$2,000,000	
SG&A	500,000	
Depreciation	400,000	
Interest	100,000	
Total expense	3,000,000	3,000,000
Profit before tax		3,000,000
Tax		1,500,000
Net profit		$1,500,000
EPS (500,000 shares outstanding)		$3.00/share

The explosion, however, destroyed a plant that had an original cost of $5 million and had been depreciated down to a book value of $2 million. (That is, the accumulated depreciation on the plant, from when it was built until the explosion, was $3 million.) Since the plant was destroyed, it had to be removed entirely from the books. Thus, the $5 million cost was removed from Gross PP&E, and the $3 million of accumulated depreciation and the $2 million of Net PP&E were also removed. The Fixed assets portion of the balance sheet, then, looked like this:

Fixed assets:
    Gross property, plant, and equipment .. $7,000,000
        Accumulated depreciation 4,000,000
    Net property, plant, & equipment 3,000,000

Since the book value of the destroyed plant was $2 million, the company has incurred a $2 million loss. This loss must be expensed, or written off against earnings. It can either be included in Cost of goods sold, or depreciation, or handled separately as an extraordinary item. The latter two methods will be shown.

BBD COMPANY
Income Statement for 1995
(Plant write-off included in Depreciation)

Sales		$6,000,000
Expense:		
CGS	$2,000,000	
SG&A	500,000	
Depreciation	2,400,000	
Interest	100,000	
	5,000,000	5,000,000
Profit before tax		1,000,000
Tax		500,000
Net profit..............................		$ 500,000
EPS (500,000 shares outstanding)		$1.00/share

By including the plant destruction in depreciation, the reported earnings of $1 per share look a lot worse that the $3 per share the company is capable of earning when it is operating normally. While BBD may not be capable of earning $3 per share next year without the plant, it may be able to earn closer to $3 per share than $1 per share, and retain its customers by working more in the remaining plants, and possibly temporarily buying dynamite from competitors to service its customers, until a new plant can be built. Once the new plant is built, earnings can be expected to return to around the $3 per share level. Therefore, including the plant write-off in depreciation does not give the financial-statement reader a fair picture of what actually happened and may be misleading by implying that earnings are more likely to stay at the $1 per share level, rather than springing back to the $3 level when the new plant is opened. The following presentation, with the plant write-off handled as an *extraordinary* or *nonrecurring item*, would be preferable.

BBD COMPANY
Income Statement for 1995
(Plant write-off handled as extraordinary item)

Sales...		$6,000,000
Expense:		
CGS	$2,000,000	
SG&A	500,000	
Depreciation	400,000	
Interest	100,000	
	3,000,000	3,000,000
Profit before taxes		3,000,000
Taxes		1,500,000
Profit before extraordinary item		$1,500,000
Extraordinary loss		
(net of tax at 50%)		$1,000,000
Net profit...............................		$ 500,000
EPS (before extraordinary loss)		$3.00/share
EPS (including extraordinary loss)		$1.00/share

Note how the tax is handled. According to the Internal Revenue Service, the plant write-off is deductible when calculating taxes. Therefore, as a result of the $2,000,000 loss, $1,000,000 was saved in taxes. The $1,000,000 tax savings, however, is deducted from the extraordinary loss that caused it, rather than from the normal earnings of the company. This is because the purpose of presenting the extraordinary item separately is to show what the company's results would have been with and without the extraordinary loss. Thus, *taxes* are listed as $1,500,000 even though only $500,000 was paid. Similarly, the extraordinary loss (net of tax) is listed as $1,000,000, even though the loss was actually $2,000,000.

EFFECT ON STOCK PRICE

The important point here is that when an extraordinary or nonrecurring event occurs, the investor must attempt to find out what caused it, what temporary or lasting effects it will have on the company's operations, and what financial hardships it may cause the company. If the effect is expected to be temporary, one should try to reconstruct the income statement as it would have been without the extraordinary item, in order to determine what progress the company may have been making in the normal course of business. In the case of BBD, the $3 per share earnings figure is probably more representative of the company's future earnings than the $1 per share. Thus, what would probably happen is that, when the news of the plant explosion got out, the stock would go down briefly, as investors were initially uncertain about what long-term effects it would have on the company's ability to generate earnings and dividends. But as investors learned that the company's earnings progress would only be temporarily hurt and not permanently impaired, the stock would probably return to near its former level.

The extraordinary write-off in this example resulted from unexpected destruction of plant and equipment. An extraordinary or nonrecurring write-off can also occur when a company manufactures a large inventory of a product and then discovers that the product cannot be sold. In such a case, the inventory would have to be written off or written down to scrap value.

15

Cash Flow

A company's ability to generate earnings and pay dividends over a period of time is perhaps the most important factor affecting its stock price. To have a more complete picture of a company, however, and to be better able to forecast stock moves, investors must look beyond earnings and also look at a company's cash flow.

Over a period of time, *cash flow from operations* will be the most important source of cash; but cash flow, into or out of the company, can also arise from other sources. In most companies' annual reports you will see, in addition to the income statement and balance sheet, a *statement of cash flow*. The cash flow statement is usually broken into three categories: cash flow from operations; cash flow from financing activities; and cash flow from investing activities. Let's first look at each of these categories separately and then look at some cash flow statements to see what they can tell us about a company.

CASH FLOW FROM OPERATIONS

As we saw in Chapter 13, *cash flow from operations* refers to the cash that flows into the company from selling its products or services, less the cash that flows out of the company to pay for raw materials, wages, and other items necessary to run the company on a day-to-day basis, such as record keeping and secretarial supplies. We also saw that cash flow from operations is not the same thing as earnings. This is because depreciation (and amortization) expense are subtracted from *sales* when calculating earnings, but are not subtracted from sales when calculating cash flow. Thus, the easiest way to calculate the cash flow from operations is to start with the earnings and *add back* depreciation, amortization, and any increase in deferred taxes. A typical cash flow from operations statement might look like this:

Cash flow from operating activities:	
Net profit	$10,000,000
Add back:	
Depreciation and amortization	2,000,000
Deferred tax	600,000
Net cash flow from operations	$12,600,000

In practice there will also be a number of other, usually smaller items, such as changes in accounts receivable, accounts payable, inventory, and other accounts, which add or subtract cash, and are included in the cash flow from operations calculation. For a company with financial problems, these other additions to, or subtractions from, cash flow may be very important. For healthy companies, however, investors can usually make a reasonable judgment of cash flow from operations from just the items shown here, and we will limit ourselves to these in this book.

Keep in mind throughout this chapter that the figure for net cash flow from operations is not just the cash coming in from sales. It is the net result of subtracting the day-to-day operating expenses (wages, raw materials, interest expense, and so on) from sales. If a company is not generating enough cash to meet these day-to-day operating needs, it will be out of business quickly. Thus, when we talk about what a company might do with its cash flow from operations, we are referring to the cash flow *after* those day-to-day operating needs have been met.

CASH FLOW FROM FINANCING

Cash flow from financing activities is straightforward. Cash flow-in from financing occurs when the company raises money by issuing new common or preferred stock, or by borrowing. Borrowing includes selling a new issue of bonds or borrowing from a bank, insurance company, or other financial institution. Cash flow-out from financing can arise from repaying the principal amount of a loan or a bond at maturity, or buying bonds back under a sinking fund or call provision, or just buying bonds on the open market and retiring them. Note that the interest payment on a loan or bond is not considered cash flow-out from financing. Interest is more appropriately included in the cash flow from operations because interest is paid on a regular basis.

Cash flow-out from financing activities would also include both the payment of common and preferred dividends and money spent to repurchase shares of the company's outstanding preferred or common stock.

CASH FLOW FROM INVESTING

Cash flow from investing activities usually does *not* mean buying stocks and bonds, although that is what investing means to most people. From a company's point of view, investing means buying new plant and equipment in order to make either more product, or to make it faster, better, or cheaper. New plant and equipment can refer to buildings, machines to make products, trucks to ship the products, cars to drive salespeople to customers, computers to keep the books, and even the company's kitchen and cafeteria equipment. If a company happens to buy stock or bonds of other companies, that would also be investing activity, but that is not what is primarily meant by investing activity in this context. In this chapter, investing activity will usually refer to a company's purchasing new plant and equipment, unless otherwise specified.

Cash flow-out from investing activities might also include buying another company. Suppose JMC bought the Swift Rat Trap company, or the XYZ Dog Food Company. The cost of purchasing these companies would be cash flow-out from investing activity. Alternatively, suppose JMC had owned the XYZ Dog Food Company for a number of years, but decided to get out of the dog food business. If XYZ were sold to another company, the money JMC received from the sale would be considered cash flow-in from investing activities. In this case it might be considered disinvesting. Similarly, if a company sells any of its property, plant, and equipment, no matter how much it has been used and depreciated, the money received from the sale would be disinvesting, or cash flow-in from investing activities.

Review of Terminology

When a company buys new plant and equipment it is called *capital spending*, or we can say the company is making *capital expenditures*. Keep in mind the distinction between capital spending and spending for inventory. Capital *spending* refers to spending for plant, equipment, tools, and other things that will be used to make the company's products. Capital *equipment* will remain in the company.

Inventory refers to the materials that will be used up and become part of the product that is being sold. In the case of JMC, wood, metal, and labor costs incurred to make mousetraps are all inventory costs. Spending for inventory would be part of the cash flow-out from operations; not cash flow from investing.

At JMC, the cost of screwdrivers, saws, and other tools, as well as the building in which the traps are made, would be *capital spending*, or *capital costs*.

In the language of Wall Street, purchases for inventory are *expensed*, meaning that they will usually be deducted from sales in the period (year or quarter) that the cost was incurred. However, as previously discussed, this is not strictly true. Purchases for inventory go on the balance sheet in raw materials and then finished goods, and don't really get "expensed" (i.e. become Cost of Goods Sold expense) until the goods are actually sold. We as investors, however, can usually "round off" a little and simply think of inventory purchases (costs) as being expenses.

Capital spending, on the other hand, is not expensed, but rather is *capitalized*, meaning its cost is put on the balance sheet and will be depreciated over a number of years. Thus, capital spending (spending for new plant and equipment) would be cash flow-out from investing activities.

To review, a company's cash flow, in or out, can arise from either operations, financing, or investing. Whether a company survives and prospers, and therefore how its stock will behave, will depend in great measure on how much cash flow comes in, how it comes in, and how the company spends or uses its cash flow. A company's cash flow from operations is its most important source of cash flow. If cash flow from operations is sufficient to meet all the company's basic needs, plus have enough left over for expansion and growth, or to pay increasing dividends to shareholders, then the company is in good shape and its stock is probably rising. If the company is unable to generate enough cash flow from operations to meet basic needs, then the stock is likely to be declining, or will have already declined.

USES OF CASH FLOW—SURVIVAL NEEDS

We will look first at what the company *must* do with its cash flow to survive, and later look at what it *may* do with its excess cash after survival needs have been met. Once again, keep in mind that *cash flow from operations* is the cash available after day-to-day spending needs for inventory, labor, interest expense, and the like have been met.

Debt Retirement

A company must repay its debt obligations on time. This includes bank loan repayments, bond sinking fund and maturity repayments, for example. If the company is unable to meet these obligations, the lenders can usually have the company declared bankrupt. Recall that interest payments on debt are treated as part of day-to-day operating requirements, not as part of the principal repayments.

Maintenance Level of Capital Spending

The maintenance level of capital spending is the minimum amount of spending necessary for the company to replace old or worn out machinery, or to replace obsolete machinery with new and better equipment to make the company's products. If JMC did not keep up with the latest manufacturing equipment, other mousetrap companies might be able to make traps cheaper, sell them for a lower price than JMC, and put JMC out of business. Maintenance capital spending does not include buying additional machinery to expand the plant and grow the company. That is *discretionary* capital spending. Also, maintenance capital spending does not include the cost of oiling machinery and making minor repairs or adjustments. These costs, which occur on a regular basis, are part of day-to-day operating expenses and are included in the cash flow-out from operations.

Preferred Dividends

Preferred dividend payments may not actually be a survival need because failure to pay the preferred dividend cannot result in bankruptcy, but the obligation is so strong that failure to pay it is usually a sign that a company is in trouble. Further, if the company is unable to pay its preferred dividend, it is certainly not going to pay a common dividend, and most likely does not have any excess cash to use for growth.

In sum, investors must look at the cash flow from operations and see if it is adequate to meet: (1) debt principal repayment requirements, (2) a maintenance level of capital spending, and (3) preferred dividends. If cash flow is not adequate to meet these minimal needs, the company's stock is probably going down. If it appears that the company will be cash-short for just a year or two, then the company may be able to issue new stock or new bonds to get past the bad year or years.

THE SIMPLIFIED CASH FLOW STATEMENT

Although most company annual reports break cash flow into the three categories (cash flow from operations, cash flow from financing activity, and cash flow from investing activity), it is usually easier to focus on the whole picture by recasting the cash flow statement into what is called the *sources and uses of funds* statement. In this statement, shown below, investors can see the pattern of increases or decreases over time for each source or use of cash flow. A more detailed cash flow statement will be explained later in this chapter. For this simplified statement, assume the dollar figures are in millions of dollars, so, for example, the depreciation and amortization for the company grew from $21 million in 1993 to $24 million in 1995.

Company ABC Cash Flow Statement						
	Actual			Forecast		
	1993	1994	1995	1996	1997	1998
Sources						
1. Net income	$50	54	59			
Add back:						
2. Depreciation and amort.	21	23	24	25	25	25
3. Incr. in deferred tax	4	5	5	5	5	5
4. Cash flow from operations	$75	82	88			
Uses						
5. Debt principal repayments	$25	15	30	30	150	22
6. Maintenance capital spending	15	15	20			
7. Preferred dividend	5	5	5	5	5	—
8. Cash flow uses	$45	35	55			

Company ABC appears to be doing well. Net income has been growing (line 1), and total cash flow from operations (line 4) has been sufficient to meet all the survival needs (line 8) and still have cash left over for additional capital spending for growth, or payment of common dividends. But notice that in 1997, the company will have a large debt repayment of $150 that cannot be met from cash flow from operations unless net income almost doubles, something that does not seem likely based on the past few years' history. It is possible, however, that Company ABC could *refinance* this debt repayment—that is, issue new bonds (or stock) to obtain the money necessary to repay the old debt. If investors felt that ABC was likely to continue to do well—that is, earnings were likely to continue rising—then most likely the $150 debt repayment in 1997 could be refinanced. But what if the level of debt repayment was scheduled to stay at $150 for another three years? Then it is less certain that investors would be willing to buy new stock or bonds of this company. Further, what if earnings had been trending down, not up, or were expected to fall sharply? Let's look at the cash flow statement using those assumptions.

Company ABC Cash Flow Statement						
	Actual			Forecast		
	1993	1994	1995	1996	1997	1998
1. Net income	$50	54	46	20	10	0
Add back:						
2. Depreciation and amort.	21	23	24	25	25?	25?
3. Incr. in deferred tax	4	5	5			
4. Cash flow from operations	$75	82	88	45	35?	25?
5. Debt principal repayments	$25	15	30	30	150	150
6. Maintenance capital spending	15	15	20			
7. Preferred dividend	5	5	5	5	5	5
8. Cash flow uses	$45	35	55			

Under these assumptions, without even guessing at deferred tax, it is clear that the company's cash flow from operations (line 4) will fall far short of what is needed to meet debt principal repayments (line 5), and this does not even consider anything for maintenance level capital spending. The cash flow shortage, combined with the rapidly deteriorating earnings outlook, would make investors very skeptical about refinancing ABC's debt. The company would need to say or do something to convince investors that the downturn in earnings was only temporary, and that earnings were likely to come back very strongly. In the absence of such assurance, it is unlikely that investors would want to buy any new bonds from the company, and with the earnings outlook as bad as it is, it is likely that the stock is so low that the company could not sell enough new shares of stock to raise the required money. Under these assumptions, Company ABC appears unable to meet the debt repayment due in 1997 and is clearly in trouble. Although the company can survive until then, investors can see the trouble coming and the stock would probably be falling now.

OBTAINING CASH FLOW INFORMATION

It is the job of security analysts and investors to obtain estimates or forecasts from the company, or to make their own forecasts of the cash flow numbers presented here, and then to make investment judgments from them as we just did. When estimating a company's earnings, the first line in the cash flow statement is usually the primary and most difficult job of the analyst or investor, encompassing knowledge of the state of the economy, the outlook for the company's products within the economy, and the competitive nature of the company, among other factors. The other cash flow items are usually easier to obtain or forecast. *Depreciation and amortization* usually do not change much from year to year. If total capital spending is rising, depreciation is likely to rise in the following years. If capital spending is declining, then depreciation is more likely to decline in the following years. In any case, most companies are willing to give investors their estimate of depreciation and amortization for the current and perhaps following year. Similarly, companies often make public forecasts of their capital spending budget for the year, or are willing to give it to investors who call and ask. Companies may also be willing to say how much of the capital spending budget is for expansion and how much is for maintenance, although sometimes it is hard to distinguish. For instance, a new plant or piece of equipment might be purchased both to replace an old, inefficient piece, but also be able to produce many more parts per day.

The required debt repayment schedule for the next five years is almost always available in the footnotes to the financial statements in the annual report, or is readily available from the company. Similarly, the preferred dividend requirements usually do not change from year to year unless the company issues more shares or retires some shares, either under a sinking fund or buying them back on the open market.

FREE CASH FLOW

Now that we have seen the things that a company must do with its cash flow in order to survive, we are able to define *free cash flow*. Free cash flow is the cash flow from operations that the company is free to spend on whatever it wants after it has met its basic survival needs of debt repayment, maintenance-level capital expenditures, and possibly preferred dividends. In the example of company ABC on page 212, free cash flow can be calculated by subtracting line 8 from line 4. Thus, ABC had free cash flow of $30 in 1993, $47 in 1994, and $33 in 1995.

DEFINITION

• **Free cash flow**—is cash flow from operations, less debt repayment requirements, less preferred dividends, less the maintenance level of capital spending.

Some investors or financial services might define free cash flow slightly differently, perhaps not deducting preferred dividends because failure to pay the preferred dividend cannot cause the company to be declared bankrupt; or perhaps excluding maintenance-level capital spending, because it is not a contractual obligation like debt repayment; or perhaps including or excluding some other minor items. But the concept of free cash flow—cash that can be used at management's discretion after all survival requirements have been met—should be clear.

USES OF FREE CASH FLOW: INCREASING SHAREHOLDER VALUE

A company with free cash flow has a number of choices of what it can do with its free cash to increase shareholder value. Several common uses are described here.

Increase Capital Spending

The company can buy new plant and equipment above what is needed for maintenance. Expanding manufacturing capacity enables the company to make more product, which can generate more sales, which can generate more profits, and the value of the company grows. Sooner or later this should be reflected in a rising stock price.

Increase the Dividend to Common Stockholders

Dividends, of course, pass value to the shareholders immediately. Also, investors usually see an increased common dividend as a sign that the company is confident about the future. Companies generally do not like to raise the dividend if they are afraid they will have to lower it again shortly. Increases in the common dividend can sometimes have an immediate impact on the company's stock price. Other times, however, when a company has substantial free cash flow, investors can see the likelihood of a dividend increase ahead of time, and the stock may move up before the dividend increase is actually announced. In such cases, the stock may then actually decline shortly after the dividend increase is announced. Such a decline right after the company announced a dividend increase would, of course, be a surprise to investors who had not been watching the company's free cash flow, and realized ahead of time that a dividend increase was highly probable. This is an important lesson that we will see again in Chapter 18: *The stock market anticipates. That is, stock prices often react to events, such as dividend changes, before they actually occur.* On the other hand, if the dividend increase had not been expected, the stock would be likely to rise when the dividend increase was announced.

Similarly, if free cash flow was large enough that investors had been anticipating a large dividend increase, but the company announced only a small dividend increase, then investors might be disappointed and take that as a sign that things were not quite as good as they thought, and the stock might decline. For this reason, investors carefully follow a company's past dividend policy, as well as watching its cash flow. That is, they look at past history to see when and by how much the company has typically raised or lowered the common dividend in response to changing business conditions and company earnings. This enables them to better anticipate future changes and therefore forecast stock price moves.

Repurchase Company Bonds or Prepay Other Debt

By prepaying debt to banks or other lenders, or buying back the company's bonds on the open market (even if there is no sinking fund requirement), the company can often lower its interest expense. This, in turn, adds to earnings, which further enhances shareholder value. Also, if an issue of debt is completely retired, it will free the company from any restrictions placed on it by the covenants in the loan agreement.

Hoard Cash

Allowing cash balances to build also increases shareholder value. First, the cash will probably be invested in marketable securities that are earning interest, which adds to earnings. But more importantly, investors can anticipate that the cash will be used when company management sees an attractive opportunity. This might include broadening the company's product line, diversifying into a different business, buying another company, becoming more automated to reduce manufacturing costs, or expanding overseas.

When a company allows its cash to build, the appearance of the cash or marketable securities on the balance sheet may call attention to the company, and it may itself become a takeover target of larger companies. As those larger companies bid to acquire the cash-rich company, its stock goes up—a direct increase in shareholder value.

Because the members of management of most companies do not want their company to be taken over, they do not want to attract unwanted attention by letting cash build on the balance sheet. For this reason, another use of free cash flow that has become more common in recent years is buying back some of the company's outstanding common stock.

Repurchase the Company's Outstanding Preferred or Common Stock

Companies with free cash flow will sometimes buy back their common stock if, as a result of having fewer shares outstanding, earnings per share will be higher. When a company announces its intention to repurchase some of its stock, the stock often goes up; first, because the company's buying can directly lift the price, second, because the resulting increase in earnings per share makes the stock look cheaper, and third, because the announcement probably reflects management's confidence that business is strong and that they expect free cash flow to remain strong for a while. On the other hand, company managers and directors know that the announcement of the intention to repurchase the company's stock can push the price up, and some managements may announce their intention to repurchase company stock even if they never intend to do it. Thus, when investors see a company announce a stock repurchase program, they should look at the company's cash flow and see if the company will realistically have enough free cash flow to enable them to buy back a meaningful amount of stock.

Repurchasing the company's outstanding preferred stock may also increase earnings per share by eliminating the preferred dividend. Recall that the preferred dividend (not the common dividend) is deducted from net earnings in calculating earnings per share.

In sum, it is the presence of free cash flow that creates these opportunities. The greater the free cash flow, the greater the opportunities to increase shareholder value and for the stock to go up. Free cash flow does not, of course, automatically add to shareholder value. If JMC used its free cash flow to expand its capacity to make more mousetraps, but then could not sell the additional traps, then the cash it used to expand the plant may have been wasted. If a company uses free cash flow to go into a new business, but fails in that new business, and loses money rather than making money, then again the shareholders will not have benefited, and in fact probably will have lost value.

There are many ways that company directors or management can use free cash flow to add to shareholder value. They have the option of buying back stock or bonds, increasing the dividend, increasing capital spending for growth, or any combination of these. Investors, on the other hand, will notice how management is using its free cash, and will make their own decisions as to how management's decisions may impact near and future earnings, and hence shareholder value and the price of the stock.

CASH FLOW STATEMENTS: WHAT TO LOOK FOR

In the cash flow statements earlier in the chapter, we looked at the cash flow from operations to see if it was adequate to meet survival needs. Now let's look at some more complete cash flow statements. The statements are set up in a slightly different format, which should better show whether the company is generating free cash or needs to raise new cash.

Company BCD's cash flow statement is shown on page 219. Assume it is early 1996. All the dollar figures are in millions of dollars, but we will leave out the zeros so the numbers are easier to follow.

Line 1. Net income grew from 1992 through 1995 and is forecast to keep growing in 1996 and 1997. 1998 is too far away to forecast but at this time there is no reason to expect any major changes, so we can project that net income will be somewhere near the 1997 level.

BCD Cash Flow Statement ($ millions)							
	Actual				Forecast		
	1992	1993	1994	1995	1996	1997	1998
1. Net income Add back:	$10	12	12	15	17	18	
2. Depr. and amort.	5	6	7	7	8	9	9
3. Deferred tax	1	2	2	3	3	3	3
4. Cash flow from ops.	$16	20	21	25	28	30	
minus:							
5. Debt repayments	0	2	10	2	2	20	4
6. Preferred div.	1	1	1	1	1	1	1
7. = Free cash flow	15	17	10	22	25	9	
minus:							
8. Common div.	4	5	5	6	6	6	
9. Capital spending	10	10	12	14	15	12	12
10. = Net cash flow before external financing	1	2	–7	2	4	–9	
plus:							
11. External financing	–	–	11	–			
12. = Net change in cash[1]	1	2	4	2			

Line 2. Depreciation and amortization have been rising along with capital spending (line 9), because the increased spending means there is more equipment to depreciate. As capital spending declines in 1997 and 1998, the depreciation should level off and then decline.

Line 3. Deferred tax is a hard number to forecast, but for this company it has generally risen with earnings. In any case it is a small number compared to the other sources of cash flow from operations, so we can guess that it will remain steady at $3 a year.

Line 4. Cash flow from operations has been growing steadily for this company and is projected to continue. But we cannot be certain that it is adequate to meet all needs until we examine the rest of the cash flow statement.

---

1 Line 12 will not be exactly the net change in cash. Recall that to simplify, we excluded changes in cash that resulted from changes in accounts receivable, accounts payable, inventory, and the like. Thus, line 12 would be closer to correct if we called it the *Net change in working capital* rather than the change in Cash. Working capital, which is defined as current assets minus current liabilities, encompasses any increases or decreases in cash due to increases or decreases in accounts receivable, accounts payable, inventory, and so on.

Line 5. The company had a large debt repayment in 1994 and has another large one due in 1997. The cash flow from operations in 1994 was big enough to cover that year's debt repayment. Based on the 1997 forecast, the cash flow from operations in 1997 ($30) should be large enough to meet the 1997 debt repayment ($20). But that alone does not tell the whole investment story, and we need to look further down the cash flow statement.

Line 6. The preferred dividend is a small item for this company and does not have a major impact on the cash flow statement.

Line 7. The company has been able to generate free cash flow every year, which investors like to see. But we also see from lines 8 and 9 that BCD apparently likes to maintain or raise the common dividend every year, as well as maintain a high level of capital expenditures. This meant that in 1994, the year when the big debt repayment was due, the company needed to resort to an outside financing.

Line 8. Between 1992 and 1995, the dividend rose each year except in 1994, which was the year of the cash shortfall that required external financing. From this we might infer that the company will not raise the dividend in 1997 when it appears that another cash shortfall will necessitate another external financing. In fact, it is always possible that the company will cut the dividend and reduce capital spending in 1997 in order to avoid having to do an external financing, but based on the 1994 experience, this does not seem likely. It would be nice if we had a longer history to look at in order to judge what the company might do. Investors should ask the company: "Would you cut the dividend in order to avoid an external financing in 1997?" Companies usually give vague answers filled with "maybe's" and "if's," but analysts can nevertheless get a sense of how management is thinking. After following a company over a period of time, investment analysts become better able to judge company actions and comments.

Based on past history we could forecast a small dividend increase in 1996 and then no change in 1997, but note that capital spending will still be rising in 1996. So possibly the company directors will decide not to raise the dividend.

Line 9. Management indicated that they expected capital spending to peak at $15 in 1996 and then decline modestly. But they also said that the maintenance level of capital spending was only about $3 to

$6 million per year, so they could cut way back on spending in 1997 if they preferred to reduce the size of, or avoid doing, an external financing.

Line 10. This line clearly displays whether the company's net cash flow is positive or negative, thereby showing the years when investors must be concerned about the possibility of new financing, or might expect reductions or increases in the dividend.

Looking down the 1994 column, it is clear that the cash flow from operations was adequate to meet the scheduled debt repayment, but was not enough to meet all the cash outflows (the debt repayment, *plus* the common dividend, *plus* the company's capital spending budget). Line 10 shows that the cash shortfall in 1994 was $7 million. From Line 11 we can see that the company did an external financing to cover the shortfall, and thus did not need to reduce the common dividend or reduce capital spending. From this we might judge that as long as the earnings outlook remains strong, the company will probably prefer to do another external financing in 1997 rather than cutting the dividend or reducing capital spending. Whether they actually choose to do this in 1997 will depend on a number of factors, including the company's outlook at that time and the condition of the financial markets; that is, how much interest the company would have to pay to do a debt financing, or the price at which new stock could be sold.

Line 11. This shows the size of the external financing, and we can see that the company raised more cash than apparently was needed to meet the shortfall. Companies may do this for a number of reasons. First, when they go to all the time and expense of doing a financing, it often makes sense to raise a little extra cash to assure they do not need to come back and do it again in the immediate future. On the other hand, they would not want to raise too much extra, because there is a cost to raising money. In the case of a debt financing, there will be additional interest costs. In an equity financing (new stock) there will likely be earnings dilution. Whether the company decides to do an equity financing or a debt financing will depend on which appears most attractive at the time. If the company's price-earnings ratio is high (which means there will be little or no dilution), the company will most likely do an equity financing and be likely to raise a little extra cash, or possibly a lot of extra cash. If the company's price-earnings ratio is low (implying a lot of dilution) but interest rates are low, then the company may be more inclined to do a debt financing, because the additional interest expense will have a lesser impact on earnings per share than the dilution from an equity financing.[2] If the price-earnings ratio is low and interest rates are high, then the company would probably only raise the least amount of money it needed, in order to avoid either dilution or too big an increase in interest expense.

Another reason that a company will raise more than the apparent shortfall is the need for increased *working capital* as the company grows. Working capital means money that is tied up in inventory and accounts receivable and the like. In order to keep the cash flow statement easy to read, we have not included the cash flow changes from these items. But if the company is growing, it is reasonable to assume that it will need more working capital—that is, it will need to carry more inventory and pay more wages, which means more cash is tied up while waiting for inventory to be sold and customers to pay their bills. A growing company, therefore, has need for cash for both capital expenditures for new plant and equipment and for working capital needs.

In sum, BCD appears to be a stable, growing company. The cash flow statement tells us that the company is not afraid to spend its money for capital expenditure while paying a dividend of about 40% of earnings. The company did not cut capital spending or dividends when it was cash short in 1994, but instead chose to do an external financing. With earnings expected to continue growing in 1996 and 1997, there seems to be no reason why the company would choose to cut capital spending or dividends this time (in 1997) if the stock price remains high enough or if interest rates are low enough to make an new financing attractive. Nevertheless, we as investors would be wise to assume there will be no dividend increase until BCD is past the new financing.

A Less Predictable Cash Flow Statement

Now let's look at a company with more erratic net income, Low Flying Airlines. Again, assume it is now early 1996 and all the dollar figures are in millions. Because net income is less predictable for this company, we do not make any attempt to project the 1998 cash flow. Rather, it is more

---

2 To go through the calculations to determine the impact on earnings per share of a debt or an equity financing, see Chapter 8.

useful to make two forecasts for 1997, a *low* and a *high* forecast. In the low-end forecast, we estimate minimal earnings and the lowest we think likely for depreciation and deferred taxes. This way we can see what the worst case is likely to be for the company. Our high-end forecast shows the best we think cash flow may be. While the results will probably come in between the extremes, having the low-end and high-end forecasts gives us a good feel for the company.

Low Flying Airlines Cash Flow Statement ($ millions)							
	Actual				Forecast		
	1992	1993	1994	1995	1996	1997 low	1997 high
1. Net income	$12	30	–12	8	15	6	30
Add back:							
2. Depr. & amort.	20	22	20	18	16	20	24
3. Deferred tax	3	2	0	2	2	1	3
4. Cash flow from ops.	$35	54	8	28	33	27	57
minus:							
5. Debt repayments	10	24	11	11	8	7	7
6. Preferred div.	–	–	–	–	–	–	–
7. = Free cash flow	25	30	–3	17	25	20	50
minus:							
8. Common div.	4	4	1	2	2	2	4
9. Capital spending	21	20	12	10	14	40	50
10. = Net cash flow before External financing	0	6	–16	5	9	–22	–4
plus:							
11. External financing	–	–	16	–	–	?	–
12. = Net change in cash	0	6	0	5	9		

Line 1. Net income has been very erratic for this company. Because it costs about the same amount of money to fly a plane between two cities regardless of how many passengers are on it, a small increase in the average number of passengers per flight can produce a large change in the airline's earnings. This makes it very hard to forecast airlines' future earnings, and therefore investors would be wise to use a wide range of forecasts. Our high end, or best-case estimate for

1997, shows how good things are likely to be if all goes well; and the low end, or worst-case estimate, reflects where we think earnings are likely to be if business turns down.

The process of making an earnings estimate is beyond the scope of this book. It is the job of professional securities analysts, so for this discussion we will assume that the earnings estimates for 1996 and 1997 were obtained from our stockbroker, who checked with the analyst at her brokerage firm who follows airlines. For 1996 the analyst is forecasting earnings to be about twice the 1995 level, probably between $15 million and $20 million. We will be conservative and use the low end of that range, $15 million. Forecasting 1997 earnings is more difficult because it is further away and a lot can change between now and then, and the airline analyst is using a wide range for his earnings forecast. For the best-case estimate in 1997 he is assuming that earnings return to the 1993 level of $30 million. For the worst likely case, he is forecasting that earnings drop to $6 million. This is a wide range of possible earnings, but since either end of the range is possible, we as investors must look at the consequences for the company and stock if either end comes to pass.

Line 2. Depreciation for this company is a much more important part of cash flow than it was for BCD above. This is generally true for *capital intensive companies*.[3] Depreciation has been declining in recent years, probably reflecting the declining capital expenditures from 1992 to 1995 and the declining depreciation on the company's older airplanes. Note that depreciation is forecast to jump in 1997, reflecting the sharp increase in capital spending that year.

Line 3. Deferred tax is hard to forecast but is a small part of the total cash flow from operations.

Line 4. Like *net income*, cash flow from operations in this company is very volatile, and the annual figure itself does not mean much until we see what it needs to be used for.

---

3 *Capital intensive* means that a large portion of the company's costs are for capital equipment; that is, the company is dependent on a lot of expensive machinery or equipment. Companies like automobile or appliance manufacturers that fabricate a lot of metal are capital intensive because they need a lot of machinery, presses, forges, and the like to work the metal. Airlines and railroads and electric power companies are also capital intensive because of the cost of the equipment. These capital intensive companies will have a high level of depreciation, reflecting the expensing of the capital cost to buy that equipment. In contrast, service companies such as brokerage firms, advertising agencies, and insurance companies are *labor intensive*, meaning that labor costs are the largest part of their total costs. Service companies do have some capital costs, such as their offices and computers, but the depreciation of these items is far less important than their labor costs. Capital intensive companies also have labor costs, but they are less significant than the capital costs.

Line 5. Debt repayments consistently run at a high level in this company, probably indicating that the company maintains a high level of debt. Fortunately, in 1993 when the company had a very large repayment, earnings were strong and the company was able to meet the debt repayment from cash flow from operations. On the other hand, in 1994, even with a smaller debt repayment, the company was unable to generate enough cash flow from operations to meet the debt repayment, and needed to do an external financing. Debt repayments appear minor in 1996 and 1997, and reference to the footnotes in the annual report shows that they stay low in 1998 and 1999 as well. Thus, debt repayment, while important, does not appear to be the major factor in the company's finances in the next few years.

Line 6. The company has no preferred stock.

Line 7. Free cash flow went negative in 1994, meaning the company would either have to use its cash reserves, if any, or would require an outside financing. The company did the latter (line 11). Our forecasts show that free cash flow will remain positive in 1996 and 1997 but will not be adequate to meet 1997 capital spending needs.

Line 8. The common dividend was cut sharply in 1994 when the required debt repayment (line 5) was greater than the cash flow from operations (line 4), and outside financing was required. The company could have chosen to maintain the $4 million dividend, as it was not a very large figure, but with the company losing money and some uncertainty at that time as to when the company might become profitable again, the company directors decided it was prudent to reduce the dividend. On the other had, the fact that they did not eliminate the dividend altogether suggests that they did not feel that the company was in serious trouble. When earnings recovered in 1995, management cautiously began to raise the dividend again, a sign that they were optimistic about the potential for continued recovery of earnings. Another dividend increase in 1996 or 1997 seems unlikely, however, because the company would probably prefer to save cash for the big capital spending program that is scheduled to begin in 1997 (line 9). Or, management might reason that they are most likely going to need to do an external financing in late 1997 or 1998 and therefore by raising the dividend early in the year, they might be able to get the stock up so that an equity financing could be done with minimal dilution. We will assume that if earnings return to the old high level of $30 million (our high-end estimate), the dividend might be increased back to the $4 million level.

Line 9. It is typical of capital intensive companies to have a big capital spending program for a few years that substantially modernizes or expands the plant and equipment, and then have capital spending decline sharply to a low maintenance level for a period. For airlines, a big spending program would reflect upgrading or expanding their fleet of planes. In fact, the company had stated in its annual report that it would be buying a new generation of airplanes to replace more than half its fleet, and that the spending program was projected to cost between $40 million and $50 million in 1997 and somewhat less in 1998. We will use the low end of management's range for the 1997 low-end estimate. This assumes that if earnings are poor that year, the spending program may be delayed—that is, the delivery of some of the planes may be pushed back a year.

Line 10. Given the company's capital spending needs and debt repayment schedule, net cash flow has never been very big, and in fact went negative in 1994, and appears likely to be negative again in 1997 and possibly 1998, depending on the size or timing of the capital spending program. If earnings appear likely to come in near the low end of the 1997 range, then cash flow will be very negative and a large financing will be necessary unless the company is able to delay a large part of its capital spending program, and possibly reduces or eliminates the dividend. Even if earnings come in at the high end of the 1997 forecast range, the company will have negative cash flow for the year, but in this case the amount would be small and the company should have no trouble financing it, possibly with just short-term bank borrowing.

From line 10, therefore, investors can see that the earnings level in 1997 will be critical. If earnings are down from the 1996 level, a large outside financing will be necessary, and that could be very expensive. In a debt financing (borrowing) the company would probably have to pay a high rate of interest, first because this company already has a lot of debt, and second because with its erratic earnings, bond investors would consider this a high-risk company. An equity financing would probably also be expensive (in terms of dilution) because if earnings are at a low level and the company needs a lot of money, the stock will almost certainly be down, which means a lot more shares will need to be sold to raise the money.

Thus, the stock is likely to go down unless earnings are coming through at a high level. Since a low stock price could make it impossible to do an equity financing, it is possible that the company could be unable to fund (pay for) its new planes, and the company might be forced sell out to another airline, or just use its old planes until they wear out and perhaps go out of business.

Since investors are generally cautious, the stock will probably not rise while investors wait to see if earnings will be strong. If earnings are disappointing, the stock may then decline sharply, but if earnings are strong, the stock could move up sharply. Thus, investors will be closely watching each quarter's report to see how the company is doing. They will also be watching other airlines' earnings for indications of how airlines in general are doing, and watching industry statistics that show whether air travel is increasing or decreasing. They will also be watching the newspapers for price wars on tickets, which would hurt company earnings even if the volume of ticket sales is rising. In sum, investors will be watching everything they can to anticipate the earnings level before it is reported.

In this chapter we looked at two companies where debt repayments were critical items on the cash flow statements and one company where a major capital spending program was a critical item. Every company's situation is slightly different. The important lesson here is that the investor must look beyond the income statement and look at the cash flow statement to see if cash flow from operations is sufficient to meet all requirements and still have enough left over to provide for company growth, increased dividends, or whatever the company's directors may choose. Cash flow projections can show us, in advance, whether a company's cash flow from operations will be sufficient to meet its upcoming debt repayment and capital spending needs and will thus give us an indication of whether the company may need to do an outside financing or may be inclined to cut the dividend. These facts will usually have a direct bearing on whether the stock is going up (or down).

16

Inventory Accounting—Impact on Company Earnings

We saw in Chapter 1 that when Jones Mousetrap Company sold a mousetrap, the cost of manufacturing the mousetrap was removed from *Finished goods inventory* on the balance sheet and added to *Cost of goods sold* expense on the income statement. In that simple example, we were able to calculate the exact cost of each mousetrap, which was the combination of the raw materials cost plus the labor cost that went into making the trap. In many companies, however, keeping track of the inventory cost of each item manufactured is either not practical or not possible, so certain assumptions must be made. We will see in this chapter that different, but reasonable, assumptions can cause reported earnings to be either higher or lower than they otherwise would be. Since stock prices are directly related to earnings, investors must be aware of how these inventory valuation assumptions may have impacted past earnings and how they will impact future earnings.

LIFO AND FIFO INVENTORY VALUATION ASSUMPTIONS

When an automobile dealer sells a new car from the inventory in the back lot he can tell exactly how much it cost him by looking at the invoice or the check he used to pay the manufacturer. So when a sale is made, the dealer removes the cost of the car, say $11,200, from Inventory and adds it to Cost of goods sold expense. He also adds the selling price, perhaps $14,000, to both Sales and either Cash or Accounts receivable. In this easy case, as in the Jones Mousetrap illustration, the precise value of the inventory is known and no assumptions need be made. Now let's look at a case where it is not possible to know exactly what the cost was, and an assumption must be made. Consider a copper company that buys raw copper ore, smelts and processes it, and then sells finished copper. In this case the inventory cost is more difficult to compute because new ore is continuously being added to the melting furnace and mixed with the old ore already there.

Assume that on January 1, the Dirty Copper Company (DCC) bought 1,000 pounds of raw copper at $6 per pound and put it into a smelting furnace or vat for processing. On February 1, DCC added another 1,000 pounds of raw copper to the vat but this time DCC paid $7 per pound. On March 1, DCC added another 1,000 pounds at $8 per pound. There were now 3,000 lbs. of copper all mixed up in the vat at a total cost of $21,000.

January 1	1,000 lbs. at $6/lb.	=	$ 6,000
February 1	1,000 lbs. at $7/lb.	=	7,000
March 1	1,000 lbs. at $8/lb.	=	8,000
			$21,000

On March 31, DCC sold 2,500 pounds of finished copper at $10 per pound, for a total sale of $25,000. How much did the 2,500 pounds cost DCC? That is, what cost should be taken out of *Inventory* and added to *Cost of goods sold*? Did DCC sell all of January's $6 copper plus all of February's $7 copper, plus half of March's $8 copper? Or did DCC sell all of March's $8 copper, all of February's $7 copper, and half of January's $6 copper? There is no way to know since all the copper was mixed evenly in the vat. Thus, one of three assumptions must be made. First, it can be assumed that the *first* copper that came in was the first that was sold. Using this assumption, all the January, February, and half of the March copper was sold. This method of inventory accounting is called FIFO—*first in, first out*. Second, it can be assumed that the *most recent* copper to come in was the first copper to go out. That is, all the March, February, and half the January copper was sold.

This method of inventory accounting is called *LIFO—last in, first out*. Third, it can be assumed that the copper was sold at an average price of the three. While some companies keep inventories on an average-cost basis, this takes quite a bit of paperwork because new raw materials are usually coming in at different prices throughout every working day, and goods are usually being sold throughout every working day. Thus, most companies find it more practical to use either the FIFO or the LIFO method. Which of the two methods is chosen can have a meaningful effect on reported earnings, as shown here.

FIFO Cost of 2,500 lbs.		LIFO Cost of 2,500 lbs.	
1,000 lbs. @ $6/lb. =	$ 6,000	500 lbs. @ $6/lb. =	$ 3,000
1,000 lbs. @ $7/lb. =	7,000	1,000 lbs. @ $7/lb. =	7,000
500 lbs. @ $8/lb. =	4,000	1,000 lbs. @ $8/lb. =	8,000
2,500 lbs.	$17,000	2,500 lbs.	$18,000

Income Statement Using FIFO Inventory Accounting		Income Statement Using LIFO Inventory Accounting	
Sales	$25,000	Sales	$25,000
Cost (FIFO)	17,000	Cost (FIFO)	18,000
Profit	$ 8,000	Profit	$ 7,000

Left in Inventory at March 31		Left in Inventory at March 31	
500 lbs. @ $8/lb. =	$ 4,000	500 lbs. @ $6/lb. =	$3,000

LIFO accounting results in Cost of goods sold being valued at most-recent cost (called *current* cost), whereas FIFO accounting results in Cost of goods sold being valued at oldest cost (called *historical* cost). Thus, in a period when the purchase price of raw copper is steadily rising (as in our example), LIFO results in a higher Cost of goods sold, hence leaving a lower profit. Also, LIFO leaves a lower cost of inventory remaining in the company. Conversely, FIFO inventory accounting results in a lower Cost of goods sold, hence leaving a higher profit, and also leaves a higher cost of inventory in the company (on the balance sheet). Note that the selling price of the finished copper has nothing to do with the LIFO/FIFO difference. Obviously, the higher the selling price the more profit; but regardless of price, the FIFO cost of goods sold in this example will always be lower than the LIFO cost of goods sold, and therefore, the FIFO profit will always be higher than the LIFO profit for any given selling price.

The statements in the last paragraph are generally true as long as the price of copper is rising. If the purchase price of raw copper were steadily falling, the opposites would be true in the last paragraph (i.e., the words *higher* and *lower* would be reversed). Work this out for yourself by making up a similar example but with prices steadily falling.

Thus, in a period of rising prices, if an investor is looking at two companies that have the same EPS and stock price, and are similar in every other way except that one uses LIFO and the other uses FIFO, the company that uses LIFO would probably be the better stock to buy because, if it decided to change to FIFO, it would suddenly be showing better earnings and the stock might go up. If these two companies were truly similar except for the LIFO/FIFO accounting difference, the company using LIFO would probably sell at a slightly higher price-earnings ratio, reflecting that potential earnings difference.

ADJUSTING THE INVENTORY VALUE AT YEAR-END TO LOWER-OF-COST-OR-MARKET

At the end of the year, if the price for which the finished goods inventory can be sold has fallen to a level below its value on the balance sheet, most companies will automatically lower the inventory value of the goods by the difference and charge (add) the same amount to Cost of goods sold for the year. This is called *adjusting the inventory to lower-of-cost-or-market* (LOCOM). *Cost* in this case means what the inventory cost to make, whether using LIFO or FIFO assumptions. *Market* means what the goods can be sold for on the open market today. Of course, if the price for which the goods can be sold is higher than the inventory cost, whether determined by LIFO or FIFO, there is no inventory adjustment to be made.

To illustrate when a LOCOM inventory adjustment might occur, and how big it might be, suppose DCC's only sales and purchases of copper during the entire year were those in January–March, shown on pages 230-231. DCC's inventory accounting policy is to use FIFO and adjust the year-end inventory on a LOCOM basis, if necessary. When the treasurer of DCC was initially putting together the financial statements for the year, they looked like this:

Income Statement (1/1/95 to 12/31/95)

Sales		$25,000
Cost of goods sold	$17,000	
SG&A	3,000	
Depreciation.................	1,000	
	21,000	21,000
Profit before tax		4,000
Tax		2,000
Profit after tax..............		$ 2,000

Balance Sheet 12/31/95
Company Using LIFO Inventory Accounting

Assets		Liabilities	
Current assets:		**Current liabilities:**	
Cash	$ 1,000	Short-term debt.............	$ 4,000
Inventory.....................	4,000	Taxes payable	1,000
Accts. receivable..........	2,000	Total current assets ...	5,000
Total current assets ..	7,000	Long-term debt	none
Fixed assets:		**Equity**	
		Stockholders' equity:	
Gross PP&E	20,000	Common stock	1,000
Accum. depreciation	7,000	Capital surplus..............	5,000
Net PP&E....................	13,000	Retained earnings	9,000
Total assets	$20,000	Total liabilities & equity .	$20,000

Before these statements were made final, however, the treasurer realized that the price for which the finished copper could be sold had fallen to $7 per pound. But DCC was carrying its inventory at a value of $8 per pound.

Thus, the inventory had to be written down to $7 per pound.

On balance sheet:	500 lbs. @ $8/lb.	=	$4,000
At market price:	500 lbs. @ $7/lb.	=	$3,500
	Inventory write-down		$ 500

This $500 is subtracted from Inventory to reflect a more realistic value of the inventory, and is taken as an expense on the income statement in the Cost of goods sold. The rationale for expensing it is that the decline in the price of finished copper resulted in a loss of value to the company (i.e., the finished copper was now worth less than when it was processed).

After these adjustments, the new financial statements would appear as follows. The account numbers that have changed are in italic.

Income Statement (1/1/95 to 12/31/95)		
Sales		$25,000
Cost of goods sold	*$17,500*	
SG&A	3,000	
Depreciation	1,000	
	21,500	21,500
Profit before tax		*3,500*
Tax		*1,750*
Net profit		*$ 1,750*

Balance Sheet 12/31/95
Using LIFO Inventory Accounting with LOCOM

Assets		Liabilities	
Current assets:		Current liabilities:	
Cash	$ 1,000	Short-term debt	$ 4,000
Inventory	*3,500*	Taxes payable	*750*
Accts. receivable	2,000	Total current assets	4,750
Total current assets	$ 6,500	Long-term debt	none
Fixed assets:		**Equity**	
Gross PP&E	20,000	Stockholders' equity:	
Accum. depreciation	7,000	Common stock	1,000
Net PP&E......................	13,000	Capital surplus..............	5,000
		Retained earnings	*8,750*
Total assets	$19,500	Total liabilities & equity ..	$19,500

In addition to the change in Inventory, note also the changes in Taxes payable and in Retained earnings.

Because this write-down was taken, *Profit before taxes* was lower, hence *Taxes* and *Net profits* were also lower. Therefore, *Taxes payable* on the balance sheet is lower; and, since *Net profit* was down, *Retained earnings* is down.

Note that had the company been using LIFO accounting, then the inventory still on the balance sheet would have had a cost of $6 a pound, and there would have been no inventory adjustment because, in that case, the inventory would already be valued at the lower of cost ($6) or market ($7).

An important point here is that in an industry where prices have been falling, the investor always has to be aware of the possibility of year-end inventory write-downs. The semiconductor industry provides an excellent example. When transistors were first introduced in the 1950s, prices were very high. As the technology improved, prices came down. This induced more electronic goods manufacturers to use transistors in place of tubes. This larger volume of business enabled the transistor manufacturers to automate, with the result that further price declines became possible. Through the 1960s and 1970s, continuously improved transistors and then integrated circuits were introduced. Each of these new products went through a similar cycle, whereby prices started out high and gradually came down as even better transistors and integrated circuits were introduced.

In the 1980s and 1990s this process continued as more and more electronic functions were able to be put on a semiconductor chip, and again prices declined as chip manufacturers made their own products obsolete by making even better chips at lower cost. Since the declining price nature of this business is well known, chip manufacturers try to keep as little inventory on hand as possible; but, of course, there are always some products in inventory that cannot be sold. In some periods, the amount of unsold products will be larger than in other periods, leading to larger write-downs and producing an erratic pattern of earnings over time. To try to smooth out the effects of such write-downs, most manufacturers of these products write down their inventory every quarter if necessary. Thus, the adjustment at the end of the year should be no bigger than the other quarterly adjustments, and a smoother flow of earnings should result.

If the company only adjusted its inventory at the end of the year, it might show high earnings for the first three quarters and then practically nothing, or even a loss in the fourth quarter. The total earnings for the year would be the same whether the write-downs were taken each quarter or only at year-end; but if the entire write-down were done at year-end, it would create a false impression of high profits during the first three quarters. With high profits in the first three quarters, investors might be misled to believe that the company's outlook was better than it really was, and they would bid up the price of the stock. Then, when the disappointing earnings were reported in the last quarter, the stock would plunge as people saw their mistake. More important, the fear that this may happen again might cause investors to avoid this stock in the future. Thus, by having an earnings adjustment quarterly, the quarterly stream of earnings would be smoother, bad surprises would be avoided, and more people would be willing to buy the stock. Such stocks, then, over a period of time, would probably sell at a higher average price than if bad surprises were continually recurring.

In the case of semiconductors, where prices are continually falling and the companies make the adjustments regularly, they are seldom noticed. A classic example of where a bad surprise did occur (a large, unexpected write-down) was in the CB radio business. When CB radios were first introduced, they quickly became very popular. Sales rose rapidly and prices were more or less steady. Within a year, however, sales declined suddenly and sharply, and CB radio manufacturers were caught with large inventories they could not sell. The manufacturers stopped making more CB radios and cut prices drastically in order to sell the large inventories they still had. This hurt earnings in two ways. First, the CBs that were sold were sold at a loss, and second, most of the excess inventory that could not be sold had to be written down to the new low price. Since the inventory was large and the price cut was drastic, the write-down was large. Earnings, therefore, came in much lower than previously expected, and the stocks fell sharply as a result. Smart investors, however, did not wait for a bad earnings report. As soon as they learned that CB sales were falling, they sold their stock immediately in anticipation of falling profits.

An important lesson that will be repeated many times in this book is that the stock market *anticipates future events,* which really means that smart investors anticipate future events. If the "smart investors" had been wrong and CB sales only dipped temporarily, and then resumed rapid growth, the stocks would probably have gone up. But the smart investor does not wait around to find out, preferring to take the risk of missing a rise in the stock rather than being caught in a rapid decline.

Inventory write-downs are almost always added to Cost of goods sold since they occur as part of the normal operations of the business. Sometimes, however, they are recorded as an extraordinary loss. An occasion where this might occur is when a company is closing down a plant and dropping a product line. In this case, any inventory left over after the plant closing would probably be sold at distress prices. Since the inventory write-down in this case only occurred because the company dropped the product line, it is reasonable to include the inventory loss as part of the extraordinary plant-closing loss.

To summarize, determining the value of Inventory and Cost of goods sold is rarely as easy as in the case of JMC or the automobile dealer discussed at the beginning of this chapter. Fluctuating prices of raw materials, as well as selling prices of finished goods, can combine with LIFO or FIFO accounting techniques and LOCOM inventory write-downs to produce distortions in a company's reported earnings that can be misleading to investors who are trying to determine a company's ability to generate future earnings growth. Investors must pay close attention to footnotes in a company's financial statements and management's comments in press releases and quarterly and annual reports to shareholders.

PART 4

Why Stocks Go Up (and Down)

17

Listing and Trading on the Stock Exchange

In Chapter 7 we saw how stocks are traded in the NASDAQ and over-the-counter markets. Stock exchange trading is somewhat different. One difference is that most stock exchange trading is done in one place, at the stock exchange. A stockbroker wishing to sell an over-the-counter or NASDAQ traded stock might have to make a number of phone calls to market makers to find the best price for the customer; but to get the best price for an exchange-listed company, the broker would only have to make one phone call, to the stock exchange. A stock exchange is simply a place where buyers come to meet sellers, or more precisely, brokers representing people who want to buy stock come to buy that stock at the lowest priced offering, and brokers representing people who want to sell stock come to sell that stock to the higher bidder. Each stock listed on the exchange is traded at a *trading post* on the floor of the exchange. At that post, the buying and selling brokers meet in front of the *specialist* who is in charge of trading that stock. The specialist essentially holds an auction for the stock. Thus, stock exchange trading is often referred to as *agency auction trading,* where the brokers are the agents representing their customers and the auction is the interaction of all the brokers and the specialist. With agency auction trading, most stock that trades on the exchange is sold directly from the seller to the buyer, with the brokers only taking a commission. This is in contrast to over-the-counter and NASDAQ trading, where *market makers* buy the stock from customers and own it themselves before selling it to other customers. On the stock exchange, the specialist, or firms who are members of the exchange, will also sometimes act like market makers and buy and sell stock for themselves, but this is the exception. More than 80% of all trades on the New York Stock Exchange (NYSE) are sales directly from the buyer to the seller. The reason why a specialist buys or sells stock, rather than just acting as an agent, is discussed later.

The stock exchange itself neither buys nor sells stock, nor, usually, does the company whose stock is being traded. There are some exceptions. Companies will sometimes buy some of their own stock to give or sell to employees under incentive or stock option plans, or for other purposes. Also, some companies occasionally buy back large amounts of their own stock to reduce the number of shares outstanding and increase earnings per share. For the most part, however, a company is not a buyer or seller of its own stock.

When you read that 120,000 thousand shares of IBM were traded yesterday between $93 and 93\frac{1}{2}$ per share, it means that some individuals (or institutions such as mutual funds, trust funds, and the like) bought them from some other individuals (or institutions). The company whose stock is being traded, IBM in this case, has nothing to do with it and has no say in the matter. All purchases and sales on a stock exchange (or over-the-counter) are *secondary* transactions of already outstanding registered stock between individuals. The only time IBM would be involved in the sale of its stock would be if IBM wished to raise some money by selling *new* stock. This, of course, is normally done through investment bankers, or a brokerage firm acting as an investment banker, and would not involve the exchange. Thus, if IBM had a primary offering, the new shares of IBM would be delivered from IBM to the initial purchaser via the underwriter, and their purchase price would be remitted to IBM via the underwriter.

Once those newly issued shares (which were registered with the SEC) are sold from IBM to their first owner, they are then free to be traded among the public. Since IBM already has other outstanding shares listed on the NYSE, all the company needs to do is file a *listing application* with the NYSE for the new shares. As soon as the new owners receive the new shares, they can then sell them on the New York Stock Exchange if they wish. IBM, or any other already-listed company, usually files the listing application before the new stock offering, and thus the newly issued shares are tradable on the exchange immediately after the offering. It would not be necessary to first trade the new shares over-the-counter, as was the case with JMC, Inc., which was not yet listed on an exchange.

If the relationship between the stock exchange, the company whose stock is being traded, and the buyer and sellers of the stock is not clear, the following analogy to the automobile business should help to clarify it.

Automobile business

When Mr. Driver buys a new Ford automobile he is buying from Ford Motor Company through a dealer. This is a "primary" transaction. Driver's money goes to Ford, via the dealer.

A year or two later, Driver no longer needs his car. Not knowing anyone who wants to buy it, he brings it to a used car dealer, where it is eventually purchased by Ms. Foehle. This is a "secondary" transaction. The money has, in effect, gone from Foehle (buyer) to Driver (seller) with the used car dealer keeping a "commission." Ford Motor Company has nothing to do with this secondary transaction and no say in the matter.

Stock brokerage business

When Mr. Driver buys some new shares of IBM stock he is buying from IBM Company through an underwriter. This is a "primary" transaction. Driver's money goes to IBM, via the underwriter.

A year or two later, Driver no longer wants his investment in IBM. Not knowing anyone who wants to buy it, he brings it to a stock exchange (via his broker), where it is eventually purchased by Ms. Foehle. This is a "secondary" transaction. The money has in effect gone from Foehle (buyer) to Driver (seller) with the brokers keeping a commission. IBM has nothing to do with this secondary transaction and no say in the matter.

The analogy is not perfect, but it should serve to clarify the idea that the company whose stock is being traded and the stock exchange are essentially separate. To recapitulate: a stock exchange is simply a place where people come to buy and sell registered stock in secondary transactions.

There are many stock exchanges in the United States. The New York Stock Exchange (NYSE), with about 2,600 companies listed, and the American Stock Exchange (ASE), with about 830 companies listed, are the biggest. The NASDAQ system, with about 4,100 companies listed, actually has more companies listed than the ASE and the NYSE combined. But the NYSE is still the biggest in terms of number of shares traded and the dollar value of shares traded each year.

In addition to the NYSE and the ASE, there are a number of smaller exchanges around the country, including the Chicago, the Cincinnati, the Boston, the Pacific, and the Philadelphia Stock Exchanges. The stocks traded on these exchanges include both smaller regional companies that are not traded on the NYSE or the ASE and many larger stocks that are also traded on the NYSE or ASE.

When a company's stock is traded on a stock exchange, we say it is *listed* on that exchange. When a stock is traded on more than one exchange, we say it has a *multiple listing*. Where multiple listing occurs, the price on each exchange is usually the same or adjusts very quickly. This is because specialists and traders on each exchange can see others' bids and offers on the *Composite Quotation System*. The Composite Quotation System is a communications network that links all the exchanges. Specialists on each exchange are required by law to show their latest bid and offer on each stock on this network. If a specialist or trader on the Boston exchange has an order to buy a stock for a customer, and sees that the lowest offered price is on the Philadelphia exchange, the Boston specialist can buy the stock from the Philadelphia exchange automatically over another computer-linked communications network known as the *Intermarket Trading System,* or *ITS* for short. After the Boston specialist, or others, buy up this cheaper stock on the Philadelphia Exchange, the Philadelphia specialist will quickly raise the offering price so it is in line with the other exchanges. With these two networks enabling traders on each exchange to see each others' bids or offers, and to buy almost instantaneously from each other, price differences disappear quickly.

LISTING REQUIREMENTS

A company desiring to have its stock listed on a given exchange must have the approval of that exchange. While that approval is based on a number of subjective factors including the historical record, nature of the business, reputation of management, future outlook, and more, the exchanges do provide numerical guidelines. The American Stock Exchange, for example, requires that a company applying for listing must meet the following requirements:

1. Stockholders' equity must be at least $4,000,000.
2. Pretax income must have been at least $750,000 in its last fiscal year, or two of its last three fiscal years.
3. There must be a public float of at least 500,000 shares of stock, and these shares must be held by at least 800 public stockholders (that is, not including shares held by company officers, directors, or other concentrated family holdings); alternatively, there may be a 1,000,000 share float with a minimum of 400 public shareholders.
4. The stock must have market value of at least $3,000,000 and a stock price of $3.

For companies that do not meet these criteria, there is an alternative set of guidelines that is more subjective, but these numbers give a good approximation of the minimum size of ASE-listed companies.

NYSE listing requirements are more stringent, including:

1. Net tangible assets of $18 million.
2. Pretax income of at least $2,500,000 in the most recent year and $2,000,000 in each of the preceding two years.
3. A public float of at least 1,100,000 common shares, and 2,000 stockholders.
4. A market value of publicly held shares of between $9 million and $18 million depending on market conditions.

Like the ASE, these are general guidelines. The exchange looks at the whole picture of a company and can make exceptions to any of these guidelines.

If a company that is listed on an exchange falls below one or more of these requirements, it is not automatically delisted. The question of when to delist a stock is more subjective than when to list. Typically, a stock must fall below more than one of the listing requirements for two or more years before the exchange votes to delist it.

In 1995 about 2,600 companies had their common stock listed on the New York Stock Exchange. Since some of these companies also have preferred stock issues traded on the exchange, there were closer to 3,200 issues in total traded there. Illinois Power, for example, has more than 11 different issues of preferred stock traded on the NYSE, in addition to its common stock. Illinois Power's preferred stocks are not traded as actively as its common, and frequently one or more of them do not trade on a given day. When this occurs, the issues that did not trade will not appear in the usual stock market listings in the next day's newspapers.

MECHANICS OF TRADING

The trading of each stock, General Motors for instance, is supervised by one person called an *assigned dealer* or a specialist in that stock. The best way to describe the specialist's role is to look at an example of how a trade might take place. Let's assume it is 11:15 A.M. and the stock market is quiet. The specialist in charge of trading General Motors is standing at his post waiting for orders. The last trade in GM stock occurred four minutes ago at 46^{1}/_{4}$; that is, some individual bought some GM stock at 46^{1}/_{4}$ per share (plus commission) from some other individual, who received the 46^{1}/_{4}$ per share (less the commission his broker kept). At 11:16 A.M., Mr. Sellers in Chicago decides to sell 5,000 of his shares of GM. He calls his stockbroker, Mr. Smith, who works for the brokerage firm of Goldman Sachs & Co. Mr. Smith has a display screen on his desk that is wired directly to the stock exchange, or more accurately is wired directly to the Composite Quotation System. By pressing certain letters on his keyboard he can instantly see on his screen that the last price at which GM traded was 46^{1}/_{4}$. He tells Sellers this, and Sellers in turn tells him to sell his 5,000 shares "at the market." This means that Sellers wants to sell 5,000 shares of stock immediately and, even if the price should fall in the next few minutes while the order is being transmitted to the trading post and executed, it is OK to sell it at the lower price. At this point, Smith might write the sell order on a slip of paper and send it to a trader at his office, or in some cases, he might enter the order directly on his computer screen through the NYSE's SuperDot System,[1] where it would go directly to the specialist's trading post, and probably be executed in seconds. If Smith sends it to his trader, the trader would then typically enter the order by calling the floor of the exchange and giving the order to a Goldman Sachs *floor broker*. The floor broker then walks it over to the GM trading post and participates in the auction in front of the

---

1 In recent years, the NYSE has seen increasing use of its Dot or SuperDot system. This system enables many orders, especially orders of under 2,100 shares, but in some cases much larger orders, to be entered directly to the specialist from the broker's office. These SuperDot orders are sometimes executed by the computer, and after review by the specialist, the report of the completed trade is immediately sent back to the brokers to tell their customers. Elapsed time: seconds.

specialist. If the Goldman Sachs floor broker is busy, he may give the order to an *independent broker* who will take it to the GM specialist. Elapsed time: a few minutes. In this case, let us assume a Goldman Sachs floor broker is walking the order to the specialist.

At about the same time, Mr. Buyer in Miami decides to buy 5,000 shares of GM. He calls his broker, Mr. Murphy, who works for Merrill Lynch and tells him to buy 5,000 shares of stock at $46. Mr. Buyer likes to buy and sell stocks frequently even if the profits are small, and consequently he considers every fraction of a dollar important. He also knows that stock prices will fluctuate and, even though the stock is selling at 46\frac{1}{4}$ now, he thinks that the stock will get down to $46 at some point during the day, so he asks his broker to put in an order to buy at only $46 or lower. This is called a *limit order*. Mr. Buyer's broker has wired the order to one of the Merrill Lynch floor brokers on the floor of the New York Stock Exchange who, in turn, acts as Mr. Buyer's agent and carries the order to the post where GM is traded. In this case, both floor brokers, one with an order to buy 5,000 shares at $46 and one with an order to sell 5,000 "at the market," approach the GM specialist together.

Since there are orders to buy 5,000 shares at $46 and to sell 5,000 shares "at the market," (i.e., at the best available price) the specialist could simply direct the Goldman Sachs broker to sell his customer's 5,000 shares to the Merrill Lynch broker for $46 per share. If that were the case, both the Merrill Lynch broker and the Goldman Sachs broker would go back to their booths and wire or call the stock brokers, who in turn would call Mr. Buyer and Mr. Sellers and tell them that their trades were done and at what price.

As it happens, however, when the specialist heard that there was an order to buy at $46 and an order to sell "at the market," he decided to check his *book*. The specialist's book is where he keeps a record of all the buy and sell orders that have not yet been filled. Upon checking his book, he discovered that there was an order to buy 3,000 GM at 46\frac{1}{8}$. Thus the specialist was obligated to buy 3,000 of the Goldman Sachs broker's 5,000 GM shares at 46\frac{1}{8}$ for the customer on his book. Remember that the Goldman Sachs order to sell "at the market" obligated both Goldman and the specialist to obtain the highest possible price for Mr. Sellers. This is why the stock exchange calls itself an "auction" market. Mr. Sellers's shares were auctioned off to the highest bidder. In this case, the highest bidder for 3,000 of the shares was an order (representing a customer) on the specialist's book. The specialist may now direct the

Goldman floor broker to sell his remaining 2,000 shares to Merrill Lynch, who is the second highest bid in this auction.

Mr. Sellers's order has now been executed—3,000 shares sold to the specialist for $46\frac{1}{8}$ and 2,000 shares sold to Merrill Lynch at $46. The Goldman Sachs floor broker will go back to his booth and call the stock-broker who, in turn, will call Mr. Sellers and inform him that he sold his 5,000 shares: 3,000 at $46\frac{1}{8}$ and 2,000 at $46. Also, the specialist will look on his book to see who the broker was who bought the 3,000 shares at $46\frac{1}{8}$. The specialist will then call or wire that brokerage firm so the broker can tell its customer that he or she bought GM at $46\frac{1}{8}$.

Also, immediately after the trade was executed, the selling broker enters into a computer that 3,000 shares of GM were traded at $46\frac{1}{8}$ and that 2,000 shares were traded at $46. That computer entry will appear on the tape seconds later, as well as appearing on the computer screens of all brokers and others around the world who happen to be monitoring GM stock. The symbol that appears on the tape for the first trade is: "30s GM $46\frac{1}{8}$." The 30s means 3,000 shares traded. Since 100 shares is considered to be the basic trading unit, the last two zeros are dropped. So "60s" would mean 6,000 shares traded. Sometimes when trading is very active and the tape cannot keep up with all the trades, the exchange will not show the volume of shares traded if it is less than 5,000 shares, and will drop the first digit of the stock's price. In that case, the symbol for the trade would be "GM $6\frac{1}{8}$," and people who watch GM would know that $6\frac{1}{8}$ really means $46\frac{1}{8}$.

The Merrill Lynch broker who bought 2,000 of Mr. Sellers's shares is still looking to buy an additional 3,000 shares of stock at $46. He can either wait at the GM trading post until someone comes along who is willing to sell at $46, or he can leave his order to buy 3,000 GM at $46 with the specialist.

THE SPECIALIST

It is the specialist's job to make sure that the auction remains fair to all. If a broker with an order to buy GM and a broker with an order to sell GM at the same price meet in front of the GM trading post, they will not trade until checking with the specialist because the specialist may have a priority order to be executed first. There are a number of rules determining priority. First, of course, is the price at which a buyer or seller is willing for the trade to be done. The person willing to pay the highest price gets the first available stock, as in any auction. For orders at the same price, the time the order was entered and the size of the order will also determine its priority.

The specialist also has the responsibility to make an orderly market. This means the following: Suppose a large number of orders to sell at the best available market price came in at the same time, and there were few available buyers at the current market price. The specialist would then have to substantially lower the price of the stock to reach the lower-priced buy orders that were on his book and to attract more buyers. As the specialist lowered the price of the stock and these trades were printed on the tape, other holders might panic and sell their stock "at the market," forcing the stock price to fall even further. At some point the stock would look so cheap that buyers, upon discovering that there was no bad news about the company, would rush in and probably bid the price of the stock right back up to where it started. Similarly, suppose a flood of buy orders came in at another point in the day. This might produce a sharp but temporary move upward in the stock. This excessive volatility is considered undesirable, because it can result in stock price movements that in no way reflect what is happening in the company. Also, it would enable manipulators to come in and intentionally produce such fluctuations to their own ends. Therefore, the specialist is charged with the responsibility of preventing such activity. To accomplish this, the specialist is obligated to buy stock for his own account if there is an influx of sell orders with no matching buy orders, and to sell stock from his own account if there is an influx of buy orders with no offsetting sell orders. If some bad news should come out about the company that would make the stock worth substantially less, the specialist is still required to buy some stock as the price goes down, but, in extreme cases, he can get permission of the exchange to temporarily stop trading in that stock until enough matching buy and sell orders come in to start trading again at a lower level. But the possibility of fluctuations caused simply by an imbalance of buy and sell orders because sellers coincidentally chose to sell at one point in the day and buyers coincidentally chose to buy at another point in the day can easily be prevented. Obviously, this leaves specialists in a position where they might be able to manipulate the market for their own benefit, but the stock exchanges have rules and procedures to prevent this. The activity and profit of the specialist are also monitored by the Securities and Exchange Commission.

COMPARING NYSE STOCK EXCHANGE TRADING WITH NASDAQ

There is a difference of opinion on Wall Street as to whether the agency-auction system of the stock exchanges or the market maker system of NASDAQ is preferable. Some believe that the auction system of the stock exchanges guarantees the customer the fairest price because most of the stock traded in this system is sold directly from the seller to the buyer, with no market maker in the middle trying to make a small profit. Also, almost every broker is at the same auction in front of the specialist and has access to the same information about who is selling or buying.

Proponents of the NASDAQ "dealer-driven" or market maker system believe NASDAQ is a superior system because with many dealers competing for business in the same stock, there is a better chance that one will be bidding higher, or offering lower, than others. NASDAQ also believes that there is better liquidity in the NASDAQ Stock Market because with more dealers (market makers) willing to use their own capital to buy stock, it is more likely that large blocks of stock can be bought or sold without moving the price of the stock.

Many public companies believe there are advantages to being listed on the NYSE or the ASE, and others prefer to be listed on the NASDAQ. One perceived advantage to being listed on the NYSE is that there is usually more information disseminated about exchange-listed companies than over-the-counter or NASDAQ-listed companies. Many newspapers, for example, publish only NYSE-listed stock prices, and perhaps a handful of NASDAQ-traded stocks. Also, big brokerage firms in many cases are more likely to assign a securities analyst to follow an exchange-listed company than a NASDAQ company, although this is not true of the larger NASDAQ-traded companies, which are just as closely followed by Wall Street research. From the company's point of view, the more brokers that follow a company, and the more information that is disseminated about the company, the more likely the company is to attract investors, and therefore have a higher stock price. Some companies also like the prestige element to being listed on the NYSE, while others prefer the rapid growth image of the NASDAQ Stock Market.

18

The Price / Earnings Ratio: When Is a Stock High or Low?

Ask a professional investor why stocks go up and down, and you will be told that each situation is different. That statement is probably correct, but it is not very useful. In this chapter, we will try to provide some background understanding and a framework from which to view and understand stock price behavior. First, we will discuss the price-to-earnings ratio, which is the most common way investors value or measure stock prices in relationship to a company's earnings. We will then discuss one way to determine when a stock is "high" or "low." We will see how stock prices often move up or down in anticipation of events, rather than reacting after the event. We will also look at the price-to-cash-flow ratio, a second way investors try to value stocks. Included is a one-sentence explanation of why stocks go up or down. This explanation is not useful by itself, but points to what investors should watch for in relationship to their stockholdings. Taken together, all these points should give the reader a good feel for why stock prices go up and down.

STOCK PRICES RELATE TO A COMPANY'S
LONG-TERM EARNINGS OUTLOOK

A company's ability to generate a profit over time is ultimately what creates increasing value for shareholders and will be reflected in rising stock prices. The converse is also true. A company that is losing money is losing value for its shareholders, and its stock is likely to be declining. In Chapter 4 we showed why the price of a share of stock can best be related to the dividends the company is currently paying, and potentially could be paying in the future. While this is true, the best measure of the company's ability to pay dividends in the long run is its ability to generate earnings.[1] A company that has cash on the balance sheet can always choose to pay a dividend, or for that matter a company may be able to borrow money to pay its dividend, but eventually the company's cash gets spent, and the ability to borrow more money dries up as the company takes on too much debt. Thus, the best measure of the ability of a company to pay dividends in the long run is the company's ability to continuously generate enough earnings to meet all company needs and have enough left over to pay dividends.

If a company is earning enough to pay a dividend, it often does not matter much whether the company is actually paying the dividend. The stockholders benefit whether there is a current dividend or not. Whatever earnings are not being paid as dividends are being retained in the company, and can be spent on such things as new plant and equipment, more inventory and employees, or new product development, which enable the company to grow faster. This could result in even larger dividends in the future.

This is why small, rapidly growing companies usually do not pay dividends. These companies expect that by reinvesting earnings back into the company now, it will lead to a higher level of earnings in the future, which can result in higher dividends then, or a higher stock price reflecting the potential for higher dividends.

THE PRICE/EARNINGS RATIO

The price/earnings ratio, or P/E, is probably the most important single tool used by investors to determine whether a stock price is high or low.

---

1 Since we are interested in the price of a *share* of stock, we talk about the company's earnings on a *per share* basis. One seldom hears investment people say "XYZ Corp earned $20,000,000." Rather, we divide it by the number of common shares outstanding (assume 4,000,000) and say, "XYZ earned $5.00 per common share." Also, investors usually do not bother to say, "earnings per common share." The "per common share" is understood, and people often just say "earnings." You will usually know from context whether "earnings" means the total earnings or the earnings per share.

This ratio is simply the price of a share of stock divided by the earnings per share of that company.

$$\text{P/E ratio} = \frac{\text{Stock price per share}}{\text{Earnings per share}} = \frac{\$30}{\$2} = 15\times$$

Company JKL is earning $2 a share and its stock is selling at $30 a share. Thus, it has a P/E of 15×. That is, its stock is selling at 15 times its earnings per share. On Wall Street, one might hear just, "JKL is selling at fifteen times." The words *earnings per common share* are assumed and do not need to be said. One might also say, "The stock is selling at a 15 multiple," or "The market is capitalizing JKL's earnings at 15 times." These all say the same thing and are used interchangeably. Other abbreviations for the price/earnings ratio are P.E.R., P.E., P-E, or just PE.

When talking about a company's price/earnings ratio, it is important to specify which year's earnings you are talking about. With JKL's stock at $30 in September 1996 and the earnings forecasts shown as follows, we can determine JKL's P/E ratio for each year. In Table 18.1, the "A" beside 1995 means *actual*. That year has been completed and earnings were $1.75 per share. The "E" beside 1996 and 1997 means *estimated,* and the "P" beside 1998 means *projected*, implying a lesser accuracy than the nearer years' estimates. "nmf" means "no meaningful figure." There is no meaning to a P/E that uses a current price but uses past earnings. Investors are deciding what they will pay for a stock based on current or future earnings, not past earnings; although the pattern of past earnings is often a good starting point in trying to forecast future earnings levels.

Table 18.1   Calculating JKL's Price/Earnings Ratios with JKL Stock at $30/Share

	1995A	1996E	1997E	1998P
Estimated earnings per share (EPS)	$1.75	$2.00	$2.20	$2.42
Implied price/earnings ratio (P/E)	nmf	15×	13.6×	12.4×

Assuming it is September 1996, we would say JKL Company is selling at 15 times this year's estimated earnings, 13.6 times next year's estimated earnings, and 12.4 times 1998 projected earnings. Instead of writing

"15 times," we usually just write "15×," which is read, "15 times." So we can say JKL sells at 15× this year's earnings, 13.6× next year's earnings, and so on. The terminology used thus far is very important to stock price discussions and the reader should become familiar with it quickly.

STOCK PRICE CHANGES CAN REFLECT CHANGES IN EARNINGS OR CHANGES IN THE PRICE/EARNING RATIO

If the price/earnings ratio stays the same over a period of time, then a stock's move will be entirely the result of the changes in earnings. Look at JKL again, assuming it is September 1996.

September 1996 stock price	1996 EPS est.	P/E	1997 EPS est.	P/E
$30	$2.00	15×	$2.20	13.6×

JKL is selling at 15× the current year's (1996's) earnings estimate. A year later, in September 1997, if the P/E remains the same, 15×, then the stock price will be up 10%, from $30 to $33; the same percentage gain as the earnings.

Expected September 1997 stock price	1997 EPS est.	P/E
$33	$2.20	15×

If JKL is a company that generally has steady earnings growth and little change in its P/E, investors can expect the stock to go up or down in line with the earnings. The stock price will still fluctuate over time because different investors will have different earnings forecasts and slightly different ideas of what price/earnings ratio ought to be paid, and will choose different times of year to start putting the 15× P/E ratio on the next year's earnings.

Alternatively, if earnings do not change, a stock can go up or down because investors decided that the company deserves a higher or lower P/E. Look again at JKL in September 1996.

September 1996 stock price	1996 EPS est.	P/E	1997 EPS est.	P/E
$30	$2.00	15×	$2.20	13.6×

Although JKL had been growing steadily in the past at about 10% a year, in September 1996 the company announced that it was diversifying into computer software, which company management expected to generate substantial earnings growth beginning in 1997. Two months after the announcement, the stock had moved up to $44 and earnings estimates for 1997 were raised to around $2.40 per share. As a result, the P/E went up from 15× to 22× this year's earnings, and from 13.6× to 18.3× next year's estimated earnings.

November 1996 stock price	1996 EPS est.	P/E	1997 EPS est.	P/E
$44	$2.00	22 ×	$2.40	18.3 ×

The higher P/E that investors were willing to pay for JKL reflected anticipation of more rapid growth beginning in 1997 and beyond. It did *not* reflect investors deciding that the $2 earnings estimate for 1996 deserved a higher P/E by itself. The higher P/E based on 1996 earnings was a byproduct of the stock's price move to reflect the more rapid growth expected in 1997 and beyond.

Changes in P/E generally occur much faster than changes in earnings. Investors who buy stocks where they see slow, steady earnings growth in stable companies such as utilities can generally expect slow, steady stock performance. Investors who buy companies where they anticipate changes in the P/E ratio can generally expect faster and bigger stock price moves, both up and down, as different investors change their minds about the company's future prospects and what P/E they care to pay for the stock.

It is also important to note that JKL's stock moved up immediately after the company announced that it expected more rapid growth. Investors did not wait until the faster growth was actually occurring. This *anticipation* by the market is a key concept and will be discussed later in the chapter.

THE PRICE LEVEL OF A STOCK DOES NOT DETERMINE WHETHER THE STOCK IS "HIGH" OR "LOW"

How often have you heard someone say, "I am not going to buy that stock. The price is so high that I cannot buy enough shares to matter?" The following example illustrates the fallacy in that statement.

Suppose it is October 1996 and an investor calls his broker and says he has $1,200 to invest. The broker recommends buying ABC Industries, which is currently selling at $60 per share. The broker estimates ABC's earnings for this year, 1996, to be $5. Therefore, the stock is currently selling at 12x this year's earnings. The broker also expects earnings to be up 50% next year to $7.50 a share, and thinks the P/E ratio should remain about 12x in the future. Thus, the broker is assuming the following:

	Estimated EPS		P/E ratio		Stock price
Current: 1996	$5.00	×	12x	=	$60
Expected: 1997	$7.50	×	12x	=	$90

The investor with $1,200 would currently be able to buy "only" 20 shares at $60 each. A year from now, if the broker was right about earnings jumping 50% and the P/E remaining at 12x, then the investor would make a profit of $600, or 50%.

	Number of shares		Price per share		Total dollars
Bought:	20	×	$60	=	$1,200
Sold:	20	×	$90	=	$1,800
Profit:					$ 600

Now consider what would happen if ABC had had a 5-for-1 stock split in October, just before the investor bought the stock. In the event of a stock split (review in Chapter 6) the stock price and earnings per share are divided by the amount of the split. So after the split the stock price and earnings would look like this:

	Estimated EPS		P/E ratio		Stock price
Current: 1996	$1.00	×	12x	=	$12
Expected: 1997	$1.50	×	12x	=	$18

After the split the stock would still be selling at 12x earnings, but now the investor with $1,200 can buy 100 shares. ABC's earnings are still expected to grow at 50% in 1997; but as a result of the 5-for-1 stock split, the new EPS estimate for 1997 is $1.50 per share ($7.50 ÷ 5). The P/E ratio does not change because of the stock split. Therefore, the investor with $1,200 would now have the following projected investment results:

	Number of shares		Price per share		Total dollars
Bought:	100	×	$12	=	$1,200
Sold:	100	×	$18	=	$1,800
Profit:					$ 600

Notice that the projected profit to the investor is the same with or without the stock split. That is, the profit is the same whether the investor bought 20 shares of the higher-priced stock or 100 shares of the lower-priced stock. What determines the gain (or loss) in a stock is not the initial absolute price level of the stock, but is either (1) the percentage change in earnings if the P/E stays the same, as was the case here, or (2) the change in the P/E if the earnings level stays the same. Usually, of course, it is a combination of the two, but in any case, the total profit earned by the investor is independent of the absolute price level at which the stock began, or the number of shares the investor was able to buy.

THE P/E, NOT THE ACTUAL PRICE, DETERMINES WHEN A STOCK IS "HIGH" OR "LOW"

To understand this, let's look at Company A and Company B. Both are in the same business, have the same expected growth rate of earnings, and both pay out 50% of earnings as dividends. But Company A sells at a lower price/earnings ratio.

	Earnings per share	P/E ratio	Price of stock	Dividend per share at 50 percent of earnings	Yield to investor per share of stock
Company A	$10	10×	$100	$5	5.0%
Company B	2	25×	50	1	2.0

An investor with $100 could buy one share of Company A and get a 5% yield on his money.

$$1 \text{ share Company A:} \quad \frac{\$5 \text{ Dividend}}{\$100 \text{ Investment}} = 5\%$$

If the same $100 were used to buy two shares of Company B, the investor would receive $2 in dividends ($1 per share), or a 2% yield on his investment.

$$\text{2 shares Company B:} \quad \frac{\$2 \text{ Dividend}}{\$100 \text{ Investment}} = 2\%$$

Therefore, although a share of Company A (selling at $100) costs twice as much as a share of Company B (selling at $50), we can say Company A is really the *cheaper* or lower priced stock, because it is yielding more dividends to the investor per dollar of investment. This higher dividend yield is a result of Company A's lower price/earnings ratio.

To see this another way, look again at the comparison of Company A and Company B, but this time, assume Company B's price/earnings ratio has fallen from 25× to 10×, equal to that of Company A. Each company still has the same EPS it had before, but since investors are now only willing to pay 10 times earnings for Company B, its stock has fallen to $20. Let's see how much dividend the investor can get for a $100 investment in Company A or Company B.

	Earnings per share	P/E ratio	Price of stock	Dividend per share at 50 percent of earnings	Yield to investor per share of stock
Company A . . .	$10	10×	$100	$5	5.0%
Company B . . .	2	10×	20	1	5.0

An investor with $100 could still buy one share of Company A and therefore receive one dividend of $5, for a yield of 5%.

$$\text{1 share Company A:} \quad \frac{\$5 \text{ Dividend}}{\$100 \text{ Investment}} = 5\%$$

Or, with Company B's stock having declined to $20, the investor could now buy five shares of Company B, and since each share of Company B pays a dividend of $1, the investor would now receive a total of $5 in dividends, also a yield of 5%.

$$\text{5 shares Company B:} \quad \frac{\$5 \text{ Dividend}}{\$100 \text{ Investment}} = 5\%$$

What has happened is that Company B's lower P/E ratio resulted in a lower stock price, which enabled the investor to buy more shares of the stock and hence receive more dividends. Now, with the P/Es the same, a

$100 investment in either company yields the same amount of dividends, and we could say that both stocks, Company A and Company B, are "equally priced" or "equally valued" in terms of dividends earned per dollar of investment. This is true even though Company A still sells at a much higher price ($100) than Company B ($20). Other things being equal, an investor should now be indifferent between buying one share of Company A or five shares of Company B.

Note that in this example Company A and Company B were equally valued based on their equal dividends and equal P/Es. But equal P/Es should only reflect equal valuation when both companies are growing at the same rate. If Companies A and B both have the same earnings today, but Company A's earnings are growing at a faster rate than Company B's earnings, then Company A should sell at a higher P/E (and therefore higher price), reflecting the fact that earnings or dividends received by Company A shareholders in the future are expected to be higher than the earnings or dividends received by Company B shareholders in the future.

WHETHER A STOCK'S P/E IS "HIGH" OR "LOW" IS SOMETIMES BETTER JUDGED ON FUTURE EARNINGS THAN PRESENT EARNINGS

If two companies were identical today except that they were expected to have different earnings growth rates, the P/E would still be the best way to judge which stock is cheaper, but now the comparison is more difficult. In this case it may be easier to determine which stock is cheaper by comparing the current price to the expected earnings a few years out.

Let's look at Company C and Company D. Both have EPS in the current year of $10 and a dividend payout ratio of 50% of earnings. Company C's earnings are expected to grow at 2% a year and Company D's earnings are expected to grow at 25% a year. This difference in growth rates is extreme, which makes the example easy to follow, but the same ideas would apply even if the growth rates were only slightly different. Both companies are expected to continue to pay out 50% of earnings as dividends. The earnings growth will look as follows.

	Earnings in 1996	1 year out	2 years out	3 years out	4 years out	5 years out
Company C .... (2% growth)	$10	$10.20	$10.40	$10.61	$10.82	$11.04
Company D .... (25% growth)	$10	$12.50	$15.60	$19.50	$24.40	$30.50

Note that Company D's growth each year is 25% *above the immediately prior year's EPS.* It is *not* a $2.50 increase each year (which would be 25% of the original $10 each year). Investors always look at growth the former way. Similarly, Company C's growth each year is 2% above the immediately prior year's earnings.

Now, using today's stock prices of $100 for Company C and $160 for Company D, let's compare the price/earnings ratio and the dividend yield for the two companies, both this year and three years out.

Current Year—1996

	Stock price	EPS	P/E	Current dividend	Dividend yield
Company C	$100	$10	10×	$5	5.0%
Company D	$160	$10	16×	$5	3.1

Based just on the current year, Company C appears to be the cheaper stock. It has a lower P/E and a higher dividend yield. But the P/E ratios and dividend yield comparisons look different based on the EPS and dividends expected three years out.

Expected 3 years out

	EPS	Expected dividend at 50% payout	Stock price	Expected yield	P/E
Company C	$10.60	$5.30	$100	5.3%	9.4×
Company D	$19.50	$9.75	$160	6.1%	8.2×

At three years out, Company D appears to be the cheaper stock: it has a lower P/E and a higher yield. Now lets look at five years out.

Expected 5 years out

	EPS	Expected dividend at 50% payout	Stock price	Expected yield	P/E
Company C	$11.04	$5.52	$100	5.5%	9.1×
Company D	$30.50	$15.25	$160	9.5%	5.2×

If the stock prices stay the same, Company D will be selling at a much lower P/E and have a much higher yield despite its faster growth rate. This suggests that Company D is really the cheaper stock today (in

1996) even though its P/E based on the 1996 earnings is higher than Company C's, and its yield based on the current dividend is lower than Company C's.

To see why Company C is the cheaper stock, let's assume that five years out, both companies are selling at a P/E of 10x that year's earnings.

Expected 5 years out	EPS	P/E	Stock price
Company C..................	$11.04	10x	$110
Company D	$30.50	10x	$305

Company C would then be selling at $110 and Company D at $305. Now let's look at the percentage gain in each stock.

	Stock price today	Stock price in 5 years	Percentage gain
Company C........	$100	$110	10%
Company D	$160	$305	91%

Comparing these expected stock price gains, we can now say that Company D clearly appears to have been the cheaper stock in 1996, and thus we can see that Company D's faster EPS growth justified its higher P/E ratio in 1996. *Because Company D was growing faster, it was a better buy in 1996 at a P/E of 16x than Company C was at a P/E of 10x.* Or, to state it another way, Company D's stock was *lower,* or *cheaper,* in 1996 despite its higher P/E ratio at that time. In fact, Company D was so much cheaper in 1996 (based on the expected future gains) that investors would probably have bought the stock in 1996 and pushed the price, and therefore the P/E ratio, even higher.

In addition, if Company D deserved to be selling at a higher P/E than Company C in 1996 because of its faster growth rate, then it should also be selling at a higher P/E five years out, if its faster growth rate were expected to continue. If that were the case, Company D would be selling at a lot higher than $305 a share, and the percentage gain in Company D's stock price would be even greater.

In sum, when attempting to determine what you think a stock is worth based on its price/earnings ratio and dividend yield, it is important to look not just at this year's earnings and dividend, but at future expected earnings and dividends as well.

THERE IS NO SUCH THING AS A CORRECT PRICE/EARNINGS RATIO, BUT THERE ARE WAYS TO HELP DETERMINE AN APPROPRIATE LEVEL

We just saw that if two companies are growing at different rates, the company with the faster growth rate should have the higher P/E. But there is no absolute measure of what P/E one should pay for a given growth rate. There have been many studies attempting to determine what P/E should be paid for a given growth rate of earnings or dividends, but in my opinion there have always been too many "other" factors for such studies to be very useful. This does not mean that investors should not try to compare growth rates to P/Es. Studying this relationship for a number of stocks you follow is an excellent way to increase your comfort level with those stock prices, even though you probably will not find the perfect formula.

In practice, most investors do not try to calculate a mathematically "correct" P/E. Rather, by watching the prices, earnings, and P/Es of a group of stocks over a period of time, they develop a feel for how the stocks behave, both individually and compared to each other.

In addition to watching prices and earnings over time, there are other steps that can be taken to help judge what P/E should be paid for a given stock. A good place to start is to look at the company's P/E ratios in prior years. If the company's growth rate in the past is expected to be about the same in the future, and if market conditions in general are about the same, then the past P/E ratios may be a good guide in helping to decide what P/E should be appropriate today. After looking up the company's past P/Es, one should then consider what might be different to cause the stock to sell at a higher or lower P/E today. That is, what might happen to the company, or the industry it serves, or in the economy in general, to cause an increase or decrease in the company's growth rate? What might happen to change investor's confidence that the forecasted growth rate can be achieved? For example, if a major competitor went out of business, investors might expect a company's future growth rate to be faster. In addition, investors would have more confidence in their forecasts of company earnings because there is less fear of competition. Conversely, if a company were dependent on a raw material that was hard to obtain and subject to unexpected price increases, then investors' confidence in their earnings estimates would be lower and the stock might sell at a lower P/E.

Another step in trying to determine a P/E for a company is to look at the P/Es of similar companies and then consider what is different between the two companies and why one should have a higher or lower P/E than the other. Looking at the computer software industry for example, some small companies with one or two good products might be growing very rapidly now, but when they get bigger they will find themselves competing against the big software companies that have a larger market share. As the smaller companies find they cannot compete successfully against the larger, dominant companies, their growth might come to an abrupt halt. So the smaller companies, although growing rapidly now, may deserve a lower P/E than the companies with the dominant market share.

P/Es are also affected by broad market conditions. In the 1960s when interest rates were low, P/Es in general were high. A broad rule of thumb at that time said that the P/E should be twice the expected growth rate of earnings. For example, if a company's earnings had been growing at a rate of 10% a year and were expected to continue to grow at that rate, a P/E of 20× would be considered reasonable. If the company were growing at 15%, then a P/E of 30× would be reasonable. Of course, companies never grow at exactly the same rate each year, and in fact growth rates often come in spurts and then slow down. So even if a company's growth rate had "averaged" 10% a year, investors would still have had to make a judgment as to whether they felt comfortable paying a P/E of more than or less than 20×.

From the mid 1970s to the early 1980s, when inflation was a concern and interest rates were higher, stocks generally sold at lower P/Es than in the 1960s. Stocks often sold at P/Es that were less than their growth rate. For example, a company that had been growing at 10% a year might have a P/E of 9× or less. In the late 1980s and mid-1990s, with interest rates declining, P/Es started rising again, and perhaps the old rule of thumb will come back into vogue.

In sum, investors trying to decide what P/E to pay for a stock can look at the company's past P/Es and similar companies' P/Es as a guide. They should also look at broad market trends to see if P/Es in general are rising or falling. By comparing past conditions with current conditions, investors will often have a good basis for determining an appropriate price/earnings ratio today.

PRICE/EARNINGS RATIO ANALYSIS: WHEN IS A STOCK "HIGH" AND WHEN IS IT "LOW"?

To see how past P/Es can help determine whether a stock is high or low, let's look at Diversified Manufacturing Inc. (DMI). DMI's earnings growth has averaged about 10% a year.[2] As Table 18.2 shows, the growth has not actually been 10% in any year. That is unrealistic, but over a period of time it has averaged about 10%, or more relevant, has *compounded* at 10%.

Table 18.2 Earnings Growth for DMI

Company DMI	Earnings per share	Percent increase over previous year
1991	$ .91	
1992	.96	5.5%
1993	1.11	15.6
1994	1.25	12.6
1995	1.33 est.	6.4
		10.025% average increase

The stock's price range and P/E ratio range for the same period are shown in Table 18.3. Assume it is now December, 1995 and the stock price is $27.

Table 18.3 Stock Price Range and P/E Ratio Range for DMI

	EPS	Price High	Low	P/E High	Low
1991	$ .91	$23	$13	25x	14x
1992	.96	27	15	28x	16x
1993	1.11	28	17	25x	15x
1994	1.25	34	20	27x	16x
1995	1.33 est.	37	23	28x	17x
1996	1.60 est.				

Table 18.3 shows that the stock price has typically fluctuated in a wide range each year, and the P/E has reached at least 25x each year and has typically been as low as 15x–16x each year. This does not necessarily mean that it will be this high or this low each year, or that it cannot go higher or lower in any future year, but the historical range is still a good first guidepost to forecasting the future P/Es.

2 Actually, the average growth rate is 10.025 percent per year. To be mathematically correct, it is the *compound* growth rate that is exactly 10 percent per year. Compound growth rate is defined as the growth rate that would be necessary so that *if* the company grew at exactly the same percentage rate each year, it would grow from a specified level ($.91 in 1991 in this case) to another specified level ($1.33 in 1995 in this case). The compound growth rate is not concerned with the earnings levels in the middle years. They could be anything. The compound growth rate for Company E , then, is exactly 10 percent. Unfortunately, there is no simple way to calculate a compound growth rate, so if you don't have a calculator that can do it, you can approximate it with an "average" growth rate by adding up the growth rates for each year and dividing the total by the number of years.

With the stock at $27 in December 1995, investors will probably be focusing on 1996 earnings. This is because investors typically buy a stock today focusing on where they think it will be 6 to 12 months in the future. With 1996 EPS estimated at $1.60, and the stock at $27, it would then be selling at 16.9x 1996 earnings and would look "low"—that is, it is selling at the low end of its historical P/E range. Let's try to estimate the upside potential of the stock, and the downside risk.

Unless the stock market is depressed in 1996, or there is some development suggesting a decline in the company's expected growth rate, it is reasonable to assume, based on the stock's history, that at some point during the year the stock price will reach 25x earnings or more. This suggests the stock could reach as high as $40 per share.

$$\frac{\text{1996 EPS estimate}}{\$1.60} \times \frac{\text{Assumed P/E}}{25\times} = \frac{\text{Expected stock price}}{\$40}$$

With the stock currently at $27, we can see a possible $13 upside move to $40, or 48% gain. On the other hand, the downside risk, based on the historical P/E range, is that stock could get as low as 15x 1996 earnings.

$$\frac{\text{1996 EPS estimate}}{\$1.60} \times \frac{\text{Assumed P/E}}{15\times} = \frac{\text{Expected stock price}}{\$24}$$

Thus, we can also see a downside risk of $3, to $24, or an 11% loss. Looking at an expected upside gain of 48% and a downside risk of only 11%, the stock looks "low," or attractive based on historical P/Es, and should be bought.

Now let's assume the stock has appreciated to $32 by March 1996. Assume, also, that the 1995 earnings came in at $1.35, slightly above the estimate, and the $1.60 estimate for 1996 remains unchanged.

	EPS	Price	P/E
1995	$1.35	$32	
1996	$1.60 est.	$32	20.0x

At this point, then, the stock is selling at 20x estimated 1996 earnings, about the middle of its historical P/E range of 16x–25x, and the expected gain and risk appear to be as follows.

	1996 EPS	Expected P/E	Expected price	Gain or loss from $32
Upside:.............	$1.60 est.	25×	$40	$8 gain
Risk:	$1.60 est.	16×	$26	$6 loss

With the stock at $32, the appreciation potential now appears to be about $8, a 25% gain, and the downside risk is about $6, from $32 to $26, a 19% loss. One might now say the stock is *fairly valued* based on 1996 estimated earnings.

If the market as a whole was expected to fall, DMI might be expected to fall with it, and the stock should be sold. But if the market were expected to rise, the stock should be held, or more purchased, because in a strong up market, stocks often go to the high end of their historical P/E range, or higher.

This analysis assumed the P/E range would stay about the same. But since the 1996 growth rate is expected to be about 20%, much higher than the company's historical average of 10% growth, and somewhat higher than even the 15.5% growth in 1993, it may be that DMI's growth rate is going to remain higher, and it is possible that the market will begin to value the company at a higher P/E.

By August 1996 the stock reached $41, a new high. The earnings estimate for 1996 was still $1.60, so the stock was selling at 26× expected 1996 earnings, near the high end of its historical range. But at this point, even if the stock went to 28× earnings, or $45 per share, there would only be $4 further upside per share, whereas the downside risk from $41 could be to 15× earnings, or $24 per share, a $17 decline ($41 − $24 = $17) if the market went down, or if some unexpected bad news came out about the company. The likelihood of a decline all the way to $24 does not seem too great, however, since by early fall investors may begin to focus on 1997 earnings, which, if higher, will make the P/E look lower. In fact, analysts' earnings estimates for 1997 were around $1.80 per share, a 12½% increase from the 1996 level. So the P/Es looked as follows:

	Estimated EPS	Stock price	P/E
1996	$1.60	$41	26×
1997	$1.80	$41	23×

Based on the 1996 earnings estimate, the stock at $41 looked "fully valued" and there seemed to be a lot more room for a decline than there was for a gain. But based on the 1997 estimate, the stock was selling at 23x, closer to the mid-point of the historical range. Still, however, the stock seemed to have more downside risk than upside potential, and a cautious investor would probably sell it. This is because with the stock at the high end of its historical P/E range, any disappointing news about company earnings could have a substantial downside impact on the stock, whereas good news might have only a limited favorable impact on the stock. In the language of Wall Street, the stock was *fully valued* or *fully priced*, and left little room for disappointment.

Suppose that in November 1996, with the stock at $39, the company made announcements that caused analysts to lower their earnings estimates for 1996 from $1.60 a share to around $1.40, and to lower their estimates for 1997 from $1.80 to $1.55 a share. Based on the lower earnings estimates, the P/Es would look higher, and once again be at the high end of the historical P/E range.

	Estimated EPS	Stock price	P/E
1996	$1.40	$39	28x
1997	$1.55	$39	25x

In addition, having been surprised by the company announcements in November, investors would have a lot less confidence in their earnings estimates, and may only be comfortable buying or holding the stock at a lower P/E than previously. Also, the growth rate of earnings would suddenly look a lot lower, also causing investors to revise downward the P/E they might be willing to pay for the stock. At this point we might say the stock appears to be *overpriced* based on the new 1996 and 1997 earnings forecasts, and should be sold.

The lowering of the earnings forecasts in November points to a problem with using past year's P/Es as a guide to the future. Recall that the stock had reached a high of $41 in August when 1996 earnings were forecast to be $1.60. But assuming that 1996 earnings eventually came in at $1.38, the historical record would show the high price of $41 during the year, and the actual EPS of $1.38, which implies a price/ earnings ratio of 29.7x. This would appear to be a new high P/E. But investors did not actually think they were paying 29x earnings for the stock. At the time the stock reached $41, the 1996 earnings forecast was $1.60 and the apparent P/E was 25.6×. The historical record does not reflect the change in investors' EPS forecasts. For this reason, historical P/Es, especially extremely high or low figures, must be treated skeptically.

We will now define, with qualifications, *low* and *high*.

DEFINITIONS

- **Low**–When a stock is selling at the lower end of its normal or expected P/E range (or below), it is *low*, or *undervalued*, or *underpriced*.

- **High**–When a stock is selling at the upper end of its normal or expected P/E range (or higher), it is *high*, or *overvalued*, or *overpriced*.

The qualifications are these. The historical P/E range of a stock can only be considered a reasonable guide to the future P/E range if: (1) the growth rate of earnings is expected to remain about the same as it was; (2) nothing has changed in the company or the industry it serves, or the economy in general to affect one's confidence in his earnings estimates; and (3) the whole market's evaluation of P/Es has not changed.

In the case of DMI, the stock sold in a normal P/E range of 16×–25× while it was achieving a growth record averaging 10% a year. When it looked like the company was going to achieve a higher growth rate, its P/E tended to be higher, 26×–28×. If the growth rate is expected to return to about 10%, the P/E range of 16×–25× might again be considered more likely. But if the recent lowering of earnings estimates reflects an expected decline in the growth rate for an extended period, then the stock may be more likely to trade at the lower end of the P/E range, perhaps 14×–17×, or even lower.

Words such as *overpriced, fully valued, undervalued, cheap,* and the like, are constantly used on Wall Street and are best thought of in terms of the price/earnings ratio. The distinctions between overvalued and fairly valued, or fairly valued and undervalued, are fuzzy and subject to individual interpretation. Nevertheless, Table 18.4 might help put some perspective on these words.

Table 18.4   Historical Record for DMI

	EPS	Price High	Price Low	P/E High	P/E Low
1991	$ .91	$23	$13	25×	14×
1992	.96	27	15	28×	16×
1993	1.11	28	17	25×	15×
1994	1.25	34	20	27×	16×
1995	1.35	41	23	30×	17×

P/E range	Evaluation
Over 26	High, overpriced, overvalued
26–23	Fully priced, fully valued
23–19	Fairly priced, fairly valued
19–16	Low, underpriced, undervalued
16–14	Cheap!
Below 14	Very cheap!

Again, these ranges are subjective. Another writer might say the stock is overpriced, or overvalued, only above 28× earnings, undervalued only below 17× earnings, and so on.

A would-be investor once asked a Wall Street magnate how to make money in the stock market. The magnate replied, "Buy low and sell high." The would-be investor walked away muttering, "Yes, but how do I know what is low and what is high except in retrospect, and then it is too late." In light of this analysis, it is evident that the would-be investor misinterpreted the answer. What the magnate meant was this: Buy a stock only if it is selling at the lower end of its P/E range relative to your best estimate of earnings. Then the probability of price appreciation as the future unfolds is greater than the probability of decline. If a stock is selling at the upper end of its historical P/E range, perhaps you should not buy it, or should sell it if you own it, not because it cannot go higher, but because the probability of its going lower exceeds the probability of its going much higher.

STOCK PRICES ANTICIPATE

One of the hardest lessons for new investors to learn is that *stock prices frequently anticipate future earnings or events—sometimes correctly and sometimes incorrectly—rather than reacting after the event.* Investors expecting improved earnings from a company, or a major new product announcement, for example, will buy the stock well ahead of the time they expect the improved earnings or new product to be announced. They will buy the stock even knowing that the expected improvement in earnings may never come to pass, or that the product announcement may be disappointing, and then the stock might go down. But they also know that if they wait, others will have purchased the stock and pushed it up in anticipation of the expected good news. Thus, stocks often move up *in anticipation* of improved earnings, and decline *in anticipation* of disappointing or declining earnings. Investors who wait until a company has reported improved earnings will usually have missed much or all of the stock's rise. How a stock behaves when earnings are actually reported, then, *is likely to depend on whether the earnings were more or less than was expected,* not whether they were more or less than the prior year's earnings. For this reason, investors who do not make earnings estimates for companies they follow, or do not have access to other investors' or analysts' estimates, are often surprised when stocks go down after reporting an earnings increase, or go up after a bad earnings report.

For example, if a company had earnings per share of $2.00 in 1995 and investors were generally expecting the company to earn $3.00 a share in 1996, the stock would most likely move up during the year 1996 in anticipation of the $3.00 earnings level. When the company reports its actual earnings for the year, if earnings were near the forecast $3 level, the chances are the stock would not move very much, if at all, because the stock had already moved up to a level that reflected investors' anticipations of $3.00 earnings a share. On the other hand, if the company reported earnings of $3.50 a share, then the stock would probably move higher, reflecting the $.50 surprise above the $3.00 that had been anticipated. Conversely, if the company had reported earnings at $2.50, the stock would probably fall. It would not fall because the company reported a gain from $2.00 to $2.50; it would fall because the stock price had moved up in anticipation of earnings of $3.00 (incorrectly, as it turned out), and when only $2.50 a share was reported, the stock was, in retrospect, too high. The price decline represents the disappointment between the $2.50 actually earned and the $3.00 anticipated.

For investors who are active traders and who try to catch each move up or down in a stock, it is therefore important not only to have a good feel for the company's expected earnings, but also to know what others are thinking. This information is usually best obtained from a stockbroker who works for a firm with a large research department. You should ask your broker what the firm's analyst is estimating for earnings, and also ask if the analyst knows what is the "consensus" estimate, that is, what most investors are expecting. Surprisingly, consensus estimates are often available from industry sources. You should also ask your broker what the firm is anticipating in the way of other important events, such as the timing of a major new product introduction, or the nature of a new product introduction. Stock prices will generally anticipate most events that can be reasonably predicted in advance. These can include earnings changes, product announcements, dividend changes, government regulatory changes, competitors' actions, and more.

VALUING A STOCK BY THE PRICE-TO-CASH-FLOW RATIO

Although the price/earnings ratio is the most common way that stocks are valued, some investors also like to look at the price-to-cash-flow ratio. Cash flow in this case can be the cash flow from operations, or the free cash flow, or any other cash flow figure one cares to use. The important thing is to be consistent and use the same type of a cash flow figure when comparing different companies. Whichever cash flow figure is chosen should be divided by the number of common shares outstanding to put it on a per-share basis. Let's look at Cross Country Railroad (CCR). CCR's cash flow statement, shown in Table 18.5, is in the same form as we used in Chapter 15.

Table 18.5   Cash Flow Statement of Cross County Railroad

CCR Cash Flow Statement	(all figures are in millions of dollars)					
	Actual			Forecast		
	1993	1994	1995	1996	1997	1998
Sources						
1. Net income	$21	23	25	27	29	30
Add back:						
2. Depreciation and amort.	50	54	58	58	56	56
3. Deferred tax	4	5	5	5	5	5
4. = Cash flow from operations	$75	82	88	90	90	91
Uses						
5. Debt principal repayments	$24	10	20	40	22	22
6. + Maintenance cap. spending	16	16	16	18	18	20
7. + Preferred dividend	5	5	5	5	5	5
8. = Cash flow uses	$45	31	41	63	45	47
9. Free cash flow (line 4 minus line 8)	$30	51	47	27	45	44

CCR has 12 million shares outstanding. In Table 18.6, we calculate the earnings per share, the cash flow from operations per share, and the free cash flow per share, by dividing each of the earnings or cash flow figures in lines 1, 4, and 9 from the cash flow statement by 12 million shares.

Table 18.6   Cash Flow and Earnings Per Share Calculations for CCR (12 million shares outstanding)

	Actual			Forecast		
	1993	1994	1995	1996	1997	1998
Earnings per share	$1.75	$1.92	$2.08	$2.25	$2.42	$2.50
Cash flow from operations per share	$6.25	$6.83	$7.33	$7.50	$7.50	$7.58
Free cash flow per share	$2.50	$4.25	$3.92	$2.25	$3.75	$3.67

With the stock selling at $32, we can now calculate the price/earnings ratio, the price-to-cash-flow-from-operations ratio, and the price-to-free-cash-flow ratio. These ratios are in Table 18.7.

Table 18.7   Calculating Price Ratios for CCR (stock at $32/share)

	Actual			Forecast		
	1993	1994	1995	1996	1997	1998
Price/earnings ratio	18.3x	16.7x	15.4x	14.2x	13.2x	12.8x
Price/cash flow from ops.	5.1x	4.7x	4.4x	4.3x	4.3x	4.2x
Price/free cash flow	12.8x	7.5x	8.2x	14.2x	8.5x	8.7x

CCR's *price-to-cash-flow-from-operations* ratio looks a lot lower than the *price-to-earnings* ratio. This is because CCR's large depreciation figure reduces the net earnings, but does not affect the cash flow.[3] Whenever there is a large depreciation figure (or deferred tax figure) that causes the net earnings to look very low compared to the cash flow from operations, the *price-to-cash-flow-from-operations* ratio may be a better basis for comparing the stock prices of two companies than the price/earnings ratio. This is because the low earnings figure does not really reflect the benefit to the shareholders of all the cash flow.

Thus, it is appropriate to use the price-to-cash-flow-from-operations ratio (which from here on we will simply refer to as *price/cash flow*) whenever the earnings are low relative to the cash flow. A rule of thumb

---

3 If this concept is not familiar, it can be reviewed in the "Cash Flow" section in Chapter 13.

might be to calculate the price/cash-flow ratio whenever a company's annual earnings are normally less than the annual depreciation. It would be particularly appropriate to use the price/cash-flow ratio when the company is either losing money, just breaking even, or only making a very small profit. In any of these three cases, the price/earnings ratio would be meaningless.

Finally, the price/cash-flow ratio might be better than the price/earnings ratio when comparing two or more companies that use different depreciation techniques. By simply comparing the price to the cash flow, you would be comparing the companies on an equal footing, and the differences in depreciation technique would be irrelevant.

We saw earlier in the chapter that there is no mathematically correct P/E ratio for a company. Similarly, there is no correct level for price/cash flow. Investors should use price/cash-flow ratios just as they would use the P/E ratios; that is, to compare similar companies, or to watch one company's ratios over time. This is true whether you are looking at the price-to-cash-flow-from-operations ratio, or the price-to-free-cash-flow ratio. Comparing similar, or even totally different companies' price/ earnings and price/cash-flow ratios will often reveal interesting patterns that will help investors decide when a stock is high or low.

Some investors prefer to look at the price-to-free-cash-flow ratio, because, as we saw in Chapter 15, the free cash flow is really what is available to be spent to increase shareholder value. The price/free-cash-flow ratio, however, is more likely to be distorted by unusual cash flow items such as the big debt repayment in 1996. On the other hand, investors can easily see that the big debt repayment is distorting that ratio in 1996 and that, in general, the price-to-free-cash-flow ratio is more typically about 8×, and that 8× would be a good figure to compare against other companies to see which is cheaper.

VALUING A STOCK BASED ON EARNINGS POWER

Did you ever wonder why shares of small companies that have no earnings sometimes sell at high prices? The answer is that investors are pricing the stock based on how much the company could possibly earn if all goes well.

For example, consider Universal Biotek (UB). UB was founded by three doctors who discovered a medicine that looked like a sure cure for a previously incurable disease. The company went public, selling new shares at $12 to raise money to build a plant to make the new medicine. Shortly after going public, as UB's story became well-known on Wall Street, the stock moved up sharply to about $60. This is why: Investment analysts who specialize in medical stocks did some research and discovered that about 100,000 people get this disease each year. They assumed that about 80,000 of them would have access to the new medical treatment. UB indicated that it expected to sell about $4,000 of medicine for the typical treatment. Thus, analysts could estimate that once the plant was up and running and the treatment was widely used by doctors, UB could generate sales of about $320,000,000 a year (80,000 patients times $4,000 per patient.) Analysts also assumed that UB could attain a profit margin of 5% after tax. This is actually a low profit margin for a drug company with a monopoly on a needed product. A 5% net profit on sales of $320 million is equal to $16 million net profit. With 2 million common shares outstanding, we would say the company has *earnings power* of $8 a share ($16 million profit divided by 2 million shares.)

It might take three or four years before UB is earning anywhere near that amount, or it might never earn that much. Someone else could discover a better or cheaper medicine. But right now, UB has a patented medicine and no known competition in the marketplace, and investors can see the potential to earn $8 a share. To say it another way, the company has earnings power of $8 a share. If we also assume that investors will be willing to pay a price/earnings ratio of 10x when the company earns that amount, then the stock would be worth about $80 at that time. More likely, however, the stock will be selling at 20x or higher, because by then the company will probably have discovered other applications for its patented medicine, and earnings will have the potential to keep growing beyond the $8 a share level. Rapidly growing drug companies often sell at P/E ratios of 20x or more. At 20x, the stock would be selling at $160.

Again, it is much too early to say that UB can actually earn $8 a share, so the stock is not likely to get anywhere near $160 for a few years. The medicine might turn out not to work, or have undesirable side effects. But right now, the medicine looks very promising and the earnings power is so high that with the stock at $12 after the public offering, the potential gain was so great that many investors jumped in and bought the stock and pushed it up to $60. From this high level, however, as enthusiasm waxes and wanes for UB's potential, the stock can be expected to be very volatile; that is, it will have sharp swings up and down as news comes out about the company's progress toward its $8 earnings power.

WHY STOCKS GO UP AND DOWN: A WORKING EXPLANATION

With our understanding of P/E ratios, price/cash-flow ratios, and how stock prices anticipate future events, we can now attempt a working explanation of why stocks go up and down.

> *Stocks go up and down in response to changes in perception of a company's ability to generate earnings and pay dividends, both this year and in the future.*
> *Changes in perception can arise from developments within the company, in the company's competitive environment, or in the economy in general.*

Many investors would quibble with this explanation, but I think readers will find it helpful when trying to predict stock price moves. Keep it in mind while watching stocks go up and down in response to news in the real world.

Note that this explanation only addresses why stocks go up and down. It does not attempt to explain why a stock sells at a particular level. In fact, it is a lot easier to understand why stocks go up and down than it is to understand why they sell at a particular price. In the language of Wall Street, we sometimes say the market is *efficient.* By this we mean that the price of a stock at any time is exactly where it should be. It is neither too high nor too low: That is, the current price reflects the net result of all the buy and sell decisions by all investors based on their interpretations of all the information that is known about the company at that time. The only important question, then, is what will make the stock go up or down from the current level; and our time is better spent trying to determine what factors will cause investor perceptions about the stock to change than trying to determine what the price "should be."

Investor perceptions can be impacted by an infinite number of developments. Innumerable events happen every day throughout the world that impact companies' near-term earnings and long-term earnings growth rates and, therefore, the price/earnings ratios that investors will be willing to pay for different stocks. Events that cause favorable changes in perception would likely boost the price of a stock, whereas unfavorable changes would likely push the price down. Let's look at a few examples of developments that would change investor's perception of a company's ability to generate earnings. This list could be endless. Just a few examples are given to help sensitize you to thinking about how every bit of news can affect your stocks.

Events Creating Favorable Changes in Perception

- **Company development**—QuickFlip Burgers announced that it was consolidating its meat buying with a major supplier with a long-term contract that provided a substantial cost saving.

- **Industry development**—The government announced a major change in chicken inspection procedures that would result in higher prices for chicken meals at fast-food outlets. This would make QuickFlip's burger restaurants relatively less expensive and therefore more attractive to consumers.

- **Economic development**—Congress lowered the minimum wage by 20%. Since much of the labor in the fast-food industry is minimum wage, costs would be expected to decline sharply, producing higher than previously expected earnings.

Events Creating Unfavorable Changes in Perception

- **Company development**—QuickFlip announced that its pension expense for retired employees was going to be much higher than the managers previously thought.

- **Competitive development**—Newspapers indicated that QuickFlip was losing market share to BiggerBurger, which had opened stores near QuickFlip and cut prices. This would result in narrower profit margins for QuickFlip in addition to the market share loss.

- **Economic development**—Gasoline prices increased sharply. Higher gasoline prices cause people to eat out less often. A food chain whose restaurants were mostly on the highways would be hurt more than a company whose restaurants were mostly in the cities.

Again, this list is endless. It is necessary for successful investors both to watch for developments that might impact their stocks, and to distinguish between those that will have a significant impact and those that will have only a minor or temporary impact.

Sometimes it can be very difficult to determine how big an impact an event will have on stock prices. For example, consider a proposal by the president of the United States to lower the minimum wage by 20%. If such a proposal were to become law, labor costs at QuickFlip would decline sharply, and as we saw, this would have a favorable impact on company earnings. But if the proposal were dropped, it would, of course, have no impact. If after months of debate, Congress and the president compromised and passed a law lowering the minimum wage by only 5%, there would still be a favorable impact on earnings, but it would be greatly reduced. So when the proposal by the president was first announced, the perception of its impact on QuickFlip's earnings would depend on one's judgment of the likelihood of the full 20% wage reduction becoming law. Since different investors would have different judgments, it is difficult to say if the stock would immediately go up on the proposal, or if investors would wait until there were indications that Congress had responded favorably and that it seemed likely that the proposal would become law.

WHAT INVESTORS SHOULD WATCH FOR

There is no substitute for experience. Investors should watch a group of stocks daily and stay tuned to all the news about those companies and the environments in which they operate: the competitive environment, the labor environment, the raw materials environment, the economic environment, and so on.

By watching how stock prices respond, or do not respond, to news developments over a period of time, you will develop the experience that distinguishes the consistently successful investors from those who keep on making the same mistakes. To develop this experience, investors should read the newspapers daily, as well as reading industry newspapers and magazines that relate to their stocks. Alert investors will watch for developments that could affect their company in any way: the demand for their company's products; the cost of manufacturing the products; the price the company can charge for its products, and so on. Financial newspapers such as *The Wall Street Journal* or *Investor's Business Daily* make it their business to extract the news that they think will be of greatest interest to investors. The financial sections of local newspapers also do this, but nowhere near as thoroughly as the financial newspapers. Other sections of the newspapers are also important. Political news, local news, and even advertisements can give indications of trends to come that will impact company earnings and, hence, stock prices. For example, think what a blockbuster movie or highly rated TV series can do for a film company, or how much damage a successful new chain of retail stores can do to competing stores in the same area.

New investors would do well to go through every page of one of the major financial newspapers every day for a month. Do not read any article the first time through. Just read the headline of each article and mark those that you think are likely to impact your company's earnings. The second time through, read the marked articles and see if you still think they are meaningful. Do this every day while watching your company's stock price. After a period of time you will find yourself becoming sensitized to which factors are important and which are less meaningful or totally irrelevant. At that point you will know why stocks go up and down.

19

For New Investors: A Note on Wall Street, Brokers, and Mutual Funds

In the last chapter we looked at the price/earnings ratio as a way of measuring what someone will pay for a share of stock. We saw that P/Es and stock prices will fluctuate within or around some presumed range of value based on projections of future earnings and dividends. In this chapter we will look at some of the people and institutions who are directly involved in the investment process and make these earnings projections and P/E judgments. We will also look at the basics of how a mutual fund works, and some of the considerations in deciding whether to choose your own stocks or to buy mutual funds.

On Wall Street[1] we talk about the "buy-side of the street" and the "sell-side of the street." The sell-side refers to firms that earn money by taking commissions each time they buy or sell stocks (or bonds or options or other investments) for their clients. Stock brokerage firms are sell-side institutions. There are currently more than 3,500 stock brokerage firms in the U.S., ranging from giant Merrill Lynch, the largest, to small regional firms whose names are not even familiar to many Wall Streeters.

---

1 "Wall Street," in this context, refers to anyone who is involved in the securities business. It does not literally mean only those firms who happen to have offices on Wall Street.

Buy-side institutions, by contrast, hold their customers' money and make all the buy and sell investment decisions. Buy-side institutions typically earn their money by taking as a fee a small percentage of the total amount of money they manage for the client, regardless of how often they buy or sell securities. Buy-side institutions include mutual funds, trust companies, pension funds, endowment funds, and others. When a buy-side institution buys or sells stock for its clients, it must use a broker (a sell-side firm), and the commission for the broker is paid from the clients' funds.

SELL-SIDE INSTITUTIONS

Full-Service Brokers

The commissions that brokers make when buying and selling stocks for their customers can vary quite a lot. For example, if you bought 1,000 shares of a $30 stock from a large, full-service brokerage firm, their standard commission would be about $500. At most brokerage firms, however, the broker will be willing to negotiate a discount and the average customer may pay closer to $400. Very active clients—those who do a lot of trading—may be able to negotiate a commission as low as $200. This is still somewhat more than the discount brokers, discussed shortly. Your individual stockbroker gets part of the commission, and the rest goes to the firm. A stockbroker who deals with individuals is called a *retail broker* or a *registered representative* or some similar title. Stock brokerage firms distinguish their retail or individual customers from their institutional customers, such as mutual funds, pension funds, and the like.

Why should an individual do business with one brokerage firm or another? The best basis for choosing a broker is that you trust the broker's judgment. Perhaps stock recommendations the broker made to people you know have worked out well. Judgment in stock selection is, of course, the ultimate test of a broker. But in the stock market, good judgment requires good information.

Although brokers work to develop good sources of information, the amount of information available is far too much for any one person to digest. Consequently, many brokerage firms have staffs of people called security analysts, or investment analysts, who specialize in analyzing information to help their stockbrokers and clients make buy and sell decisions.

Most big firms have many analysts. Each specializes in one or more industries. One analyst, for example, may specialize in analyzing stocks in the automotive and tire industries, another may specialize in insurance stocks, another in computer stocks. These analysts usually devote their full time to researching stocks. They analyze a company and its industry, make forecasts of earnings and dividends for individual companies, and, based on that information, make judgments about the outlook for those stocks. In most firms the analysts write reports that are available to their stockbrokers and important clients. The reports typically give both the most relevant information and the analyst's judgment about it. Thus, the stockbroker, instead of trying to do all the research personally, can read the firm's analysts' reports. The broker can then use this information in recommending stocks to his clients. Of course, he also uses his own judgment. Just because the firm's analysts are recommending certain stocks does not mean that the broker has to recommend them to any client. The broker may disagree with the judgment of the analyst. Thus, a broker's recommendations may come from the firm's research department (security analysts) or they may come from personal resources.

Discount Brokers

Some investors do not want or need advice from stockbrokers. They have their own sources of information and just use a broker to execute their orders. In this case they may prefer to use a *discount broker.*

Discount brokers charge much lower commissions than full-service brokers because they do not keep a staff of analysts and do not offer advice. Discount brokers are also sell-side firms in that they earn money from commissions when customers buy and sell stocks; but, because they do not provide as much service, they can afford to charge lower commissions. Commissions at discount brokers can vary a lot. One large discount broker, for example, was charging about $35 for buying or selling 100 shares of a $30 stock and about $110 for a 1,000-share order of a $30 stock at the date of this writing. Another discount broker was charging about $50 for 100 shares of a $30 stock and about $150 for 1,000 shares of a $30 stock. For very active traders, some discount brokers offer even lower commission rates. In any case, these commissions are much lower than the full-service firms' commissions.

A discount broker, of course, gives you less service. A broker at a full-service firm, by contrast, usually has time to discuss your investment ideas and can often get you a lot of information about stocks or bonds that interest you. You can choose whichever broker seems appropriate for you. Obviously, if a broker is recommending stocks that go up and is consistently making money for you, you should stay with the full-service broker, because the commissions will be small relative to your profits.

BUY-SIDE INSTITUTIONS

Suppose you want to have some of your savings invested in the stock market but do not want to be actively involved in the decision of which stock or stocks to own. One way to avoid this is to give your broker discretion to buy and sell on your behalf. A second possibility, if you have enough money, is to put it into a trust company where your money or investments can be kept separately, and a person, typically called a trust investment officer, will be assigned to manage the money for you. A third alternative is to put your money into a mutual fund, where it is pooled with other people's money and invested together.

Mutual Funds as Investment Tools

Buy-side institutions, as mentioned, include mutual funds, pension and retirement funds, charitable funds, insurance companies that invest their own cash, and anyone else who has investment responsibility for managing other peoples' money. Of these, most people will have the most direct contact with mutual funds, so our discussion of buy-side institutions will be limited to those.

A mutual fund is an organization that is usually set up as a corporation or a trust that takes in money from a large number of people and invests it. Mutual funds issue a prospectus that, among other things, states the fund's objectives and the type of investments the fund will make. Some funds are created to invest in common stock, others in bonds, U.S. Treasury bills, or other investments. Some funds further specialize, investing in only over-the-counter stocks, Japanese stocks, electric utility stocks, technology stocks, and so on.

A mutual fund is typically created by a firm called a *mutual fund management company,* or an *investment advisor,* or some similar name. Although a mutual fund management company set up the fund, the fund is actually owned by the people who have money in the fund, called the fund's shareholders. Each shareholder's ownership is proportionate to the amount of money he or she has in the fund. The shareholders elect directors or trustees who are responsible to watch over the investment management firm to make sure it is investing the fund's money according to the prospectus, and doing a good job. If the trustees are not happy with the management firm, they can recommend to the fund's shareholders that they change management firms. In practice this does not happen very often, because if a shareholder is unhappy with the mutual fund, it is much simpler just to sell the fund and buy another one.

There are thousands of mutual funds and hundreds of investment management firms, or investment advisory firms, which manage mutual funds. Most investment advisory firms manage more than one fund, with some of the larger firms managing 30 or more funds. Fidelity Investments, the largest, manages more than a hundred funds. If you look in the mutual fund section of the newspaper you will typically see the name of the management firm in bold print, followed by a listing of the funds they manage. Some of these investment advisors do nothing but manage mutual funds, and some investment advisors are part of firms that are also in other businesses. For example, many banks and brokerage firms now manage mutual funds.

Mutual funds have shareholder meetings. Most shareholders do not attend these meetings, but may vote by proxy. The business at these meetings usually consists of electing trustees or directors, approving the investment advisory contract with the investment manager or voting on any proposed changes in the investment advisory contract, and approving an auditor.

Mutual fund management firms are buy-side institutions because they manage other people's money and take a fee, called an *investment management fee* or an *investment advisory fee,* as a percentage of the assets (money and investments) in the funds they manage. The amount of the fee, or fee schedule, is stated in the fund's prospectus, and cannot be changed without the fundholder's approval. The management firm uses the fee to pay for a staff of investment analysts, portfolio managers, an investment library, and so on. The annual investment advisory fee for common stock mutual funds typically ranges from 0.5% to 1.5% of the assets in the fund, with one-twelfth of the annualized fee being paid monthly. For example, assume that in June a fund had $100 million worth of cash and investments. If the fee was 0.5% a year, the annualized fee would be $500,000; so the fee for the month of June would be one-twelfth of $500,000, or $41,667. Now suppose the fund manager chose stocks very well, and six months later, in December, the fund had grown to $160 million. In that case, the annualized fee at 0.5% would now be $800,000, and the fee for December would be one-twelfth of $800,000, or $66,667. Since the investment management fee, or advisory fee, goes up with the assets, the management company has the same goal as the investors do— to make the fund go up as much as possible. Some investment advisory contracts also have an incentive fee built in. These typically say if the mutual fund's performance beats some specified market average by a specified amount, the mutual fund management company will get an extra fee.

In addition to the management fee, mutual fund shareholders also pay certain expenses of the fund. The nature and amount of those expenses is discussed in the fund's prospectus and typically includes fees for providing shareholders' services, such as communications to shareholders, custodian fees for the bank that holds the stocks belonging to the fund, and so on. Some funds also have what is called a "12b-1 fee," which is basically part of a sales charge. The "12b-1" refers to the section of the securities laws that permits the funds to charge this fee. The combination of the investment advisory fee and the expenses for which the fund reimburses the management company are easy to find in the fund's prospectus and are usually given both in dollars and as a percentage of the fund's assets. For example, if the combination of the fund's management fee and expenses came to $1 million in a year, and there was $100 million in the fund, we would say the *expense ratio* is 1%. It is easy to compare expense ratios from the data in the prospectuses, but investors should bear in mind that the cheapest fund is not necessarily the best. Newspapers and other sources publish the performance of mutual funds, typically showing their performance over the past 12 months, or for the current year from January 1 to the present, or both, and it is easy to see that differences in performance can far outweigh the differences in management fees or expense ratio.

Open-Ended Mutual Funds

Let's say that Mr. Adams, Mr. Burt, and Mrs. Cassens formed a mutual fund management company and called it ABC Investment Advisors. ABC Investment Advisors believed there were a large number of investors who would like to invest in high-technology stocks but did not know which companies to buy. So ABC Investment Advisors decided to start a new common stock mutual fund that specialized in buying high-technology stocks. They called the new fund ABC Technology Fund. Before they could accept money into the fund from the public, it was first necessary to register with the SEC and state agencies and publish a prospectus.

Assuming all the legalities have been taken care of, ABC Investment Advisors could now start advertising and selling shares of the ABC Technology Fund.

ABC Investment Advisors initially sold shares of the ABC Technology Fund at $10 per share on March 1, 1995. On that day five individuals bought some shares of the fund, as shown in Table 19.1.

Table 19.1   Investors in ABC Technology Fund

	Amount invested	Price per share March 1	Number of shares purchased March 1
Mr. Davis..................	$1,000	$10	100
Ms. Evans	500	10	50
Mr. Frank	1,500	10	150
Mrs. Gibbs	1,000	10	100
Mrs. Hunt	2,000	10	200
	$6,000 = 10		× 600 Shares

At the end of the day on March 1, there were 600 shares of ABC Technology Fund outstanding and there was $6,000 to invest. On the morning of March 2, the fund manager of ABC Technology Fund called a brokerage firm and bought the following five stocks for the fund, shown in Table 19.2.

Table 19.2   Investments of ABC Technology Fund on March 2

Stock	Price paid	Number of shares purchased	Amount invested
SFC Corporation	$50	40	$2,000
Smith Electronics.................	80	25	2,000
Super Computer	10	100	1,000
Data Electrix	50	10	500
National Robotics	25	16	400
Remaining cash*			100
Total worth of fund			$6,000

* The example ignores commissions.

Do not confuse shares of ABC Technology Fund with the shares of SFC, Smith Electronics, and so on, owned by this fund. Smith Electronics, for example, has 150 million shares outstanding, 25 of which are owned by ABC Technology Fund. ABC Technology Fund has 600 shares outstanding, 100 of which are owned by Mr. Davis, 50 by Ms. Evans, and so on. Although Davis and Evans do not directly own shares of SFC, they do own shares of SFC indirectly through their ownership of ABC Technology Fund. When people talk about owning shares of a mutual fund, they are talking about owning shares like ABC Technology Fund. They are not talking about the shares of SFC and the others held by the fund. However, an individual can certainly call a broker and buy shares of SFC or Smith Electronics for himself, which he then owns directly. Thus, it is possible that Davis can own shares of SFC both directly and indirectly through his ownership of ABC Technology Fund.

Returning to ABC Technology Fund, by the end of the day on March 2, three stocks had gone up, one had declined, and one was unchanged. Table 19.3 shows what the fund was worth at the end of the day. The amount of gain assumed in each stock is much larger than would normally occur in one day's trading, but the larger figures make the example easier to follow. Also, the cash would have been invested in something that earned interest, but the amount of interest earned in a day is small enough to be ignored in this example.

**Table 19.3   Investments of ABC Technology Fund,
                         Closing Prices of March 2**

Stock	Price at end of day	Number of shares held	Amount invested
SFC Corporation	$65	40	$2,600
Smith Electronics	100	25	2,500
Super Computer	9	100	900
Data Electrix	70	10	700
National Robotics	25	16	400
Cash			100
Total worth of fund			$7,200

At the close of business on March 2, the total net worth of ABC Technology Fund was $7,200. Since there are 600 shares of ABC outstanding, we say the *net asset value* per share of ABC Technology Fund is now $12:

$$\frac{\text{Net asset value}}{\text{Shares outstanding}} = \frac{\$7,200}{600} = \$12/\text{share}$$

Since ABC initially sold shares at $10 per share and they are now worth $12 per share, each share has appreciated by 20 percent—not surprising, since the fund's net assets appreciated by 20 percent, from $6,000 to $7,200. Thus, each of the original five investors has seen his or her investment go up by 20 percent. For example, look at Davis's account:

Original investment: 100 shares × $10/share = $1,000
Current worth: 100 shares × $12/share = $1,200 = 20% gain

ABC Technology Fund is an *open-ended fund.* This means the fund is always willing to sell new fund shares and is always willing to redeem (buy back) its outstanding fund shares. When a person calls or writes to the fund and commits to buy (or sell) shares of the fund, the price that person will pay (or receive) is the *net asset value* (NAV) at the close of the stock market that day. If the person buying or selling the ABC Technology Fund shares commits to do so after the stock market has closed that day, the price paid or received is the net asset value at the close of the market the next day.[2] Say, for instance, Mr. Frank had called ABC Investment Advisors in the middle of the day on March 2 and said to sell 100 of his 150 shares of the ABC Technology Fund. He would receive $12 per fund share (the net asset value of the fund at the close of business that day), or a total of $1,200.

When more people are buying fund shares than redeeming them, there will be an increase in the amount of cash in the fund. The fund manager can use this cash to buy more shares of stock for the fund. If there has been a net redemption of fund shares (more shares redeemed than new fund shares sold), the fund manager will have to sell shares of stock from the fund to raise cash to pay the fundholders who redeemed their shares if there is not enough cash available. In addition to buying new shares of stock when more money comes into the fund, and selling stock when shares of the fund are redeemed, the fund manager can also change stocks within the fund. For instance, the fund manager may think Data Electrix has gone as high as it is likely to go, so she would sell it and buy another stock she feels is more likely to go up. Or she may decide she was wrong in buying Super Computer and might want to sell it before it goes any lower, and reinvest the proceeds in stocks she feels are more attractive.

Open-ended funds can grow in two ways. First, new investors can put money in by buying new shares of the fund. Although this increases the size of the fund, it does not add to, or subtract from, the net asset value

---

2 The price may also include a *load,* or sales charge, discussed later.

of the fund, and therefore does not change the value of existing share-holders' investments. Second, the fund can grow (or shrink) because the value of the stocks in the fund goes up (or down). This *does* add to or subtract from the value of each fund share.

Closed-End Mutual Funds

Closed-end funds, unlike open-end funds, do not usually stand ready at any time to issue new fund shares or redeem existing fund shares. Rather, a closed-end fund's shares are usually sold only when the fund is initially created, and that number of fund shares remains outstanding indefinitely. There are some exceptions. Some closed-end funds will occasionally redeem existing shares or issue new shares at a specified date in the future, but this is unusual, and may occur only once every few years for such funds. Normally, if you want to buy shares of a closed-end fund, you have to buy already-outstanding shares from someone who owns them and is willing to sell them. Similarly, if you want to sell your shares in a closed-end fund, you must find someone to buy them. Thus, closed-end funds are usually traded on a stock exchange or over-the-counter, much like stocks, and the price of such fund shares will vary depending on what people are willing to buy or sell them for.

Closed-end funds calculate an NAV per share every day, just like open-ended funds. The price at which the closed-end fund shares trade on the exchange is usually close to that NAV, but most often is either slightly higher than, or slightly less than, the actual net asset value of the fund. In that case we would say the closed-end fund is selling at a *premium* or a *discount* to the net asset value of the fund. If a closed-end fund is selling at a discount from the fund's net asset value, investors should not automatically assume that the fund is a bargain and buy it. Two reasons why a closed-end fund may sell at a discount are as follows. First, assume Fund QRS, a closed-end mutual fund, was formed in 1993 with a net asset value of $10 a share. Now, let's assume Fund QRS continues to hold the same stocks in 1996 that it purchased in 1993, and that those stocks have appreciated to the point where the fund now has an NAV of $30 per share. Fund QRS would probably not sell at $30. This is because if the fund decides to sell the stocks it holds, it would have a capital gain on those stocks, and that capital gain would be passed on to Fund QRS's shareholders, who would have to pay tax on the gain. The investment advisory firm that manages Fund QRS is sometimes willing to tell callers about how much capital gain a closed-end fund has built in, but other times shareholders would not know. Thus, the fund would tend to sell below the $30 NAV because no one would want to pay $30 a share when they knew they were "buying" a tax obligation of uncertain size that could hit them at any time. By buying the closed-end fund at a discount from net asset value, the investor is buying the fund at closer to what it is really worth after paying the eventual capital gains tax. It is a safe guess that when the stock market has been rising, most closed-end funds will have capital gains that will eventually be passed through to the fund shareholders. Thus, after a market rise, closed-end funds will often sell at a discount to net asset value.

Another reason that closed-end funds sell at a discount to the net asset value of the stocks in the fund is that often, if the fund buys stock of very small companies, investors know that if the fund manager decided to sell one or more of these small companies, she might have to force down the price of the stock in order to sell all the fund's shares. This is called the *liquidity* problem. Liquidity refers to the ability to sell or buy shares of stock without causing the market to move up or down. General Motors is a very liquid stock, and it might be possible to sell 50,000 shares without moving the market. But if a fund owned 50,000 shares of an illiquid, infrequently traded stock, then it might have to take a price of two or more points below the currently quoted market price in order to sell all its stock. Because the NAV of the fund is based on the quoted market price of the stocks, it overstates the value of the fund compared to what it would be worth when the fund actually sells those stocks below their quoted market price. Thus, investors who see that a fund holds a lot of such illiquid stocks would know that the fund is really worth less than its NAV, and they would only be willing to buy the fund at a discount from the NAV.

Closed-end funds can also sell at a premium to their net asset value, but for different reasons. Suppose a small investor thought that the stock market in a small country, perhaps Korea, was going to go up. An individual investor would have difficulty knowing which Korean stocks to buy, and would probably also have difficulty finding a stockbroker who did. Even if the investor found a broker who knew about Korean stocks, it would be hard for an individual investor to buy enough different stocks to have diversified holdings without paying a lot in commissions. By buying a closed-end fund that specializes in Korean stocks, the investor will (1) get a diversified portfolio of Korean stocks; (2) pay lower commissions for buying and selling the Korean stocks; and (3) have a manager who specializes in Korean stocks and watches the Korean market daily, something your local broker probably cannot do. Most investors realize these benefits can help them earn a higher return, as well as perhaps avoid taking major losses, and they would prefer to own a closed-end Korean fund than try to make their own decisions on Korean stocks. Thus, there is a demand for closed-end funds that invest in countries where there is relatively little access to daily information and management expertise is needed. Many investors consider a small premium above net asset value to be a small price to pay for these advantages.

LOAD VERSUS NO-LOAD FUNDS

All mutual funds, open-end and closed-end, take a management fee, or investment advisory fee, as well as expense reimbursement from the fund. In addition, some open-ended mutual funds also charge what is commonly called a *load, sales load,* or *sales charge.* The sales load is primarily designed to compensate the salespeople and firms that sold the mutual fund to their customers. Most load funds are sold through stockbrokers, insurance salespeople, financial planners, and the like who do not work for the investment management firm that manages the fund. No-load funds, on the other hand, are primarily sold directly by the investment management firm that manages the fund, although recently a number of brokers have also begun to offer other firms' no-load funds to their customers. In addition, a number of investment management firms are also selling no-load funds managed by other management firms as well as their own.

The load, or sales charge can be structured in different ways. For some funds, the load is paid at the time the fund is purchased. These are called *front-end loads.* Front-end loads vary from fund to fund, but typically the amount of the load declines as the amount of the purchase gets larger. A typical front-end load fund might be structured so that someone who invests up to $50,000 in the fund pays a 5% load, an investment of $50,000 to $100,000 pays a 4% load, between $100,000 and $200,000 a 3% load, between $200,000 and $500,000 a 2% load, between $500,000 and $1,000,000 a 1% load, and no load, or sales charge, for purchases over $1,000,000. Other funds' loads might start at 6% or higher, and will have different breakpoints.

Suppose, for example, that you had $10,000 to invest and were considering buying shares of a mutual fund that had a net asset value of $10 a share. If you were buying a no-load fund you would pay exactly $10 per fund share and could buy 1,000 shares of the fund. If you were buying a fund with a 4% front-end load, you would have to pay $10.40 a share (including the 4% load) and thus would only be able to buy 961 shares with your $10,000. Obviously it would be preferable to have 1,000 shares, and most people who read about funds and make their own decisions would choose a no-load fund.

Because this front-end load immediately reduces the amount of money that you have invested, it tends to discourage many people from buying such funds. Thus, some fund management companies have created funds with *back-end,* or *rear-end* loads. These are typically structured so that you do not pay a load or sales charge when you buy the fund, but you pay it when you leave the fund. Usually, the amount of the back-end load declines the longer you hold the fund. For example, a fund's prospectus might specify that if you hold the fund less than one year, the management company will take out a 4% load when you sell it—that is, 4% of the value of the fund shares at the time they were sold. If you hold the fund between one year and two years, the back-end load would be 3%; between two and three years, 2%, and so on. The amount of the load and the holding period for which it is assessed will vary from fund to fund.

A back-end load would generally seem more desirable than a front-end load because you have more money invested, but this is not always so, because many back-end load funds also specify that the investor must pay a higher annual expense ratio to the management company. Thus, investors who expect to hold the fund for many years may be better off paying a front-end load once, rather than have an additional annual fee taken out of their investment every year. In fact, some loaded mutual funds give the investor the option of a front-end load or a back-end load within the same fund. Thus, they create two different classes of shareholders, and in the newspaper, you will see these funds listed twice, once with an "A" at the end of the fund name, and once with a "B." Typically, the "A" share is the front-end load share, and the "B" share is the rear-end load option.

Another reason for back-end loads is to discourage fund holders from jumping in and out of the fund too often. Without the back-end load, there will always be some investors who buy and sell shares of the fund frequently to catch short-term moves in the market. This is called *market timing.* These market timers make it difficult to run the fund and add "hidden" costs as the fund manager would constantly have to buy and sell securities as money came into or went out of the fund. Each time the fund manager has to buy or sell a stock or bond, the fund has to pay another commission. More importantly, the fund may have to pay above the last quoted price to buy a security if the market is moving up, and may have to sell at a lower-than-market price if the market is declining. This problem is most serious for funds that buy less-liquid securities, such as junk-bond funds, or some foreign funds where it can sometimes be difficult for the fund manager to buy or sell stock or bonds on short notice. The back-end load, or exit fee, discourages these "market timer" moves by fundholders and thereby saves the fund these unnecessary costs. Some funds have these exit fees only to discourage the market timers, and not as a sales commission. Exit fees are sometimes as small as 1% or 2% and are only applied if the fund is held less than some specified amount of time, typically ranging between 3 and 18 months. The details about front-end or back-end load fees vary from fund to fund and are always laid out in the fund's prospectus, or can be learned from your stockbroker or financial advisor.

There are no inherent advantages to load funds. The load is not buying you superior management. The purpose of the load is primarily (if not entirely) to pay the sales charge. Load funds are best suited to people who do not have much information about mutual funds and do not know how to select a fund that fits their needs. The load fund salesperson can bring his or her expertise to these people and help them decide what kind of fund would be most appropriate for them.

CHOOSING BETWEEN A MUTUAL FUND AND INVESTING YOURSELF

The decision of whether to choose stocks yourself, possibly with the help of your broker, or to buy a mutual fund, is a personal one and may be based on how much money you have to invest, how much time you want to devote to it, and your attitude toward risk. There are advantages to both methods of investing.

Advantages of Mutual Funds

1. *Diversification of risk.* Whereas an individual can only buy a limited number of stocks without running up big commissions, mutual funds can easily diversify substantially because of the large amount of money they manage. The advantage of diversification, of course, is that if you bought only one or two stocks and they both went down you

could incur a substantial loss. Through diversification, one or two unexpected losses will not have a major impact, and, in fact, might not even be noticed if the rest of the stocks in the fund go up.

2. *Access to expertise.* Mutual fund management company research departments devote their full efforts to working for their funds. Their research reports and stock recommendations are not available to stockbrokers or the public, as are brokerage firms' research reports and recommendations. Further, buy-side institutions have access to most brokerage firm research departments and thus can choose the best of all research available.

3. *Family-of-funds concept.* Many mutual fund management companies offer a variety of funds, including growth stock funds, income stock funds, corporate bond funds, municipal bond funds, money market funds, and so on. Such management companies usually allow you to switch your money back and forth between funds free or at minimal cost.

4. *Bookkeeping.* Most mutual funds keep track of your fund for you, and regular mailings tell you about your gain or loss, your tax consequences, and the like.

Advantages of Individual Investments

1. *Concentration of investment.* If you have a strong conviction that a certain stock is going up, you can put all or as much of your money into it as you wish.

2. *Control of investment.* Buying stocks yourself gives you total control over the nature and diversification of your stocks at all times. For example, you could quickly move from energy stocks to computer stocks or to a diversified portfolio. In addition, you can buy or sell stocks any time the market is open. Open-end mutual funds are usually bought or sold (redeemed) only at the end-of-day price.

3. *Access to information.* Individual investors are free to call their broker for information or advice on their stocks anytime. Mutual fund management companies generally do not give investment advice beyond the information provided in the prospectus.

4. *Control over timing of taxes.* When you own stocks or bonds individually, you do not pay any capital gains tax until you choose to sell them, which can be many years after your purchase. When you own a mutual fund, the fund manager decides when to sell securities; and

taxable capital gains, if there are any, are passed on to you as capital gains dividends each year. If you need to sell shares of your mutual fund to raise money to pay your tax on these capital gains dividends, you then have less money invested going forward.[3] Note that by paying some capital gains tax each year (or however often the fund declares these capital gains dividends), your taxable gain in the future when you sell the fund is being reduced. So you are probably not increasing your overall tax liability; rather, you are just paying it earlier and thereby reducing the amount of money you have invested, and thereby reducing your profits if the fund appreciates.

THE RELATIONSHIP OF BUY-SIDE AND SELL-SIDE INSTITUTIONS

As mentioned earlier, buy-side institutions are important customers for the sell-side brokers, generating far more buying or selling commissions than any individual would be likely to do. One way that brokers compete for the buy and sell orders of mutual funds and other buy-side institutions is by providing research. Most brokerage firms maintain research staffs, which include security analysts who research individual stocks and industries; market strategists who try to forecast moves in the stock market as a whole, or in segments of the market; and economic analysts, who research and make forecasts on the overall economy and on segments of the economy. This research is then made available to the buy-side institutions. The buy-side analysts and portfolio managers look at all this research material and can use as much as they feel is helpful to them. They pay for this research via commissions, by directing buy and sell orders to those brokerage firms whose research they choose to pay for.

The question arises: If buy-side institutions have their own research staffs, why do they use research from sell-side (brokerage firm) analysts? The answer is that because there is so much information available to analyze on so many stocks, buy-side analysts can cover more companies and more industries more thoroughly by taking advantage of sell-side analysts' research. This sell-side research is not absolutely necessary, but it is widely used by buy-side institutions that want to cover a broad range of stocks and still cover them in depth. As a result of the large commission business generated by the buy-side institutions, brokerage firms are

---

3 This is a particularly serious problem if the fund's investments have done well, but the fund has not recently paid any capital gains dividend. In that case, new buyers of the fund might find themselves owing a big tax on gains they never benefited from.

able to keep larger staffs of analysts than they might otherwise keep just to assist their own traders and stockbrokers who deal with individuals.

With all these investment analysts and portfolio managers doing intensive research, there is an enormous amount of information and opinion flowing around Wall Street. Since buy-side and sell-side investors are constantly on the phones with one another, it is not surprising that information, fact and rumor, tends to spread quickly in the investment community. When a well-regarded analyst changes his or her earnings estimate for a company, or recommendation for the stock, other analysts on the buy-side and the sell-side often tend to change their forecasts as well. This is partially a result of a "herd" instinct, whereby no one wants to stand out and look bad by being wrong, and partially because analysts who research their companies thoroughly often have access to much of the same information as other analysts, and therefore often come to the same conclusions. The herd instinct is not always right, but it can create big moves in stocks. For example, if many analysts were raising their earnings estimates substantially for a company, that stock would probably go up. Conversely, if the company then reported earnings that were well below what investors had come to expect, the stock could fall sharply and suddenly. Thus, short-term moves in stocks can often be caused by such changes in "consensus" thinking on Wall Street. For the individual investor who is not in touch with Wall Street information all day, it is not really possible to catch all these moves. But in the long run, stocks will continue to go up and down in response to changes in the outlook for earnings and dividends, and individual investors can still be very successful by studying their companies and industries and making judgments on whether the company's prospects are improving or deteriorating, and whether the price, or price/earnings ratio, is high or low.

SUGGESTIONS FOR READERS

It is difficult to be consistently successful in the stock market without good sources of information on which to base your judgments. Readers are encouraged to make the effort to develop good sources of information, or to rely on others, such as a broker who may be able to access information sources you cannot. If you have the time, do the following: (1) read a broad-based investment service such as the *Value Line*, (2) read two or more market letters, such as those you will find advertised in investment magazines, (3) read one or two specialized industry publications such as

Automotive News, American Metal Market, Oil & Gas Journal, Electronic News, or any of hundreds of others that you can subscribe to or find in libraries, but that do not normally appear on newsstands. Choose industries you may care to invest in, perhaps where you already have some knowledge through your job or friends, (4) try to develop contacts with people who work for companies in industries that interest you, and (5) if you have lots of time, there is also a wealth of data available from federal and state government sources on innumerable industries and products that can give valuable investment insights. And, of course, there are the basics—company annual and quarterly reports, filings with the SEC, press releases, prospectuses, and the like, and either *The Wall Street Journal* or *Investor's Business Daily.*

Whatever you choose, read it consistently and promptly. Watching markets, company data, and investment opinion changing over time is far more educational than just doing research at occasional points in time. Also, company, industry, and stock market data evolve quickly, and investors' perceptions can turn from bullish to bearish and vice versa very quickly.

Readers who do not have time to do a lot of independent investment research should try to take advantage of good Wall Street research. One way to do this is to buy mutual funds from an organization that maintains a large research department. For those who prefer to make their own investment decisions, choose a broker who works for a firm with a large research department, and who can get occasional research reports for you. Be sure to ask, because many large brokerage firms will not provide individual clients with their research reports. Also, you might split your business between two or more brokers and thereby have access to information from more than one research department. Research reports from many brokerage firms are also sometimes available from other sources that are advertised in investment magazines.

As much information as you read, you should assume that in most cases others have also seen the same information. Therefore, while a lack of information can cause you to make bad investment decisions, good information alone does not guarantee successful investing. Good judgment is still necessary to determine when a stock is too high or too low, given all the information that is known about the company. Your judgment will improve with experience and willingness to learn from your mistakes.

APPENDIX:
Short Selling

When you as an investor buy stock of a company, we say you are "long" that stock. This simply means that you own it. If the stock goes up and you sell it, you have a profit. If it goes down from where you bought it, you have a loss. Thus, you only "go long" (i.e., buy a stock) if you expect it to go up. However, if you expect a stock to go down, you can make money by selling short, or *shorting,* as it is called. Shorting essentially means borrowing a stock you do not own in order to sell it.

To see how shorting works, let's look at an example. Suppose Microsoft is selling at $100 per share. You do not own the stock and you feel certain it is going down. So you call your stockbroker and tell her to "short 10 shares of Microsoft." This means you want to sell 10 shares of Microsoft even though you do not own it. In order to sell stock you don't own, it is first necessary to borrow it. Then you can sell the shares that you borrowed. Normally, your brokerage firm will lend you the shares you want to sell. Let's assume you sold the 10 shares for $100 each, or a total of $1,000. The brokerage firm will not give you the $1,000 yet because you have borrowed 10 shares that you still owe them, and the brokerage firm wants to hold the $1,000 as collateral for the loan. Now, assume you were right and the stock declined to $70, which is as low as you think it is going. At this point, you call your stockbroker and tell her to "cover your short." This means you want her to buy 10 shares of Microsoft for you in the market and use those 10 shares to replace the 10 shares you borrowed. Since Microsoft is now selling at $70 a share, you can buy 10 shares for $700. Since the broker is holding $1,000 of your money (received when you initially sold short the 10 shares), she uses $700 of it to buy the 10 shares and then sends you the remaining $300, which is your profit. The brokerage firm, of course, also keeps the 10 shares you just bought as replacement for those it loaned to you earlier.

When selling short, what you are doing is betting that the stock is going down. You are borrowing stock in order to sell it, and hoping to buy it back later at a lower price to repay the loan.

The risk in shorting is that you might be wrong and the stock might go up. Suppose you shorted 10 shares of Microsoft at $100 per share. However, instead of declining, as you expected, the stock went up. You still have an obligation to replace the 10 shares you borrowed. But now that the stock has risen to $110, it will cost you $1,100 to buy back the 10 shares. Thus, if you "cover your short" now (i.e., buy back the 10 shares to repay the loan), then you will have lost $100. You sold the stock for $1,000 and bought it back for $1,100, so you have to pay your broker $100. The risk in shorting a stock is that if it keeps going higher, it will cost you more to buy it back. In short selling there is no limit to how much you can lose. Conversely, when you buy a stock "long" the most you can lose is what you paid for it if it goes to $0.

Why would an investor sell a stock short? Obviously, because the investor thought the stock was overpriced and was likely to come down. Specifically, he or she might anticipate or know some bad news about the company that is not generally known yet—news that, when it becomes known, will probably cause the stock to decline. For example, the investor may think that earnings are going to be lower than generally expected, or that a competitor is about to introduce a superior product. Or, as frequently occurs in market declines, some people simply short a stock because they think the stock is going down with the market and they want to make money on the decline. In doing so, of course, they add to the decline because they are selling.

GLOSSARY

A

Accelerated depreciation. A method whereby an asset is depreciated more in its early years and less in its later years.

Acceleration. The process of making an entire loan due for redemption immediately.

Accounts payable. Money that a company owes, typically to suppliers of raw materials and services.

Accounts receivable. Money that is owned to a company.

Accounts receivable-to-sales ratio. Accounts receivable divided by sales.

Accumulated depreciation. The total amount by which all the assets in the Gross plant and equipment account have been depreciated down through the years; or the total amount by which a single asset has been depreciated down through the years.

Acid test ratio. Current assets, less inventories, divided by current liabilities.

Additional paid-in capital. Paid-in capital minus the dollar amount in common stock at par value.

After market. Any trade of stock made between members of the pubic after an investment banker or underwriter has completed an offering.

Amortization. The deferred expensing of a cost incurred in an earlier year.

Antidilutive issue. A convertible issue that causes an increase in EPS as a result of the conversion process.

Asked price. The price at which a market maker is willing to sell a particular stock.

Assets. A balance sheet category reflecting anything of value that a company owns or has claim to.

Authorized stock. The total number of shares of stock a company has been permitted by its shareholders to issue, whether or not it has all been issued.

B

Baby bonds. Bonds with a face value of less than $1,000.

Back-end load. A fee that is paid when an investor leaves a mutual fund.

Balance sheet. A financial statement that reflects the financial condition of the company *at a point in time,* showing what assets are held, what liabilities are owed, what money (or capital) was initially put into the company, and how much was earned by the company.

Balloon payment. A large payment to complete the repayment of a long-term loan, e.g., the repayment of remaining outstanding bonds at final maturity

Basic earnings per share. Actual net earnings divided by the number of shares outstanding at the end of the year, without giving any consideration to convertible issues.

Basis point. One one-hundredth of a percentage point, as used in the measurement of bond interest rates and yields.

Bearer bond. A bond belonging to the person who possesses it.

Bid. The price a market maker is willing to pay to buy a particular stock.

Bond. A contract between a company that is borrowing money and the people and institutions who are lending the money.

Bond certificate. A document that says the bondholder is the lender and has the right to be paid back by the issuer on a certain date or dates, and to receive interest from the issuer on certain dates.

Bond ratings. Judgments made by rating agencies about the safety of bonds.

Bondholder. A lender to a company through the purchase of its bonds.

Book (specialist's). A record of all the buy and sell orders for a stock that have not yet been filled.

Book value. Total assets less total liabilities less liquidating value of preferred stock, if any.

Book value per common share. Book value divided by the number of common shares outstanding.

Bullet. A bond issue that has no sinking-fund payment and is completely redeemed at final maturity.

Buy-side institutions. Firms that hold their customers' money and make all the buy and sell investment decisions.

C

Call date. The date on or after which a company may redeem its bonds earlier than maturity.

Call feature, *see* **Call provision.**

Call premium. Extra money paid to bondholders to compensate them when bonds are called by a company ahead of final or sinking fund maturity.

Call price. The price the company must pay to bondholders when redeeming their bonds early under a call provision. The call price often includes a call premium in addition to face value.

Call protection. Any of a number of restrictions on the callability of bonds.

Call provision. The section of the bond indenture that states when and at what prices a company may call (redeem) its bonds ahead of maturity.

Callable bond. A bond that can be redeemed early by the issuer, at the issuer's option.

Capital. Can refer to funds used in the company (*see* **Long-term capital** and **Working capital**), or can refer to the goods (usually fixed assets) used to make other goods.

Capital intensive companies. Companies for whom capital costs are a significant part of their total costs.

Capital spending. A company's purchases of new plant and/or equipment.

Capitalization. On the balance sheet, the combination of long-term debt and stockholders' equity and possibly other long-term liabilities; or, the P/E ratio investors are willing to pay for a stock; or, the value of all of a company's stock.

Capitalizing an asset. Putting an asset's cost on the balance sheet under Fixed Assets (or some similar title); the asset will usually then be depreciated or amortized over an appropriate number of years.

Cash flow. The flow of money into and out of a company.

Cash flow from financing. The amount of cash a company generates from issuing stock or bonds, or from borrowing, less cash used to pay dividends, repay debt, or repurchase the company's stock.

Cash flow from investing. The amount of cash a company uses to buy new plant and equipment, or to buy stock of other companies, offset by cash generated selling off old plant and equipment. Cash flow from investing is usually a net outflow.

Cash flow from operations. The amount of cash a company generates from making and selling its products or services.

Cash ratio. Cash plus marketable securities divided by current liabilities.

Certificate (bond). A document that says the bondholder is the lender and has the right to be paid back by the issuer on a certain date or dates, and to receive interest from the issuer on certain dates.

Closed-end mutual funds. Mutual funds that usually sell shares only when the fund is initially created.

Combined offering. A sale of stock where some of the offered shares are primary shares being offered by the company, and some are secondary shares being offered by existing shareholders.

Common stock. A certificate that represents partial ownership in a company, and gives its owner the right to vote at stockholders' meetings.

Common stock equivalents. Convertible bonds, or convertible preferreds or other securities, that are deemed likely to be converted into common stock at some time.

Conversion rate. The number of shares of common stock a convertible bond or convertible preferred converts into.

Converted value. A convertible bond or convertible preferred's value if it were converted to common stock. Obtained by multiplying the price of the common stock times the number of shares of common stock that the bond or preferred converts into.

Convertible bonds. Bonds that can be converted into stock.

Cost of goods sold. The dollar cost of goods that have been sold. This may include materials costs, labor costs, and other costs.

Cost. Incurred by a company when it pays for something or becomes obligated to pay for something; may or may not also be an expense.

Coupon. The interest payment required by a bond.

Coupon rate. Same as **coupon yield**.

Coupon yield. A bond's coupon divided by its face amount.

Covenants. Agreements a bond issuer makes as safeguards to its bondholders.

Creditors. People or institutions that are owed money. Bondholders, for example, are among a company's creditors, as are the persons owed the money in Accounts payable.

Cumulative preferred stock. A preferred stock specifying that if the preferred dividend has been omitted for one or more quarters, no common dividend can be paid until all of the omitted preferred dividends from the past are paid.

Current assets. Cash and items that are expected to be converted into cash within one year.

Current cost. Most-recent cost.

Current liabilities. Debts due within one year.

Current ratio. Current assets divided by current liabilities.

Current yield. A bond's dollar coupon divided by the bond's current price in the secondary market.

Currently callable bond. A bond that can be called by a company at any time.

D

Debenture. A loan that is very much like a bond except it is not backed by any specific assets.

Debt to total capitalization ratio. Long-term debt divided by total capitalization.

Default. The failure of a company to make an interest payment, sinking fund payment, or final maturity payment when it is due, or a company's violating a covenant in a bond indenture.

Depreciation. An expense reflecting the wearing out of fixed assets.

Dilution. A reduction in percentage of ownership represented by a share of stock as a result of a company issuing more shares; or, a reduction in earnings per share as a result of a company issuing more shares.

Dilutive issue. A convertible issue that causes a reduction of EPS as a result of the conversion process.

Discount broker. A broker who simply executes orders for customers without providing financial advice.

Discount from par. A bond price that is lower than the bond's face value.

Discount rate. The interest rate the Federal Reserve charges when it lends money to banks.

Discount to conversion. A bond price that is lower than the bond's converted value.

Dividend. The money a company may choose to pay to stockholders, usually from the profit it earns.

E

Earnings per share. Net earnings for the year divided by the number of shares of common stock outstanding.

Earnings power. The highest projected earnings for a company if all goes well.

Effective tax rate. Actual tax paid divided by pretax profit.

Efficient market. A market where stock prices are believed to reflect all the information that investors can know about a company.

Equipment. The tools a company uses to help produce the goods that are to be sold.

Equipment Trust Certificate. A bond issued for a particular purpose, e.g, an airline borrowing money to buy an airplane.

Equity money. Money a company raises from the sale of stock, and/or money earned as profit.

Expense. Any and all dollar figures that are deducted from sales to reach net profit; always reflects a cost, although that cost may have been incurred in a different year.

Expensing. The process of deducting costs, or portions of costs, from sales to calculate earnings.

Expensing an asset. Broadly, the process of deducting all or some portion of a cost from sales to calculate earnings. Usually, however, refers to deducting an asset's entire cost from sales in the year in which the asset was purchased, as opposed to *capitalizing the asset.*

Extraordinary cost. A cost that does not occur regularly in the normal operations of the company.

F

Face value. The amount of money a company must pay back when a bond is redeemed.

Federal funds rate. The interest rate banks charge when they lend money for a day or two to other banks to help them meet reserve requirements.

FIFO inventory accounting. An inventory accounting method in which the first inventory that comes in is assumed to be the first that is sold.

Final maturity. The last date a borrower must pay back any bonds of a particular issue that are still outstanding.

Finished goods. The dollar cost of the goods that have been manufactured but not yet sold.

First-in, first-out, *see* FIFO.

Float. The number of shares that are publicly traded that are not owned by a company officer or director or by anyone who owns more than 10 percent of the company's total shares outstanding.

Floating rate notes. Notes with a coupon payment that varies with some other specified market interest rate.

Floor broker. A stockbroker who works on the floor of a stock exchange.

Free cash flow. Cash flow from operations, less debt repayment requirements, less preferred dividends, less the maintenance level of capital spending.

Front-end load. A fee that is paid when an investor purchases a mutual fund.

Fully diluted earnings per share. The earnings per share figure that results from converting all convertible issues, whether or not they are likely to ever be converted.

G

Goodwill. An intangible asset that reflects the difference between what a company paid to acquire another company (or perhaps a patent or mailing list, etc.) and the book value of the acquired company (or asset).

Gross plant and equipment. The initial cost of the plant and equipment.

H

Historical cost. The oldest cost.

I

In arrears. Refers to a preferred stock that has omitted (not paid) its dividend for one or more quarters.

Income statement. A financial statement that shows the revenue (sales) that the company has made, the expenses that have been incurred to make those sales, and the profit or loss derived therefrom.

Indenture. The complete detailed agreement between bondholders and an issuer.

Initial public offering. The first time that any stock of a company is being sold to the public.

Insider. One who has access to information about a company that the general public does not have.

Intangible asset. A non-physical asset, such as a patent, brand name, or copyright.

Interest coverage ratio. Money available to pay interest (the earnings before interest and taxes) divided by total interest.

Inventory. Material or materials that will be used and will become part of the products that will ultimately be sold by a company.

Inventory-to-sales ratio. Inventory divided by sales.

Inventory turnover ratio. Sales divided by inventory.

Investment bank. A firm that helps businesses raise money by selling new stock or bonds either to the public or as private placements.

Investment management fee. A fee taken by mutual fund management firms as a percentage of the assets in the funds they manage.

Issued stock. The number of shares of stock that have been sold (or given away) by a company. The issued shares may still be outstanding, or may have been repurchased by the company.

Issuer (of a bond). A company that borrows money by selling bonds.

L

Labor intensive companies. Companies for whom labor costs are a significant part of their total costs.

Last-in, first-out, *see* **LIFO.**

Legend. A statement stamped on a stock certificate explaining that the stock has not been registered and may not be resold unless a registration statement (or an exemption from registration) is in effect.

Liabilities. A balance sheet category reflecting the debts a company owes.

LIFO inventory accounting. An inventory accounting method in which the last inventory that comes in is assumed to be the first that is sold.

Limit order. An order from an investor authorizing purchase of a stock only at or below a certain price, or sale of a stock at or above a certain price.

Liquidating value. The amount of money each preferred share receives when a company is liquidated.

Liquidation. Terminating a company by selling all its assets and paying its liabilities.

Liquidity. The ability to buy or sell shares of stock without causing the market to move up or down.

Listed stock. Stock that is traded on a stock exchange.

Listing application. An application to list and trade a stock on a stock exchange.

Load. A fee charged by mutual funds to compensate the salespeople and firms that sell the mutual fund to their customers.

LOCOM, *see* **Lower-of-cost-or-market.**

Long-term assets. Assets a company is expected to retain for more than one year, such as tools, buildings, and vehicles.

Long-term capital. Refers to the long-term debt and equity which are the sources of funds used, for the most part, to buy long-term assets.

Long-term debt. Loans that must be repaid after one year.

Long-term liabilities. Debts due after one year.

Lottery. A random selection of bonds in order to make a required sinking-fund redemption.

Lower-of-cost-or-market. An inventory adjustment wherein a company lowers the value of its finished goods inventory by the difference between the price for which the inventory can be sold and its value on the balance sheet, and adds the same amount to Cost of goods sold for the year.

M

Market capitalization. The value of all of a company's stock.

Market makers. Individuals or firms who post bids and offers on over-the-counter or NASDAQ stocks, and who are committed to buy and sell those stocks at any time.

Market size. The number of shares a market-making firm will buy or sell at its posted bid and offered prices.

Market timers. Investors who buy and sell shares of mutual funds frequently to catch short-term moves in the market.

Market value of the float. The number of shares in the float multiplied by the current stock price.

Maturity. The date a bond must be paid back by the issuer.

Mortgage bonds. A bond in which one or more specific pieces of property are "pledged" to the bondholders.

Multiple listed stock. Stock that is traded on more than one stock exchange.

Mutual fund. An organization, usually set up as a corporation or trust, that takes in money from a large number of people and invests it.

N

Net plant and equipment. Gross plant and equipment less Accumulated depreciation. May also be referred to as the book value of the plant and equipment.

Net profit margin ratio. After-tax profit divided by total sales.

New issue. Any offering of stock or bonds that has not previously been issued. A new issue may be a private placement or a public offering. A new issue will always be a primary offering, and it may be an initial public offering.

Noncallable (NC) bond. A bond that cannot be called by a company at the present time.

Noncumulative preferred stock. A preferred stock specifying that as long as the preferred dividend is not paid, the common dividend cannot be paid.

Nonrecurring costs. Costs that do not occur regularly in the normal operations of the company.

Note. A loan of typically less than 10 years.

O

Omission. The non-payment of a dividend.

Offered price. The price at which a market maker is willing to sell a particular stock.

Open-ended mutual fund. A mutual fund that is willing to sell new fund shares or redeem outstanding fund shares every day.

Outstanding stock. Stock that has been issued and not repurchased by the company.

Over-the-counter market. Specifically, the market where stocks that are too small to qualify for trading on the NASDAQ market are traded; broadly, *all* trading not done on the New York or American Stock Exchanges.

Overhead costs. Costs a company incurs that are not attributed directly to making goods.

Overpriced stock. A stock that an investor thinks is too high and is likely to come down. This may be because the investor thinks the price/earnings ratio is too high, or because he thinks the company's earnings are likely to fall unexpectedly.

Ownership equity. A balance sheet category reflecting the combination of the amount of money put into a company by the owners plus the total amount of profit the company has earned through the years, less any dividends the company has paid through the years.

P

Paid-in capital. The amount of money paid into the company by stockholders for stock.

Par value. An arbitrary figure set by a company that distinguishes one of the two components of paid-in capital.

Participating preferred stock. A preferred stock specifying that the dividend moves up or down with the company's earnings or with the common stock dividend.

P/E ratio, *see* **Price-to-earnings ratio.**

Period expense. An expense deducted from sales in the period in which the cost is incurred.

Perpetual preferred stock. A preferred stock that may be outstanding forever unless the company buys it back on the secondary market and retires it.

Preferred stock. A stock with priority over common stock in both the right to receive dividends and in the division of assets in the event of a liquidation.

Premium to conversion. A convertible bond or convertible preferred's price that is higher than its converted value.

Premium to par. A bond price that is higher than the bond's face value.

Pretax profit margin ratio. Pretax profit divided by total sales.

Price-to-cash-flow ratio. Cash flow divided by the number of common shares outstanding.

Price-to-earnings ratio. Stock price divided by earnings per share.

Primary earnings per share. The earnings per share figure that results from converting any convertible issues that, according to a decision

rule, are likely to be converted to stock at some time.

Primary offering. The creation and sale of new stock by a company. The company receives the money from the sale of the shares.

Prime rate. The interest rate that banks usually charge their safest business borrowers.

Private company. A company which has no stock registered with the SEC, or sold to the public. Usually has only a small number of investors and has no obligation to publish financial statements or report to the Securities and Exchange Commission.

Private placement. The sale of unregistered stock or bonds.

Profit margin. Profit, either before tax or after tax, divided by sales.

Prospectus. A summary of a company's most relevant financial information, compiled to help potential investors make a proper evaluation of the risks involved in buying the company's stock. It is part of the company's registration statement with the SEC.

Proxy. An absentee ballot by which shareholders who do not attend a company's annual shareholder meeting can vote for directors and other matters.

Proxy fight. A battle between opposing groups of shareholders who are each trying to get other shareholders to vote their "proxies" for a particular group of candidates for company directors.

Public company. A company which has registered some or all of its stock with the SEC, and has sold at least some of the registered stock to the public.

Public offering. Broadly, any sale of registered stock, whether a primary or secondary offering, but usually refers to a company doing a primary offering.

Q

Quick ratio. Current assets, less inventory, divided by current liabilities.

R

Ratably. An equal amount each year.

Rating agencies. Independent companies that analyze and issue judgments about the safety of bonds.

Rear-end load. A fee that is paid when an investor leaves a mutual fund.

Redemption. Returning a bond certificate to the company or trustee in exchange for the amount of money due.

Refinancing. Issuing new stock or bonds to obtain the money necessary to repay old debt.

Refunding. The issuance of new bonds at a lower interest rate to pay back old bonds that have a higher interest rate.

Registered bond. A bond that belongs to the person in whose name it is registered; there is no risk if it is lost.

Registration statement. The complete filing a company must make with the SEC before it can have a public offering of stock or bonds.

Reorganization. Mostly for bankrupt companies, a procedure wherein a company and its creditors try to make a plan for partial repayment of debt and for issuance of new stock to creditors who were not paid back in full.

Reset bonds. Bonds that specify that the coupon rate will change at some point, usually at a specified time.

Residual value. A small book value of an asset left over at the end of the asset's expected life, or after the asset is no longer being depreciated.

Restructuring cost. A write-off that sometimes occurs when a company either sells off or closes a division, or makes some other substantial change in the company.

Retail broker. A stockbroker who deals with individuals.

Retained earnings. Total profits earned by a company for all years since its inception, less any losses in any years since inception, less all of the dividends paid since inception.

Retirement (of an asset). The disposal of an asset.

Retirement (of a bond). The withdrawal of a bond from circulation, either through redemption or because the issuing company buys the bond back in the secondary market.

Return. Can refer to a company's profit, or a shareholder's gain, either by dividend or by stock price appreciation.

Return on capital ratio. Profit divided by total capitalization. Can be either before tax or after tax profit.

Return on sales ratio. Profit divided by sales. Same as *Profit margin*.

Return on stockholders' equity ratio. Profit divided by stockholders' equity.

S

Secondary offering. A sale of already-outstanding stock from one investor to another; the investor who sells the stock receives the money from the sale of the shares.

Sell-side institutions. Firms that earn money by taking commissions each time they buy or sell stocks (or other investments) for their clients.

Selling group. All dealers, such as investment bankers and stockbrokers, participating in a stock offering.

Serial redemption. The retirement of certain numbered bonds in certain years, thereby constituting the sinking fund.

Shareholder. A person who owns one or more shares of a company.

Short selling. Borrowing a stock you do not own in order to sell it. Usually done with the expectation of buying the stock back later at a lower price, to replace the borrowed stock, and keep the dollar difference as profit.

Short-term debt. Loans that must be repaid within one year.

Sinking fund. A required partial repayment on a long-term loan, e.g., an obligation to retire a certain amount of bonds on or before specified dates ahead of final maturity.

Sole proprietorship. A company that is owned by one person and is not yet incorporated.

Specialist. An individual on a stock exchange who is in charge of trading a particular stock.

Split rating. A difference of opinion regarding a bond's risk as judged by different rating agencies.

Spread. The difference between a bid price and an offered price.

Statement of cash flow. A financial statement detailing the categories of cash flow into and out of a company.

Stock, *see* **Common stock** and **Preferred stock.**

Stock exchange. A place where people come to buy and sell registered stock in secondary transactions.

Stock options. The right to purchase a company's stock for the price stated on the option, any time within the period stated on the option. Companies sometimes give such options to employees as an incentive. Also, there are options on many companies' stock that any investor can purchase on the option exchanges. These latter options are sold from one investor to another and do not come from the company.

Stockholder. A person who owns one or more shares of a company.

Stockholders' equity. A balance sheet category reflecting the combination of the amount of money put into a company by the stockholders plus the total amount of profit the company has earned through the years, less any dividends the company has paid through the years. Same as Ownership equity.

Straight-line depreciation. A method whereby an asset is depreciated evenly over its estimated useful life.

T

Tangible book value. Total assets less intangible assets less total liabilities less liquidating value of preferred stock.

Term bond. A bond issue that has no sinking-fund payment and is completely redeemed at final maturity.

Term loan. A loan of typically three to seven years.

Trading post. A place on the floor of a stock exchange where the buying and selling of stock occurs.

Trading stock. The sale of stock from one person to another.

Treasury stock. Stock a company has bought back from shareholders; it no longer represents partial ownership of the company.

Trustee. A person or institution who looks out for the rights of bondholders.

U

Underpriced stock. A stock that an investor thinks is too low and is likely to go up. This may be because the investor thinks the price/earnings ratio is too low (compared to the company's past P/E ratios, or compared to similar companies' P/E ratios) or because the investor thinks the company's earnings are likely to increase more than most other investors expect.

Underwriting. A guarantee by an investment bank to sell an issue of stock.

V

Variable rate notes. Notes with a coupon payment that varies with some other specified market interest rate.

W

Waive. To make an exception.

Widely held company or stock. A company whose stock is owned by a large number of investors.

Working capital. Money that is tied up in inventory, accounts receivable, and the like. Defined as total current assets, less total current liabilities.

Write off. Usually refers to the immediate and complete expensing of some cost, rather than expensing it gradually over a number of years through depreciation or amortization. More broadly, it may mean expensing any cost.

Y

Yield. Usually refers to the interest or dividend return to an investor expressed as a percentage of the price of the bond or stock.

Yield on a common stock. Dividend divided by the price of the stock.

Yield spread. The difference in yield between any two bonds or other securities being examined.

Yield to call. A bond yield similar to yield to maturity, except that it uses the bond's call price and call date rather than the bond's face value and final maturity date.

Yield to maturity. A bond yield that includes both the annual coupon and any capital gain or loss an investor may have on the difference between what she paid for the bond and its face value at maturity.

Z

Zero coupon bond. A bond that pays no interest to bondholders; all of the return to bondholders comes at maturity when the bond is redeemed.

INDEX